GLOBAL DEPRESSION AND REGIONAL WARS

GLOBAL
DEPRESSION
and
REGIONAL
WARS

JAMES PETRAS

CLARITY PRESS, INC.

ISBN: 0-932863-68-X
       978-0-932863-68-3

In-house editor: Diana G. Collier
Cover: R. Jordan P. Santos

Library of Congress Cataloging-in-Publication Data

Petras, James F., 1937-
  Global depression and regional wars / James Petras.
      p. cm.
  Includes index.
  ISBN-13: 978-0-932863-68-3
  ISBN-10: 0-932863-68-X
  1. War--Economic aspects. 2. International economic relations--
Political aspects. 3. Capitalism--United States. 4. Zionism--United
States. 5. Imperialism--Economic aspects. 6. United States--Foreign
relations--2009- 7. Israel--Military policy. 8. United States--Foreign
relations--Latin America. 9. Latin America--Foreign relations--United
States. I. Title.

JZ6401.P48 2010
330.9--dc22

                                                    2009024439

                            Clarity Press, Inc.
                   Ste. 469, 3277 Roswell Rd. NE
                          Atlanta, GA. 30305
                                USA
                     http://www.claritypress.com

To Robin Eastman Abaya

ACKNOWLEDGMENTS

I would like to acknowledge the fine editorial support of Diana Collier.

TABLE OF CONTENTS

PART I

GLOBAL DEPRESSION

CHAPTER 1

THE FINANCIAL CRISIS AND WORLD DEPRESSION
A SYSTEMIC PERSPECTIVE

Introduction

All the idols of capitalism over the past three decades have crashed. The assumptions and presumptions, paradigms and prognosis of indefinite progress under liberal free market capitalism have been tested and have failed. We are living the end of an entire epoch: experts everywhere witness the collapse of the US and world financial system, the absence of credit for trade and the lack of financing for investment. A world depression, in which upward of a quarter of the world's labor force will be unemployed, is looming. The biggest decline in trade in recent world history—down 40% year to year—defines the future. The imminent bankruptcies of the biggest manufacturing companies in the capitalist world haunt Western political leaders. The 'market' as a mechanism for allocating resources and the government of the US as the 'leader' of the global economy have been discredited.[1] All the assumptions about 'self-stabilizing markets' are demonstrably false and outmoded. The rejection of public intervention in the market and the advocacy of supply-side economics have been discredited even in the eyes of their practitioners. Even official circles recognize that 'inequality of income' contributed to the onset of the economic crash and should be corrected. Planning, public ownership, nationalization are on the agenda while socialist alternatives have become almost respectable.

With the onset of the depression, all the shibboleths of the past decade are discarded. As export-oriented growth strategies fail, we see the re-emergence (actual and potential) of import substitution policies and the panoply of developmentalist models which had been forced into academic and political obscurity by the IMF-enforced restructuring and Friedmanite economics that have assailed developing countries since the early 1980s. As the world economy 'de-globalizes' and capital is 'repatriated' to save near bankrupt head offices—"national ownership" is proposed. As trillions of dollars/Euros/yen in assets are destroyed and devalued, massive layoffs extend unemployment everywhere. Fear, anxiety and uncertainty stalk the offices of state, financial directorships, management suites of the factories, and the streets...

We enter a time of upheaval, when the foundations of the world political and economic order are deeply fractured, to the point that no one can imagine any restoration of the political-economic order of the recent past. The future promises economic chaos, political upheavals and mass impoverishment. Once again, the specter of socialism hovers over the ruins of the former giants of finance. As free market capital collapses, its ideological advocates jump ship, abandon their line and verse of the virtues of the market and sing a new chorus: the State as Savior of the System—a dubious proposition, whose outcome will not be socialism, but only a prolongation of the pillage of the public treasury and postponement of the death agony of capitalism as we have known it.

The Demise of the Economic Expert

The failed economic policies of political and economic leaders are rooted in the operation of markets—of capitalism, in short. To avoid a critique of the capitalist system itself, writers are blaming the leaders and financial experts for their incompetence, 'greed' and individual defects, or indeed, extending that greed and guilt to cover "all of us".

Psycho-babble has replaced reasoned analysis of structures, material forces and objective reality, which drive, motivate and provide incentives to investors, policy makers and bankers. When capitalist economies collapse, the gods drive the politicians and editorial columnists crazy, depriving them of any capacity to reason about *objective processes* and sending them into the wilderness of subjective speculation.

Instead of examining the real systemic operations of global capitalism—in particular, 1) the processes by which enormous surpluses of capital were accumulated (i.e. the relentless capitalist exploitation of labor and shedding of collateral costs of production onto society at large), and 2) the systemic reasons why capitalist elites channeled this over-accumulation (reinvestment of profits) into the host of opportunity structures fashioned by finance rather than into the real economy (in the US or elsewhere via domestic production or domestic consumption)—we are told the financial crisis was due to 'the failure of leadership'.

Instead of examining the power and influence of the capitalist class over the state, in particular the selection of economic policy makers and regulators, ensuring that they in turn would only promote policies and regulations that would enable the capitalist elite to maximize their profits, we are told there was a 'lack of understanding' or 'willful ignorance of what markets need'.

Instead of looking at the real social classes and class relations—specifically the historically existing capitalist classes operating in real existing markets—the psycho-babblers posit an abstract 'market' populated by imaginary ('rational') capitalists who would never run the system into the ground in a scramble to realize short-term profits.

Instead of examining how rising profits, expanding markets, cheap credit, docile labor, and control over state policies and budgets, *create* 'investor confidence', and, in their absence, *destroy* 'confidence', the psycho-babblers claim that the 'loss of confidence' is a cause for the economic debacle. The *objective* problem of how confidence is tied to specific conditions, and how the loss of confidence is tied to the loss of these material conditions, is turned into perception of the shaken investor as the *cause* of this loss.

Confidence, faith, hope, and trust in capitalist economies derive from economic relations and structures which produce profits—when these in fact do produce profits. These psychological states are derivative from and dependent on successful outcomes: economic transactions, investments and market shares that raise value, multiply present and future gains. But when investments go sour, firms lose money, enterprises go bankrupt, and those prejudiced 'lose confidence' in the owners and brokers, when entire economic sectors severely prejudice the entire class of investors, depositors and borrowers—there is a loss of 'systemic confidence.'

Psycho-babble is the last resort of capitalist ideologues, academics, experts and financial page editorialists. Unwilling to face the breakdown of real existing capitalist markets, they write and resort to vague utopias such as 'proper markets' distorted by 'certain mindsets'. In other words, to save their failed ideology which is based on capitalist markets, they invent a moral ideal which is required to be resident in the individual and collective mindsets of the system's participants: the 'proper capitalist mind and market', divorced from real behavior, economic imperatives and contradictions embedded in class warfare. Now, it's all about *attitude!*

The inadequate and shoddy economic arguments, which pervade the writing of capitalist ideologues, parallel the bankruptcy of the social system in which they are embedded. The intellectual and moral failures of the capitalist class and their political followers are not personal defects; they reflect the economic failure of the capitalist market.

The crash of the US financial system is symptomatic of a deeper and more profound collapse of the capitalist system that has its roots in the dynamic development of capitalism over the previous three decades. In its broadest terms, the current world depression results from the classic formulation outlined by Karl Marx over 150 years ago: the contradiction between the development of the forces and relations of production.

Contrary to the theorists who argue that the nub of the problem is that 'finance' and 'post-industrial' capitalism have 'destroyed' or de-industrialized the US economy and put in its place a kind of "casino" or speculative capital, in fact, we have witnessed the most spectacular long-term growth of industrial capital, globally employing more industrial and salaried workers than ever in history. Driven by rising rates of profit, large scale and long-term investments have been the motor force for the penetration by industrial and related capital of the most remote underdeveloped regions of the world. New and old capitalist countries have spawned enormous economic empires, breaking down the political barriers of states and the cultural barriers of peoples to incorporate and exploit billions of new and old workers in a relentless process. As competition from the newly-industrialized countries intensified, and as the rising mass of profits exceeded the capacity to reinvest them most profitably in the older capitalist centers, masses of capital migrated to Asia, Latin America, Eastern Europe, and to a lesser degree, into the Middle East and Southern Africa to reap the greatest gain or (as explained to abandoned first-world workers) to remain competitive.

Huge surplus profits spilled over into services, including finance, real estate, insurance, large-scale real estate and urban lands, driving up prices and creating bubbles everywhere.

The dynamic growth of capitalism's technological innovations found expression in its greater social and political power—dwarfing the organization of labor, limiting its bargaining power and multiplying its profits. With the growth of world markets, domestic workers were seen merely as 'costs of production' not as final consumers upon whose purchasing power sales depended. Wages stagnated; social benefits were limited, curtailed or shifted onto workers. Under conditions of dynamic capitalist growth, the state and state policy became their absolute instrument: restrictions, controls, regulation were weakened. With the heads of multinationals at the helm of government, the process dubbed "neo-liberalism" opened new areas for investment of surplus profits: public enterprises, land, resources and banks were privatized.

As competition intensified, as new industrial powers emerged in Asia, US capital increasingly invested in financial activity. The financial circuits elaborated a whole series of financial instruments, which enticed investment from the growing wealth and profits generated by the productive sectors by offering even higher returns.

US capital did not 'de-industrialize' – it *relocated* to China, Korea and other centers of growth, not because of "falling profits" but because of surplus profits and greater profits overseas.

Capital's opening in China provided hundreds of millions of workers with jobs subject to the most brutal exploitation at subsistence wages, with no social benefits, little or no organized social power. A new class of Asian capitalist collaborators, nurtured and facilitated by Asian state capitalism, increased the enormous volume of profits. Rates of investments reached dizzying proportions, given the vast inequalities between the income/ property owning class and wageworkers. Huge surpluses accrued but internal demand was sharply constrained through state repression. Exports, export growth and overseas consumers became the driving force of the Asian economies. US and European manufacturers invested in Asia to export back to their home markets—shifting the structure of internal capital toward commerce and finance, and domestic purchasing power toward credit card debt. Diminished wages paid to the workers led to a vast expansion in the ability of banks to sell debt, billed as "credit". Financial activity grew in proportion to the entrance of commodities from the dynamic, newly industrialized countries. Industrial profits were re-invested in financial services or in Treasurys, facilitating the government's ongoing pursuit of war. Profits and liquidity grew in proportion to the relative decline in real value generated by the shift from industrial to financial/commercial capital. Super profits from world production, trade, finances and the recycling of overseas earnings back to the US through both state and private financial circuits created enormous liquidity. It was far beyond the historical capacity of the US and European economies to absorb such profits in productive sectors.

The dynamic and voracious exploitation of the huge surplus labor forces in China, India, and elsewhere and the absolute pillage and transfer of hundreds of billions from ex-communist Russia and 'neo-liberalized' Latin America filled the coffers of new and old financial institutions.

Over-exploitation of labor in Asia, and the over-accumulation of financial liquidity in the US led to the magnification of the paper economy and what liberal economists later called "global disequilibrium" between savers/industrial investors/ exporters (in Asia) and consumers (debtors)/ financiers/importers (in the US). Huge trade surpluses in the East were papered over by their purchase of US T-notes. The US economy was precariously backed by an increasingly inflated paper economy.

The expansion of the financial sector resulted from the high rates of return the 'liberalized' global economy imposed by the power of diversified investment capital in previous decades through its instruments, the International Monetary Fund and World Trade Organization. The internationalization of capital, its dynamic growth and the enormous growth of trade outran the stagnant wages and declining social payments from exploitation of the now huge surplus labor force. Seeking to maintain the high rates of return to which investors had become accustomed, finance capital sought to bolster its profits via inflated real estate based on expanded credit, highly leveraged debt and outright massive fraudulent 'financial instruments' (collateralized debt obligations bundling securitized mortgages whose actual value could not be ascertained by investors) The collapse of the paper economy exposed the overdeveloped financial system and forced its demise. In quick order, many of the major investment banks of the western world, and notably in the United States, Merrill Lynch, Lehman Brothers, Bank of America, Bear Sterns and others, deflated, restructured, collapsed or were absorbed.

The loss of finance, credit and markets reverberated through all the export-oriented industrial manufacturing powers. The lack of social consumption that resulted from application of the neo-liberal prescription and the resultant weakness of internal markets globally denied the industrial countries any compensatory markets to stabilize or limit their fall into recession and depression. The dynamic growth of the productive forces based on the over-exploitation of labor, led to the overdevelopment of the financial circuits, which set in motion the process of 'feeding off' industry and subordinating and redirecting the accumulation process towards highly speculative capital.

Cheap labor—the primary source of profits, investment, trade and export growth on a world scale—could no longer sustain both the pillage by finance capital and provide a market for the dynamic industrial sector. What was erroneously dubbed a financial crisis or even more narrowly at first a "mortgage", "sub-prime lending" or housing crisis, was merely the "trigger" for the collapse of the overdeveloped financial sector, awash in derivatives and credit default swaps, and a host of mechanisms which had become directed toward speculation rather than the management and insurance of real production. As a result, the financial sector, which grew out of the dynamic expansion of 'productive' capitalism, later 'rebounded' against it. But it was the historic links and global ties between industry and financial capital that led inevitably to a systemic capitalist crisis; the crisis was embedded in the contradiction between impoverished labor and concentrated capital. The current world depression is a product of the 'over-accumulation' process of the capitalist system in which the crash of the financial system was the 'detonator' but not the structural determinant: the exploitation of labor. This is demonstrated by the fact that industrial Japan and Germany experienced a bigger fall in exports, investments and growth than 'financial' US and England

According to free market theorists: the capitalist system in crisis destroys capital in order to 'purge itself' of the least efficient, least competitive and most indebted enterprises and sectors, in order to re-concentrate capital and reconstruct the powers of accumulation. However, free market ideology aside, in the real world, political conditions permitting, this re-composition of capital grows out of the pillage of state resources—so-called bailouts and other massive transfers from the public treasury (read 'taxpayers'), *which results from* the savage reduction of social transfers (read 'public services') and the cheapening of labor through firings, massive unemployment, wage, pension and health reductions and the general reduction of living standards in order to increase the rate of profit.

THE WORLD DEPRESSION: A CLASS ANALYSIS

The aggregate economic indicators of the rise and fall of the world capitalist system are of limited value in understanding the causes, trajectory and impact of the world depression. At best, they describe the economic carnage; at worst, they obfuscate the role of the leading (ruling) social classes, with their complex networks and transformations, which put into place the global trade and financial architecture, directed the neoliberal expansion and then managed the resultant economic collapse and the role of the wage and salaried (working) classes, which produced the wealth to fuel the expansive phase and now pay the cost of the economic collapse. It is a well-known truism that those who caused the crisis are also those who have been the greatest beneficiaries of government largesse. The crude and simple everyday observation that the ruling class 'made' the crisis and the working class 'pays' the cost, at a minimum, is an implicit recognition of the utility of class analyses in deciphering the social reality behind the aggregate economic data.

From Over-Accumulation to the Dominance of Finance Capital

Following the recession of the early 1970s, the Western industrial capitalist class secured financing to launch a period of extensive and deep growth covering the entire globe. German, Japanese and Southeast Asian capitalists flourished, competed and collaborated with their US counterparts. Throughout this period the social power, organization and political influence of the working class witnessed a relative and absolute decline in its share of material income. Technological innovations, including the re-organization of work, compensated for wage increases by reducing the 'mass of workers' and in particular, their capacity to pressure the prerogatives of management. The capitalist strategic position in the management of production was strengthened: they were able to exercise near absolute control over the location and movements of capital.

The established capitalist powers—especially in England and the US—with large accumulations of capital and facing increasing competition from the fully recovered German and Japanese capitalists, sought to expand their rates of return by moving capital investments into finance and services. At first, this move was linked and directed towards promoting the sale of their manufactured products by providing credit and financing toward the domestic purchases of automobiles or 'white goods'. Less dynamic industrial capitalists relocated their assembly plants to low-wage regions and countries.

The result was that industrial capitalists took on more of the appearance of 'financiers' in the US even as they retained their industrial character in the operation of their overseas manufacturing subsidiaries and satellite suppliers. Both overseas manufacturing and local financial returns swelled the aggregate profits of the capitalist class. While capital accumulation expanded in the 'home country', domestic wages and social costs were under pressure as capitalists imposed the costs of competition on the backs of wage earners via the collaboration of the trade unions in the US and social democratic political parties in Europe. Wage constraints, tying wages to productivity in an asymmetrical way and labor-capital pacts increased profits. US workers were 'compensated' by the cheap consumer imports produced by the low-wage labor force in the newly industrializing countries and access to easy credit at home.

The Western pillage of the former-USSR, with the collaboration of gangster-oligarchs, led to the massive flow of looted capital into Western banks throughout the 1990s. The Chinese transition to capitalism in the 1980s, which accelerated in the 1990s, expanded the accumulation of industrial profits via the intensive exploitation of tens of millions of wageworkers employed at subsistence levels. While the trillion-dollar pillage of Russia and the entire former Soviet Union bloated the West European and US financial sector, the massive growth of billions of dollars in illegal transfers and money laundering toward US and UK banks added to the overdevelopment of the financial sector.

The rise in oil prices and 'rents' among 'rentier' capitalists added a vast new source of financial profits and liquidity. Pillage, rents, and contraband capital provided a vast accumulation of financial wealth disconnected from industrial production. On the other hand, the rapid industrialization of China and other Asian countries provided a vast market for German and Japanese high-end manufacturers: they supplied the high quality machines and technology to the Chinese and Vietnamese factories. US capitalists did not 'de-industrialize'—they de-industrialized *the United States*. By relocating production overseas, importing finished products and focusing on credit and financing in order to achieve domestic sales, the US capitalist class and its members became diversified and multi-sectoral. They multiplied their profits and intensified the accumulation of capital, even as they fled US taxation.

On the other hand, workers were subject to multiple forms of exploitation: wages stagnated, creditors squeezed interest, and the conversion from high wage/high skill manufacturing jobs to lower-paid service jobs steadily reduced living standards.

The basic process leading up to the breakdown was clearly present: the dynamic growth of western capitalist wealth was based, in part, on the brutal pillage of the USSR and Latin America, which profoundly lowered living standards throughout the 1990s. The intensified and savage exploitation of hundreds of millions of low-paid Chinese, Mexican, Indonesian and Indochinese workers, and the forced exodus of former peasants as migrant laborers to manufacturing centers led to high rates of accumulation. The relative decline of wages in the US and Western Europe also added to the accumulation of capital. The German, Chinese, Japanese, Latin American and Eastern European emphasis on export-driven growth added to the mounting 'imbalance' or contradiction between concentrated capitalist wealth and ownership and the growing mass of low-paid workers. Inequalities on a world scale grew geometrically. The dynamic accumulation process exceeded the capacity of the highly polarized capitalist system to absorb capital in productive activity at existing high rates of profit. This led to the large scale and multiform growth of speculator capital in order to maintain the same rate of return to which investors had become addicted, leading to massive investment and price inflation in real estate and commodities, and a range of financial restructuring related to hedge funds, securities, debt-financing, mergers and acquisitions—all divorced from real value-producing activity.

Speculator-financial activity with massive liquidity offered a 'short-term solution': profits based on debt financing. Competition among lenders fueled the availability of cheap credit. Real estate speculation was extended into the working class, as wage and salaried workers, without personal savings or assets, took advantage of their access to easy loans to join the speculator-induced frenzy—based on an ideology of irreversible rising home values.

The inevitable collapse reverberated throughout the system—detonated by failures to make debt payments first occurring at the bottom of the speculative chain. From the latest entrants to the real estate sub-prime mortgage holders, the crisis moved up the ladder affecting the biggest banks and corporations, all of whom had been deeply engaged in leveraged buyouts and acquisitions. All 'sectors', which had 'diversified' from manufacturing to finance, trade and commodities speculation, were downgraded. The entire panoply of capitalists—both industrial and financial—faced bankruptcy, as German, Japanese and Chinese industrial exporters who exploited labor witnessed the collapse of their export markets.

Indicators of the Onset of Depression

Indicators of the deepening depression in 2009 are found everywhere:

- There were 330,477 filings in the January-to-March 2009 period, up 10 percent from the previous quarter and up 35 percent from a year earlier, the Administrative Office of the U.S. Courts said this week. Consumer bankruptcy filings rose 33 percent from a year earlier, while business filings rose 64 percent.[2]

- The International Monetary Fund (IMF) said on April 21, 2009 that banks around the globe will need to write down about $4.1 trillion in loans and securities. So far, about one-third of that amount has been written down.[3]
- The losses arising from banks having to mark their investments down to market prices stand at 3 Trillion dollars—equivalent to a year's worth of British economic production.[4]
- Financial *assets* worldwide have *fallen* by more than $50 trillion—a figure of the same order as *annual global output*.[5]
- The face value of all derivatives contracts across the world a measure that counts the value of a derivative's underlying assets outstanding at the end of last year (2008) totaled more than $680 trillion, according to the Bank for International Settlements in Switzerland. The biggest banks and brokerage firms, including JPMorgan Chase, Citigroup and Goldman Sachs, as well as major insurers, are all major players in derivatives.[6]
- For 2009, the US will run a budget deficit of 12.3% of gross domestic product…giant fiscal deficits…that will ultimately ruin public finances.

The world markets have been in a vertical fall:

- The TOPIX has fallen from 1800 in mid-2007 to 700 in early 2009.
- Standard and Poor from 1380 in early 2008 to below 700 in 2009.
- FTSE 100 from 6600 to 3600 in early 2009.
- Hang Seng from 32,000 in early 2008 to 13,000 at the start of 2009.[7]
- In the fourth quarter of 2008, GDP shrank at annualized rate of 20.8% in South Korea, 12.7% in Japan, 8.2% in Germany, 2.9% in the UK and 3.8% in the US.[8]
- The Dow Jones Industrial Average has declined from 14,164 in October 2007 to 6600 in March 2009.
- Year on year declines in industrial output were 21% in Japan, 19% in South Korea, 12% in Germany, 10% in the US, and 9% in the UK.[9]
- Net private capital flows to less developed capitalist countries from the imperial countries were predicted to shrink by 82% and credit flows by $30 billion USD.[10]
- The US economy declined by 6.2% in the last three months of 2008 and fell further in the first quarter of 2009 as a result of a sharp decline in exports (23.6%) and consumer spending (4.3%) in the final quarter of 2008.[11]

With over 600,000 workers losing their jobs monthly in the first three months of 2009, and many more on short hours and scheduled for axing throughout 2009, real and disguised unemployment may reach 25% by the end of the year. All of the signs point to a deep and prolonged depression:

- Automobile sales of General Motors, Chrysler and Ford were down nearly 50% year to year (2007-2008). The first quarter of 2009 saw a further decline of 50%. General Motors and Chrysler have since gone into bankruptcy.
- Foreign markets are drying up as the depression spreads overseas.
- In the US domestic market, durable goods sales are declining by 22%.[12]
- Residential investments fell by 23.6% and business investment was down 19.1%, led by a 27.8% drop in equipment and software.
- Since the recession began in December 2007, 5.7 million jobs have been lost. In April, job losses were large and widespread across nearly all major private-sector industries. Overall, private-sector employment fell by 611,000. (May 8, 2009)[13]

The rising tide of depression is driven by private business-led disinvestment. Rising business inventories, declining investment, bankruptcies, foreclosures, insolvent banks, massive accumulative losses, restricted access to credit, falling asset values and a 20% reduction in household wealth (over 3 trillion dollars) are cause and consequence of the depression. As a result of collapse of the industrial, mining, real estate and trade sectors, there are at least $2.2 trillion USD of "toxic" (defaulting) bank debt worldwide, far beyond the bailout funds allocated by the White House in October 2008 and February and March 2009. But if you take into account the credit default swaps which may be tied purely to speculation (where the owners of CDS don't even own assets whose standing they purport to be "insuring"), these have created a much huger more insurmountable hole, if these contracts are to be upheld. According to Bloomberg, the Fed has already lent or committed $12.8 trillion, an unsupervised /unauthorized by Congress expansion of the money supply, making the government programs insignificant in comparison (except that they incur debt rather than induce inflation).

Regional Impact of the Global Crisis

It has been argued that "economic development outside the process of globalization is no longer possible".[14]   However, a short review of the impact of the global crisis on other regions of the world reveals the disastrous consequences inflicted upon the regions due to their linkage to first world capital and the accelerated processes of de-globalization which are actually in progress, and leads rather to the conviction that "globalization" as an imperial project is presently moribund.

The worldwide depression has both *common and different* causes, affected by the interconnections between economies and specific socio-economic structures. At the most general-global level the rising rate of profits and the over-accumulation of capital leading to the financial/real estate/speculative frenzy and crash affected most countries either directly or indirectly. At the same time, while all regional economies suffered the consequences of the onset of the depression, regions were situated in the world economy differently and subsequently the effects on them varied substantially.

Latin America

With its free market policies in disarray and huge class divisions undermining any domestic recovery, and its high velocity fall in exports and industrial production, Brazil is heading toward a deep recession despite the boasts and claims of Wall Street and the White House favorite, President Lula da Silva.

In January 2009, industrial production fell 17.2% year to year. Gross domestic product contracted 3.6% in the last quarter of 2008.[15] All indications are that negative growth will persist and deepen during the rest of 2009. Foreign direct investment and export markets, the driving forces of past growth, are in sharp retrenchment. Lula's privatization policies have led to extensive foreign takeover of the financial sector, which has transmitted the crises from the US and EU. His 'globalization' policies increase Brazil's vulnerability to the collapse of foreign trade. Capital flows are strongly negative. Hundreds of thousands of workers lost their jobs between December 2008 and April 2009. The 5 million impoverished landless rural workers and the 10 million families living on a one-dollar-a-day food-basket handout from the government are excluded from effective domestic demand as are the tens of millions of minimum wage workers living on $250 dollars a month. The purchasing power of highly indebted family farmers is no substitute for shrinking external demand. All sectors, rural and urban, of the capitalist class are freezing new investments as private credit evaporates, overseas investors flee and local consumer spending declines in the face of the deepening recession. Lula's claims of 'decoupling' and his growth projections of 4% are seen as 'seeding illusions' to cover up the onset of a severe economic recession. Lula's blind support for globalization and the 'free market' is a central determinant of Brazil's deepening recession.

Brazil's descent into negative GDP is the pattern throughout the region. Argentina is headed for –2% growth, Mexico –3% and Chile 0% or less. Central America and the Caribbean, which are highly 'integrated' with the US and world economy are experiencing the full force of the world depression in skyrocketing unemployment resulting from the collapse of tourism, declining demand for primary commodities and a serious drop in remittances from overseas workers. There will be a sharp rise in extreme poverty, crime and a potential for popular social upheavals against the incumbent right and center-left governments.

The spread of imperial capital throughout the world—dubbed 'globalization' by its defenders (and imperialism by its critics)—led to the rapid spread of the financial crisis and breakdown among those countries most closely linked to the US and European financial circuits. Globalization tied Latin American economies to world markets at the expense of domestic markets, and increased their vulnerability to the vertical fall in demand, prices and credit witnessed today. Globalization, which earlier promoted the inflow of capital, now, with the onset of the depression, facilitates massive capital outflow.

The US, which is absorbing 70% of the world's savings in its desperate effort to borrow and finance its monstrous trade and budget deficits, has squeezed out its Latin American trading partners from the global credit market. The depression demonstrates with crystal clarity the pitfalls of imperial-centered globalization and the stark absence of any remedies for its collaborators in Latin America. The disintegration of the imperial-centered global economy is evident amidst rising protectionism and billions of dollars in state subsidies to prop up the imperial states' own capitalists in the banking, insurance, real estate and manufacturing sectors. The world depression not only reveals the intrinsic fault lines of the globalized economy, but ensures its ultimate demise into a multiplicity of competing units: nations, each depending on their own treasuries and state sectors to pull them out of the deepening depression at the expense of their former partners. The world depression is spurring the return of the nation-state, as 'de-globalization' accelerates.

Parallel and intimately related to the demise of the world market is the rise of the *capitalist state* as the center-piece for salvaging the national treasury and exacting an exorbitant tribute from the pension, health and wage funds of billions of workers, pensioners and tax-payers. Growing '*state capitalism*' in times of capitalist collapse only emerges to '*save the capitalist system from capitalist failures*' as its promoters argue. In order to do so it exploits the collective wealth of the entire people. '*Nationalization*' or '*statification*' of insolvent banks and industries is the culmination of predator capitalism—not the opening steps of a progression towards socialism. Instead of individual enterprises or even sectoral exploitation of wage and salaried workers, it is now the *capitalist state* that preys on the entire class of the producers of wealth.

Latin America's options revolve around recognizing and accepting that *globalization is dead*, that only under popular democratic control can nationalization function with a socialist orientation, with a view to generating wealth and creating employment, instead of serving to channel and redistribute resources upward and outward to the failed, bankrupt capitalist class in the developed countries.

Eastern Europe and the Ex-communist Countries

The conversion from communism to capitalism in Eastern Europe followed a process of privatization, in many cases based on widespread pillage, the illegal seizures of public resources and the precipitous fall in domestic living standards and production during the first half of the 1990s. Taking advantage of cheap labor and easy access to lucrative opportunities in all economic sectors, Western European and US capitalists took control of the manufacturing, mining, financial and communication sectors. At the same time as the barriers between East and West fell, there was a massive flow of skilled workers to Western Europe. The economic recovery and subsequent growth in Eastern Europe and the ex-communist countries was based on its dependency on the expansion of investment and credit from Western capitalism. The relocation of manufacturing, the influx of specu-lative capital in finance and real estate, the access to expanding Western markets and especially *debt financing* of consumer expenditures, which spurred Eastern growth.

As a consequence, the region has been hit from two sides during the economic crisis: unsustainable *internal speculation* and dependency on a depressed Western Europe for capital, credit and markets. The capitalist economies of the Baltic States, Eastern Europe and Russia collapsed rapidly. As Western European credit markets shriveled and large-scale multi-national disinvestment set in, the local currencies were devalued and their overseas markets disappeared. The entire pattern of 'dependent development' rooted in the disarticulation of local markets and inflows of capital undermined local efforts to counter the collapse. Their only choice was to seek massive infusions of financial aid from the IMF and banks on onerous terms, which limited options for any national fiscal stimulus plans. The regions' linkages with world markets, based on subordinate-dependent relations with Western capitalists, meant that first they lacked the internal markets and capital to cushion the fall and secondly, that the drying up of external flows would deepen and extend the depression. From the Baltic to the Balkan states, from Eastern Europe to Russia, the full force of the depression has led to large-scale, long-term unemployment, widespread bankruptcies of local satellite and subsidiary industries, services and banks.

Popular movements have emerged calling into question the free market policies of governments, and, in some cases, rejecting the export-dependent capitalist model.

Asia: The End of the Illusions of De-coupling and Autonomous Growth

The Great Depression of 2009 has adversely affected every economy in Asia, dependent on the international, financial and commodity markets. Even the most dynamic countries, like Japan, China, India, South Korea, Taiwan and Vietnam, have not escaped the consequences of drastic declines in trade, employment, investment and living standards. Two decades of dynamic expansion, high growth, and rising profit margins based on export markets and intense exploitation of labor, led to the over-accumulation of capital. Many Asian and Western pundits argued for a 'new world order', led and directed by the emerging Asian economic powers, especially China, where power would be increasingly based on their purported 'regional autonomy'. In reality, China's dynamic industrial growth was deeply embedded in a world commodity chain in which advanced industrial countries, like Germany, Japan, Taiwan and South Korea, provided precision tools, machinery and parts to China for assembly and subsequent export to US, European and Asian markets. 'Decoupling' was a myth.

Export-driven growth was fueled by savage exploitation of labor, the dismantling of vast areas of social services (namely free health care, pensions, subsidized food and lodging and education) and the extensive concentration of wealth in a tiny elite of newly rich billionaires.[16] China and the rest of Asia's growth were based on the contradiction between the *dynamic expansion of the forces of production* and the increasing *polarization of the class relations of production*. The high rates of profit led to high rates of investment and the over-accumulation of capital leading to huge budget and trade surpluses, which spilled over into the financial sectors, overseas expansion (or money-laundering) and real estate speculation.

Asia's economic edifice was precariously situated on the backs of hundreds of millions of laborers with virtually no consumer power and an increasing dependence on overseas export markets. The world crisis especially deflated the export markets, exposing the Asian economies' vulnerabilities and causing a massive fall in trade, production and a huge growth in unemployment. China and the other Asian countries' efforts to counteract the collapse of the export markets by massive injections of public capital to stimulate financial liquidity and infrastructure development has been insufficient to stem the growth of unemployment and the bankruptcy of millions of export-linked enterprises. The Asian capitalist classes and their government elites are entirely incapable of 'restructuring' the economy and social structure toward substituting domestic demand as the external market collapses. To do so would mean several profound transformations in the class structure. These include the shift from investments based on high profitability toward low profit margin productive and social services for the hundreds of millions of low-income workers and peasants. It would require the transfer of capital back from private real estate, stock markets and overseas bond purchases (like US Treasury Notes) where it presently resides, to finance universal health care, education and pensions and the restoration of land to productive use rather than to dispossession and real estate speculation.

The entire dynamic growth of Asia, built around capital concentration, high profits and low wages, is trying to survive based on deepening the impoverishment of labor via massive firing of workers, huge reverse flows of migrant labor back to the devastated countryside and the growth of the surplus labor force. The expulsion of labor, the usual capitalist solution, merely re-locates and intensifies the contradiction—heightening the conflict between urban-based industrial/finance capital and hundreds of millions of impoverished, unemployed and underemployed workers and peasants. The state's injections of capital to stimulate the economy passes through the 'filter' of regional state elites and the capitalist class, which absorbs and uses the bulk of this capital to buttress faltering enterprises—with negligible impact on the mass of unemployed workers.

Private ownership and capitalist control over the state precludes the kind of social transformation, which can restart growth by expanding the domestic economy.

China's present slowdown has, by necessity, weakened its trading partners who depend on industrial and raw material exports to China. The collapse of demand from its Euro-American markets adversely affects the architecture of China's export industries. The savage exploitation of labor and the power of China's new bourgeoisie ensure that there are limited possibilities for any revival of domestic demand from the 'interior'.

China's economic recovery is dependent on a new socialist transformation, which makes mass domestic demand the real engine of growth.

The Middle East: Depression and Regional Wars

The key to the crisis and breakdown of the Middle East is rooted in the imperial-Zionist regional wars and the collapse of commodity prices.

The oil producing countries accumulated vast 'rents', which they re-cycled into large-scale finance, real estate and military purchases in and out of the region. Profits concentrated in the hands of billionaire absolutist rulers led to highly polarized class relationships: super-wealthy rentiers and low-paid immigrant laborers limited the size and scope of the domestic markets. To break out of the crisis of over-accumulation and falling profits, the ruling elites adopted two strategies that temporarily avoided the crisis: large-scale export of capital to rent, interest and dividend-yielding sites throughout the world—first to the US and Europe and later to Asia and Africa—and the recycling of profits into real estate, tourist and banking centers of pharaonic scale and splendor in the Gulf States...leading to an enormous real estate bubble.

The collapse of the Middle East 'rentier (or non-productive) oligarchies' began with the frenzied commodity oil boom between 2004-2008, which heightened a construction and real estate boom—and the accumulation of debt and labor importation. The result was the onset of a regional economic crisis, in which budget and trade surpluses were replaced by mounting deficits. At no point did the Middle East economies diversify from their foundation based on 'rents' and create a diversified economy centered on production and the creation of a dynamic mass-based regional market. The rentier ruling classes face a growing mass of unemployed domestic and immigrant workers (who will likely be sent home), and the massive flight of thousands of expatriate European financiers, real estate professionals and other non-productive hangers-on.

No longer the beneficiaries of the petro-dollar boom—as prices, profits and rents collapsed—and no longer the powerful bankers and holders of debt, the Gulf Arab ruling class has few external and internal resources and outlets to project a 'recovery program' for the immediate future.

Worse still, in the midst of this emerging economic collapse, the militarist state of Israel serves as a regional destabilizing force projecting its power and colonial ambitions throughout the region. Through one of world history's most unique configuration of power, the economically insignificant state of Israel, operating through the activity of several tens of thousands of strategically-placed, highly organized, disciplined and ideologically committed loyalists in the Diaspora, control key levels of political power in the US government.

An Unprecedented Crisis

The depression is diminishing the worldwide economic presence of imperial countries and undermining the foreign capital-financed export strategies of Latin American, Eastern European, Asian and African regions. Among almost all conventional economists, pundits, investment advisors and various and sundry experts and economic historians, there is a common faith that "in the long-run", the stock market will recover, the recession will end and the government will withdraw from the economy. Fixed on notions of past cyclical patterns, historical 'trends', these analysts lose sight of the present realities which have no precedent: the world nature of the economic depression, the unprecedented speed of the fall, and the levels of debt incurred by governments to sustain insolvent banks and industries, leading to unprecedented public deficits, which will drain resources for many generations to come.

The academic prophets of 'long-term developments" arbitrarily select trend markers from the past, which were established on the basis of a political-economic context radically different from today. The idle chatter of 'post crisis' economists overlooks the open-ended and constantly shifting parameters, therefore missing the true 'trend markers' of the current depression. As one analyst noted, "any starting conditions we select in the historical data cannot replicate the starting conditions at any other moment because the preceding events in the two cases are never identical".[17] The current US depression takes place in the context of a de-industrialized economy, an insolvent financial system, record fiscal deficits, record trade deficits, unprecedented public debt, multi-trillion dollar foreign debt and well over $800 billion dollars committed in military expenditures for several ongoing wars and occupations. All of these variables defy the contexts in which previous depressions occurred.

Nothing in previous contexts leading up to a crisis of capitalism resembles the present situation. The present configuration of economic, political and social structures of capitalism include astronomical levels of state pillage of the public treasury in order to prop up insolvent banks and factories, involving unprecedented transfers of income from wage and salaried taxpayers to non-productive 'rent earners' and to failed industrial capitalists, dividend collectors and creditors. The rate and levels of appropriation and reduction of savings, pensions and health plans—all without any compensation—has led to the most rapid and widespread reduction of living standards and mass impoverishment in recent US history.

Never in the history of capitalism has a deep economic crisis occurred without any alternative socialist movement, party or state present to pose an alternative. Never have states and regimes been under such absolute control by the capitalist class—especially in the allocation of public resources. Never in the history of an economic depression has so much of government expenditures been so one-sidedly directed towards compensating a failed capitalist class with so little going to wage and salaried workers.

The Obama regime's economic appointments and policies clearly reflect the total control by the capitalist class over state expenditures and economic planning.

THE FAILURE TO ADDRESS THE STRUCTURAL BASIS OF THE CRISIS

The programs put forth by the US, West Europeans and other capitalist regions do not even begin to recognize the structural bases of the depression.

First, Obama is allocating huge resources to buy worthless bank assets. Over 40% of his $787 billion stimulus package goes to insolvent banks and tax breaks in order to save stock and bond holders, rather than to the productive sector, where almost 600,000 workers are losing their jobs monthly. At the same time, the Obama regime is channeling over $800 billion dollars to fund the wars in Iraq and Afghanistan to sustain military-driven empire building. This constitutes a massive transfer of public funds from the civilian economy to the military sector forcing tens of thousands of unemployed young people to enlist in the military.[18]

Instead of seeking to support the productive sector or otherwise address the structural problem reflected in the flight of manufacturing from the US, Obama's commission to oversee the "restructuring" of the US auto industry has backed their plans to close scores of factories, eliminate company-financed health plans for retirees and force tens of thousands of workers to accept brutal reductions in employee health care and pensions. The entire burden for returning the privately owned auto industry to profitability is placed on the shoulders of the wage, salaried and retired workers, and the US taxpayers. Obama's regime avoids any direct state investments in publicly owned productive enterprises, which would provide employment for the 10 million unemployed workers—even as he is accused of "socialism" for taking on non-voting shares in banks.

Obama's 'job creation' scheme channels billions toward the privately owned telecommunication, construction, environmental and energy corporations, where the bulk of the government funds go to salaries and bonuses for senior management and staff and provide profits to stock holders, while a lesser part will go to wage workers. Moreover, the bulk of the unemployed workers in the manufacturing and service areas are not remotely employable in the 'recipient' sectors. Only a fraction of the 'stimulus package' will be allocated in 2009, and even so, it's real purpose and impact will be to sustain the income of the financial and industrial ruling class and to postpone their long-overdue demise, rather than to stimulate productive growth in the US or at least address the reduction of this sector as a source for employment.

Its effect will be to heighten the socioeconomic inequalities between the ruling class and the wage and salaried workers. The tax increases on the rich are incremental, while the massive debts resulting from the fiscal deficits are imposed on present and future wage and salaried taxpayers.

The Obama regime has even failed to effectively re-regulate Wall Street in the areas that were most pernicious: derivatives, credit default swaps.[20] Structurally, while there may be a return to greater regulation of existing systemic processes, this will not address the fundamental problems related to the US economy—the manufacturing sector. Re-regulation of the financial sector is insufficient to get the US economy back in gear, presuming that meaningful regulation would/could even be introduced by his Goldman Sachs appointees.

Obama's wholehearted embrace and promotion of military-driven empire building even in the midst of record-breaking budget deficits, huge trade deficits and an advancing depression defines a militarist without peer in modern history—by actions even if inclination is denied. Despite promises to the contrary, the military budget for 2009-2010 exceeds that of the Bush Administration by at least 4%. The numbers of US military forces will increase by several hundred thousands, facilitated by the desperation of huge numbers of unemployed youth. The number of US troops in Iraq will remain close to its peak and increase by tens of thousands in Afghanistan, at least through 2009 (despite promises to the contrary). US-based military air and ground attacks in Pakistan have multiplied geometrically. Obama's top foreign policy appointees in the State Department, Pentagon, Treasury and the National Security Council, especially in any capacity involving the Middle East, are predominantly militarist Zionists with a long history of advocacy of war against Iran and with close ties with the Israeli high command.

In summary, the *highest priorities* of the Obama regime are evidenced by his actual allocation of the bulk of financial and material resources to restoring the liquidity of the banks and expanding military appropriations (despite the fillips to public needs such as projects to computerize health care, develop wind and solar power, and doubling funding of Charter schools)—whether through budget or special appropriations, or a failure to rein in the Federal Reserve—and his appointments of top economic and foreign policy-makers. These make clear which classes or interests (Israel) benefit and which lose under his administration. Obama's policies demonstrate that his regime is totally committed to saving the capitalist class and the US empire. To do so, he is willing to sacrifice the most basic immediate needs and future interests, as well as the living standards, of the vast majority of working and home-owning Americans who are most directly affected by the domestic economic depression. Obama has increased the scope of military-driven empire building and enhanced the power position of the pro-Israeli warmongers in his administration.

However, Obama's 'economic recovery' and military escalation strategies are financially and fiscally incompatible; the cost of each undermines the impact of the other and together they preclude any serious efforts to counteract the collapse of social services, rising home foreclosures, business bankruptcies and massive layoffs.

The horizontal transfers of public wealth from the Obama governing elite to the economic ruling class does not "trickle down" into jobs, credit and social services. Attempting to turn insolvent banks into credit-lending, profitable enterprises is an oxymoron. *The central dilemma for Obama is how to create conditions to restore profitability to the failed sectors of the existing US economy.*

WHAT IS NEEDED FOR RECOVERY

There are several fundamental problems with Obama's strategy:

First, the US economic structure, which once generated employment, profits and growth, no longer exists. It has been dismantled in the course of diverting capital overseas and into financial instruments and other non-productive economic sectors.

Secondly, the Obama 'stimulus' policies reinforce the financial stranglehold over the economy by channeling great resources to that sector instead of 'rebalancing' the economy toward the productive sector. Even within the 'productive sector' state resources are directed toward subsiding capitalist elites who have demonstrated their incapacity to generate sustained employment, foster market competitiveness and innovate in line with consumer preferences and interests.

Thirdly, the Obama economic strategy of 'top-down' recovery squanders most of its impact by subsidizing failed capitalists instead of raising working class income by doubling the minimum wage and unemployment benefits, which is the only real basis for increasing demand and stimulating economic recovery. Given the declining living standards resulting from domestic decay and the expansion of military-driven empire, both embedded in the institutional foundation of the state, there are no chances for the kind of structural transformation that can reverse the 'top-down', empire-absorbing policies promoted by the Obama regime. In addition the cheapening of the position of US labor serves to make capital more competitive globally while lowering living standards and purchasing power in the USA.

Recovery from the deepening depression does not reside in running a multi-trillion dollar printing operation, which only creates conditions for hyperinflation and the debasement of the dollar, particularly given the *root cause* is the over-exploitation of labor leading to the over-accumulation of capital resulting from rising rates of profit, which culminated at last in the collapse of demand. The vast disparity between capital expansion and the declining rate of worker consumption set the stage for the financial bubble.

The 'rebalancing' of the economy means:

- Creating demand (not from an utterly prostrate private productive sector or an insolvent financial system) via direct state ownership and long-term, large-scale investment in the production of goods and social services.
- Dismantling the entire financial speculative 'superstructure', which grew to enormous proportions by feeding off of the value created by labor and multiplied itself in a myriad of 'paper instruments' divorced from any use value. The entire paper economy needs to be

dismantled in order to free the productive forces from the shackles and constraints of unproductive capitalists and their entourage. Let banks return to their role of direct savings and lending institutions.

- Establishing a vast re-training program to convert the employees in the FIRE sector into engineers and productive workers, and redirecting the energies of America's best and brightest away from the finance industry.
- Massive dismantling of the US's worldwide military empire. Costly and unproductive military bases, the essential elements for military-driven empire building, should be closed and replaced by overseas trade networks, markets, and economic transactions linked to producers operating out of their home markets. Reversing domestic decay requires the end of empire and the construction of a democratic socialist republic.
- Fundamental to the dismantling of the empire is the end of political alliances with overseas militarist powers, in particular with the state of Israel and uprooting its entire domestic power configuration, which undermine efforts to create an open democratic society serving the interests of the American people (see Part II, Regional Wars).

THE BASIC PRIORITY OF PUBLIC POLICY: A BETTER LIFE FOR ALL

In order to explore the perspectives leading toward socialism in the 21st century, it is essential to recover some of the basic postulates which inform the egalitarian project. In addition, it is important to recover some of the basic advances achieved by 20th century socialist regimes as well as to critically reflect on their distorted structures and failed policies.

In the most basic sense it is important to remember that 'socialism' is a means to a *better material life* than under capitalism: higher living standards, greater political freedom, social equality of conditions, and internal and external security. 'Respect', 'dignity' and 'solidarity' can only be understood as *accompaniments* of these basic material goals, *not* as substitutes which receive only lip-service. 'Respect" and 'dignity' cannot be pursued in the face of long-term, large-scale forced deprivation, sacrifice and delayed fulfillment of material improvement. Governments claiming to be 'socialist' which idealize 'sacrifice' of material living standards in the name of abstract principles of justice, are more akin to 'spiritual socialism' of a religious order rather than to a modern dynamic socialist government.

Social transformations and the replacement of capitalist owners by the socialist state can only be justified if the new order can improve the efficiency, working conditions and responsiveness to consumers of the socialist enterprise. For example, in some socialist regimes, under the guise of a 'revolutionary offensive', the state intervened and eliminated thousands of small and medium-size retail urban enterprises in the name of 'eliminating capitalists'. The result was a disaster. The stores remained closed; the state was incapable of organizing the multitude of small businesses, the great majority of workers were deprived of vital services—and enterprising individuals and thus their society as a whole, were deprived of the opportunity for creative entrepreneurial self-expression and variety (within the context of non-exploitation) which might have added many dimensions of flavorful socio-cultural development to the productive sector.

Twentieth century socialist states built effective and successful medical, educational and security systems to serve the majority of the workers. The majority of socialist states eliminated foreign control and exploitation of natural resources and in some cases developed diversified industrial economies. On the whole living standards rose, crime declined, employment, pensions and welfare were secured. However 20th century socialism was divided by deep contradictions leading to profound systemic crises. Bureaucratic centralism denied freedom at the workplace and restricted public debate and popular governance. Public authority's over-emphasis on 'security' (albeit induced by the conditions of siege and assault maintained against socialist governments by the capitalist world) blocked innovation, entrepreneurship, scientific and popular initiatives leading to technological stagnation and mass passivity. Elite material privileges based on political office led to profound inequalities, which undermined popular belief in socialist principles and led to the spread of capitalist values.

Capitalism thrives on social inequalities; socialism deepens through greater equality. Both capitalism and socialism depend on efficient, productive and innovative workers: The former in order to maximize profits, the latter, per the twentieth century models, to sustaining an expanding welfare state. But is "welfare state" how socialists of the twenty-first century should still conceive of socialism?

Twentieth Century Lessons for 21st Century Socialists

Twenty-first century socialists can learn from the achievements and failures of 20th century socialism.

First: Policies must be directed toward improving the living as well as working conditions of the people. That means massive investment in quality housing, household appliances, public transport, environmental concerns and infrastructure. Overseas solidarity and missions should not take priority over large-scale, long-term investments in expanding and deepening material improvements for the principal internal class base of the socialist regime. Solidarity begins at home. And indeed, it could be argued that this lack of socio-economic development at home has done more, by way of example, to nullify the attractions of socialism for ordinary people who simply seek a better material life than the overseas efforts for which this was sacrificed, have done to promote it.

Second: Development policies should focus on diversifying the economy with a special focus on industrializing the raw material, making major investment in industries producing quality goods of mass consumption (clothing, shoes, and so on) and in agriculture, especially with a view to becoming self-sufficient in basic essential foods. Under no conditions should socialist economies rely on single products for income (sugar, tourism, petroleum, nickel), which are subject to great volatility.

Socialist governments should finance education, income and infrastructure policies, which are compatible with its high economic, social and cultural priorities; this means educating agronomists and skilled agricultural workers, skilled construction workers (plumbers, electricians, painters) and civil engineers, transport workers and urban and rural planners of public housing to decentralize mega-cities and substitute public for private transport. They should set up popularly-elected environment and consumer councils to oversee the quality of air, water and noise levels, and the availability, prices and quality of food.

Twentieth century socialist governments frequently alienated their workers by diverting large of amount of aid to overseas regimes (many of whom were not even progressive!). As a result, local needs were neglected in the name of 'international solidarity'. The first priority of 21st century socialism is *solidarity at home.*

Twentieth century socialists emphasized 'welfare' from above—government as 'giver' and the masses as 'receivers'—discouraging local action and encouraging passivity. Twenty-first century socialism must encourage autonomous class action to counter privileged 'socialist' bourgeois ministers and functionaries who use their office to accumulate and protect private wealth through public power. Autonomous popular organizations can expose the hypocrisy of rich ministers who attack well-paid industrial workers as 'privileged' while riding in chauffeured Mercedes and enjoying luxurious apartments, second and third 'vacation homes' and who send their children to expensive and exclusive schools at home and abroad.

Above all socialism is about social equality: equality in income, schools and hospitals; equality between classes and within classes. But without material equality, all talk of social equality via 'diversity', 'dignity' and 'respect' is meaningless. Capitalists also support 'diversity', as long as it does not affect their profits and wealth. Socialists support income and property equality which effectively re-distributes wealth and property to all workers, white and black, Indian farmer and urban worker, men and women, and young and old. There is no 'dignity' in being poor and exploited; dignity comes with struggle and the achievement of socialist goals of social equality and rising living standards.

Today as President Obama deepens inequalities by pouring trillions into the pockets of bankers while demanding that tens of thousands of autoworkers half their pay and retirees hit the streets with meager pensions, socialism takes on a new relevance as an option for the real change that Americans are now desperately seeking, but have never been effectively offered.

Endnotes

1   *Financial Times,* March 9, 2009
2   "US Bankruptcies Highest Since 2005," Reuters, June 10, 2009.
3   "No Quick Solution to Financial Crisis: IMF", Reuters, April 21, 2009.
4   *Financial Times,* March 10, 2009, p. 9.
5   The Asian Development Bank, as quoted by the *Financial Times,* ibid.
6   Stephen Labaton and Jackie Calmes, "Obama Pushes Broad Rules for Oversight of Derivatives," *New York Times,* May 13, 2009.
7   *Financial Times,* Feb 25, 2009, p. 27.
8   Ibid.
9   Ibid.
10   Ibid.
11   British Broadcasting Corporation, Feb. 27, 2009.
12   Ibid.
13   <http://www.econedlink.org/unemployment>
14   Benn Steill, "The End of National Currency", Foreign Affairs, 2007.
15   *Financial Times,* March 11, 2009.
16   *Economic and Political Weekly,* Mumbai, December 27, 2008 page 27-102.
17   *Financial Times,* Feb. 26, 2009, p. 24.
18   *Boston Globe,* March 1, 2009.
19   See Michael Hirsch, "Wall Street Digs In", *Newsweek,* April 10, 2009.

CHAPTER 2

BERNARD MADOFF: WALL STREET SWINDLER STRIKES POWERFUL BLOWS FOR SOCIAL JUSTICE

"We never thought he would do this to us,
he was one of our people."
Member of Palm Beach Country Club

Wall Street broker Bernard ('Bernie') Madoff, former president of NASDAQ, revered and respected investor confessed to pulling off the biggest fraud in history, a $50 billion dollar scam. Bernie was known for his generous philanthropy, especially to Zionist, Jewish and Israeli causes.

An Introduction to the Mega-Swindle

Wall Street broker Bernard ('Bernie') Madoff, former president of NASDAQ, revered and respected investor confessed to pulling off the biggest fraud in history, a *$50 billion dollar scam*. Bernie was known for his generous philanthropy, especially to Zionist, Jewish and Israeli causes. A one time life-guard on Long Island in the 1960s, Bernie launched his financial career by raising money from colleagues, friends and relatives among wealthier Jews in the Long Island suburbs, Palm Beach, Florida and in Manhattan, promising a modest, steady and secure return of between 10 to 12%, covering returns and any withdrawals in typical Ponzi fashion by drawing on funds from new investors who literally pleaded for Bernie to fleece them. Madoff personally managed at least $17 billion dollars. For almost four decades he built up a clientele, which came to include some of the biggest banks and investment houses in Scotland, Spain, England and France, as well as major hedge funds in the United States. Madoff

41

drew almost all of the funds from high net-worth private clients who were recruited by brokers working on commission. Bernie's clients included many multi-millionaires and billionaires from Switzerland, Israel and elsewhere, as well as the US's largest hedge funds (RMF Division of the Man Group and the Tremont).[1]

Many of the swindled super-rich clients forced their money on Madoff, who sternly imposed rigorous conditions on potential clients: he insisted they have recommendations from existing investors, deposit a substantial amount and guarantee their own solvency. Most considered themselves lucky to have their funds taken by the highly respected Wall Street…swindler. Madoff's standard message was that the fund was closed…but because they came from the same world (the financial community, board members of Jewish charities, pro-Israel fund raising organizations or the 'right' country clubs) or were related to a friend, colleague or existing clients, he would take their money.

Madoff set up advisory councils with distinguished members, contributed heavily to museums, hospitals and upscale cultural organizations. He was a prominent member of exclusive country clubs in Palm Beach and Long Island. His reputation was enhanced by his funds' record of never having a losing year—a big selling point in luring millionaire investors. Madoff shared with his super-rich clients (Jews and Gentiles) a common upper class life style, and mix of cultural philanthropy with low key financial profiteering. Madoff 'played' his colleagues with a soft-spoken but authoritative appearance of 'expertise', enhanced by a veneer of upper class collegiality, deep commitment to Zionism and long-term friendships. Bernie's mega-fund demonstrated many of the same indicators as recent high level scams: the constant high returns, unmatched by any other broker; a lack of third party oversight; a backroom accounting firm physically incapable of auditing the multi-billion dollar operation; broker-dealer operations directly under his thumb and the total obfuscation of what he was actually investing in. The obvious similarities to other fraudsters were overlooked by the rich and famous, the sophisticated investors and high paid consultants, the Harvard MBAs and the entire army of regulators from the Security and Exchange Commission (SEC)[2] because they were totally embedded in the corrupt culture of 'take the money and run' and 'if you're making it, don't ask questions'. The reputation of the superior wisdom of a seemingly successful Jewish Wall Streeter fed into the self-delusions of the wealthy and the stereotypes held by millionaire Gentiles.

The Big Swindle

Madoff's investment fund only dealt with a limited clientele of multi-millionaire and billionaires who kept their funds in for the long haul; the occasional withdrawals were limited in amount and were easily covered by the ongoing solicitation of new funds from new investors fighting to have access to Madoff's money management. The long-term big private investors looked toward passing on their investments to their kin or eventual retirement. The wealthy lawyers, dentists, surgeons, distinguished Ivy League professors and others who might need to draw from their funds for an occasional fancy wedding or celebrity-studded bar-mitzvah, could draw from their funds because Madoff faced no problem in covering the withdrawal.

Madoff was no Robin Hood. His philanthropic and charity contributions facilitated access to the rich and wealthy who served on the boards of the recipient institutions and proved that he was 'one of them', a kind of super-rich 'intimate' of the same elite class. The shock, awe and heart attacks that followed Madoff's confession that he was 'running a Ponzi scheme' reflected anger for the money lost and the fall from the moneyed class as well as the embarrassment of knowing that some of the world's biggest exploiters and smartest swindlers on Wall Street were completely 'taken' by one of their own. Not only did they suffer big losses, but their self-image of themselves as rich because they were so smart and of 'superior stock' was utterly shattered: They saw themselves as suffering the same fate as all the schmucks they had previously swindled, exploited and dispossessed in their climb to the top. There is nothing worse for the ego of a respectable swindler than to be trumped by a bigger swindler. As a result, a number of the biggest losers refused to give their names or the amount they lost, working instead through lawyers to prioritize their claims over other losers.

**The Positive Side of Madoff's Mega-Swindle
(The Inadvertent Hand of Justice)**

While it is understandable that the super-rich and wealthy, who have lost a large portion of their retirement and investment funds are unanimous in their condemnation and cries of betrayal of trust, and the editorials of all the prestigious newspapers and weeklies have joined the chorus of moral critics, there is much to praise in the results flowing from Madoff's deeds, even if such outcomes were not what he had in mind when attracting funds from rich owners of sweat shop garment factories, dangerous meat packing outfits and slumlords.

It is worthwhile to list the inadvertent positive outcomes of Madoff's mega-swindle:

1. The swindle of $50 plus billion dollars may make a big dent on US Zionist funding of illegal Israeli colonial settlements in the Occupied Territories,

lessen funding for AIPAC's purchase of Congressional influence and financing of propaganda campaigns in favor of a pre-emptive US military attack against Iran.[3] Most investors will have to lower or eliminate their purchase of Israel bonds, which subsidize the Jewish State's military budget.

2. The swindle has further discredited the highly speculative hedge funds already reeling from massive withdrawals because of deep losses. Madoff's funds were one of the last 'respected' operations still drawing new investors, but with the latest revelations it may accelerate their demise.   On its webpage on "Pink Slips on Wall Street"[4], *The Deal Magazine* maintains a list of worldwide layoffs in the financial industry that documents the truly shocking extent of the fall-out. Tens—maybe even hundreds—of thousands of dismissed promoters may finally have to perform an honest, productive day's work.

3. Madoff's long-term, large-scale fraud was not detected by the Securities and Exchange Commission (SEC) despite its claims of at least two investigations.More generally, the SEC's failure demonstrates the incapacity or unwillingness of capitalist government regulatory agencies to detect mega frauds. As a result, the regulatory system as a whole suffers from a total loss of credibility. This failure raises the question of whether alternatives to investing in Wall Street are better suited to protect savings and pension funds.

4. Madoff's long-term association with NASDAQ, including his chairmanship while he was defrauding his clients of billions, strongly suggests that the members and leaders of this stock exchange are incapable of recognizing a crook, and are prone to overlook felonious behavior of 'one of their own'. In other words, the investing public can no longer look to holders of high posts in NASDAQ as a sign of probity. After Madoff it may signal time to look for a king-size mattress for safe keeping of what remains of a family's wealth.

5. The investment advisors from top banks in Europe, Asia and the US managing billions of funds simply *could not have* carried out the most elementary due diligence of Madoff's operations, irrespective of the procedural requirements of their own institutions. Apart from severe bank losses, tens of thousands of influential, affluent and super-rich lost their entire accumulated wealth. The result is a total loss of confidence in the leading banks and financial instruments as well as the general discrediting of 'expert knowledge' leading to a weakening of the financial stranglehold over investor behavior and the demise of the world's most prominent investment banks, servicing an important sector of the parasitic 'rentier' class, which gains without producing any useful commodities or providing needed services.

6. Since most of the money stolen by Madoff came from the upper classes around the world, his behavior has reduced inequalities, making Madoff the 'greatest leveler' since the introduction of the progressive income tax. By ruining billionaires and bankrupting millionaires, Madoff has lessened their capacity to use their wealth to influence politicians in their favor—thus increasing the potential political influence of the less affluent sectors of class society...and inadvertently strengthening democracy against the financial oligarchs.

7. By swindling life-long friends, self-same ethno-religious investors, narrow ethnically defined country club members and close family members, Madoff demonstrates that finance capital shows no respect for any of the pieties of everyday life: Great and small, holy and profane, all are subordinated to the rule of capital.

8. Among the many ruined investors in New York and New England, there are a number of mega slumlords (real estate moguls), sweatshop owners (fancy name-brand clothes and toy manufacturers) and others who barely paid the minimum wage to their women and immigrant laborers, evicted poor tenants and swindled employees out of their pensions before moving their operations to China. Madoff's swindle served as a kind of secular 'divine' retribution for past and present crimes against labor and the poor. Needless to say, this 'unconscious Robin Hood' did not redistribute the money fleeced from the employers to their workers, he reinvested part of it in charities which enhanced his philanthropic image and the payout to some of his early investors to sustain the overall Ponzi scam.

9. Madoff struck a severe blow against anti-Semites who claim that there is a 'close-knit Jewish conspiracy to defraud the Gentiles', laying that canard to rest once and for all. Among Bernard Madoff's principle victims were his closest Jewish friends and colleagues, people who shared Seder meals and frequented the same upscale temples in Long Island and Palm Beach. Bernie was discriminating in accepting clients, but it was on the basis of their wealth and not their national origin, race, religion or sexual preference. He was very ecumenical and a strong backer of globalization. There was nothing ethnocentric about Madoff: He defrauded the Anglo-Chinese bank HSBC of $1 billion dollars and several billions from the Dutch arm of the Belgian bank, Fortes. $1.4 billion came from the Royal Bank of Scotland, the French bank BNP Paribas, the Spanish bank, Banco Santander, the Japanese Nomura; not to mention hedge funds in London and the US, which have admitted holdings in Bernard Madoff Investment Securities. Indeed Bernie was emblematic of the modern up-to-date, politically correct, multicultural, international... swindler. The ease with which the super rich of Europe forked their fortunes

over caused one Madrid-based business consultant to observe that, "picking off Spain's wealthiest was like clubbing seals..."[5]

10. Madoff's swindle will likely promote greater self-criticism and a more distrustful attitude toward other potential confidence people posing as reliable financial know-it-alls. Self-critical Jews are less likely to confide in brokers simply because they are zealous backers of Israel and generous contributors to Zionist fund drives. That is no longer an adequate guarantee of ethical behavior and a certificate of good conduct. In fact it may raise suspicion of brokers who are excessively ardent boosters of Israel and promise consistent high returns to local Zionist affiliates—leading potential investors to ask themselves whether this business about 'what is good for jews ' is really a cover for another scam.

11. The demise of Madoff's enterprise and his wealthy Jewish victims will adversely affect contributions to the 52 major Jewish American organizations, numerous foundations in Boston, Los Angeles, New York and elsewhere, as well as to the Clinton/Schumer militarist wing of the Democratic Party (Madoff bankrolled both of them as well as other unconditional Congressional supporters of Israel). This may open Congress to greater debate on Middle East policy without the usual high volume attacks—though the recent success of AIPAC in rolling back the nomination of America-First diplomat, Charles Freeman, as Director of the National Intelligence Council indicates the Lobby had fat to spare.

Conclusion

Madoff's swindle and fraudulent behavior is not the result of a personal moral failure. It is the product of a systemic imperative and the economic culture, which informs the highest circles of our class structure. The paper economy, hedge funds and all the 'sophisticated financial instruments' are all 'Ponzi schemes'—they are not based on producing and selling goods and services. They are financial bets on future financial paper growth based on securing future buyers to pay off earlier cash-ins. In fact, as Ellen Brown pointed out in her article, "The Wall Street Ponzi Scheme called Fractional Reserve Lending: Borrowing from Peter to Pay Paul":

> Banks themselves are involved in a sort of Ponzi scheme,
> one that has been perpetuated for hundreds of years.
> What distinguishes the legal scheme known as "fractional
> reserve" lending from the illegal schemes of Bernie Madoff
> and his ilk is that the bankers' scheme is protected by
> government charter and backstopped with government

funds. At last count, the Federal Reserve and the U.S. Treasury had committed $8.5 trillion to bailing out the banks from their follies."[6]

The 'failure' of the SEC is totally predictable and systemic: The *regulators* are selected from the *regulatees*, are beholden to them and defer to their judgments, claims and audit sheets. They are structured to 'miss the signs' and to avoid 'over-regulating' their financial superiors. Madoff operated in a milieu of a Wall Street where everything goes, where impunity or mega-bailouts for mega swindlers is the norm. As an individual swindler, he out-defrauded some of his bigger institutional competitors on the Street. The whole system of rewards and prestige goes to those best able to juggle the books, to cover the paper trails and who have willing victims begging to get fleeced. What a mensch, this Madoff!

In a few days, one individual, Bernard Madoff, has struck a bigger blow against global financial capital, Wall Street and the US Zionist Lobby/Israel-First Agenda than the entire US and European Left combined over the past half century! He has been more successful in reducing vast wealth disparities in New York than all the white, black, Christian and Jewish, reform and mainline Democratic and Republican governors and Mayors over the past two centuries.

Some right-wing conspiracy theorists are claiming that Bernie is a secret Islamic-Palestinian agent (from Hamas) who set out to deliberately undermine the financial base of the Jewish State of Israel and its most powerful, affluent and generous US backers and foundations. Others claim that he is a closet Marxist whose swindles were carefully designed to discredit Wall Street and to funnel billions into clandestine radical organizations—after all... *does anyone know where the lost billions have gone?* Unlike the leftist pundits, bloggers and protest marchers, whose earnest and public activities have had no effect on the rich and powerful, Madoff has aimed his blows where it hurts the most: their mega-bank accounts, their confidence in the capitalist system, their self-esteem and, yes, even their cardiac well-being.

Does that mean we on the left should form a Bernie Madoff Defense Committee and call for a bailout in line with Paulson's bailout of his Citibank cronies? Should we proclaim *"Equal bailout for equal swindlers!"*? Should we advocate his flight (or his right of return) to Israel to avoid a trial? It might not fly with his many Jewish victims to make the case for an Israeli retirement for Bernie.

There is no reason to mount the barricades for Bernard Madoff. It's enough to recognize that he has inadvertently rendered an historic service to popular justice by undermining some of the financial props of a class-ridden injustice system.

Postscript

Was it out of sheer admiration or because of some covert linkages with Madoff that then-current Attorney General Michael Mukasey removed himself from the investigation? Others of equal importance and influence are most certainly tied in the Madoff Affair, and not just the 'victims'. We are facing a serious case of *matters of State* ... No one can believe that a single person could by himself pull off a scam of this size and duration. Nor can any serious investigator believe that $50 billion dollars has simply 'disappeared' or been squirreled into personal accounts.

On June 29, 2009, Bernard Madoff was sentenced to 150 years in prison.

Endnotes

1   The *Wall Street Journal* made Madoff's full clientele available in a line-item list of 163 pages, (see <http://online.wsj.com/public/resources/documents/madoffclientlist020409.pdf>which included the addresses of the bilked parties, but not the amounts of their exposures. It also detailed the substantial losses of the major clients. See "Madoff's Victims", *Wall Street Journal*, March 6, 2007, at <http://s.wsj.net/public/resources/documents/st_madoff_victims_20081215.html>

2   By SEC Chairman Christopher Cox's own admission, "the agency inappropriately discounted allegations, that staff did not relay concerns to the agency's leadership and that examiners relied on documents volunteered by Madoff rather than seeking subpoenas to obtain critical information." "SEC Ignored Credible Tips about Madoff," *Washington Post,* December 17, 2008.

3   See my recent works, *The Power of Israel in the United States* and *Zionism, Militarism and the Decline of US Power* published in 2006 and 2008 respectively by Clarity Press, Inc.

4   SeeTheDeal.com at <http://www.thedeal.com/newsweekly/dealwatch/pink-slips-on-the-street.php>

5   *Financial Times*, December 18, 2008 p.16.

6   Ellen Brown, cited on GlobalResearch.ca on January 3, 2009 at <http://www.globalresearch.ca/index.php?context=va&aid=11600>

CHAPTER 3

THE ELECTION OF THE GREATEST CON-MAN IN RECENT HISTORY

"I have a vision of Americans in their 80s being wheeled to their offices and factories having lost their legs in imperial wars and their pensions to Wall Street speculators and with bitter memories of voting for a President who promised change, prosperity and peace, and then appointed financial swindlers and warmongers."
An itinerant Minister, 2008

Introduction

The entire political spectrum ranging from the 'libertarian' left, through the progressive editors of the *Nation* to the entire far right neo-con/Zionist war party and free market Berkeley/Chicago/Harvard academics, with a single voice, hailed the election of Barack Obama as a 'historic moment', a 'turning point in American history and other such histrionics. For reasons *completely foreign* to the emotional ejaculations of his boosters, *it is indeed a historic moment*: witness the *abysmal gap* between his 'populist' campaign demagoguery and his longstanding and deepening carnal relations with America's most retrograde political figures, power brokers and billionaire real estate and financial backers.

What was evident from even a cursory analysis of his key campaign advisers and public commitments to Wall Street speculators, civilian militarists, zealous Zionists and corporate lawyers was hidden from the electorate by Obama's people-friendly imagery and smooth, eloquent deliverance of a message of 'hope'. He effectively gained the confidence, dollars and votes of tens of millions of voters by promising 'change' (*implying* higher taxes for the rich, ending the Iraq war and national health care reform) when in fact the selection of his campaign advisers (and subsequent strategic appointments) pointed to a continuation of the economic and military policies of the Bush and Clinton administrations.

Even during the campaign, telltale signs of his true orientation surfaced. If Obama's obsequious message to the AIPAC convention that promised more to the Zionists than had ever been conceded by any previous US administration—inter alia, support for Israel's illegal annexation of greater East Jerusalem—liberals' enthusiasm should have been dashed by Obama's opting out of the new system of public campaign financing, which sought to limit the influence of big money on electoral campaigns, for which so many had fought. While it may have been possible to excuse Obama's appeasement of the Israel Firsters as an unavoidable necessity in any US election campaign, no such excuse was conceivable in relation to his effective destruction of public campaign financing. The assault on one of the major liberal efforts to cleanse the US electoral system of special interest influence delivered a gratuitous strike on behalf of privilege against a more egalitarian and democratic electoral system. Obama hadn't even needed the extra money.

Within three weeks of his election, he had appointed all the political dregs who brought on the unending wars of the past two decades, and the economic policy makers responsible for the financial crash and the deepening recession afflicting tens of millions of Americans today and for the foreseeable future. We can affirm that the election of Obama does indeed mark a historic moment in American history: the victory of the greatest con man and his accomplices and backers in recent history.

He spoke to the workers and worked for their financial overlords.

He flashed his color to minorities while obliterating any mention of their socio-economic grievances.

He promised peace in the Middle East to the majority of young Americans, yet slavishly swore undying allegiance to the War Party of American Zionists serving a foreign colonial power (Israel).

Obama, on a bigger stage, is the perfect incarnation of Melville's Confidence Man. He catches your eye while he picks your pocket. He gives thanks as he packs you off to fight wars in the Middle East on behalf of a foreign country. He solemnly mouths vacuous pieties while he empties your Social Security funds to bail out the arch financiers who swindled your pension investments. He appoints and praises the architects of collapsed pyramid schemes to high office while promising you that better days are ahead.

Yes, indeed, "our greatest intellectual critics", our 'libertarian' leftists and academic anarchists, used their 5-figure speaking engagements as platforms to promote the con man's candidacy: they described the con man's political pitch as "meeting the deeply felt needs of our people". They praised the con man when he spoke of 'change' and 'turning the country around' 180 degrees. Indeed, Obama went one step further: he did it twice, turning the full 360 degrees, bringing us back to the policies and policy makers who were the architects of our current political-economic disaster.

The Self-Opiated Progressive Camp Followers

The contrast between Obama's campaign rhetoric and his political activities was clear, public and evident to any but the mesmerized masses and the self-opiated 'progressives' who concocted arguments in his favor. Indeed even after Obama's election and after he appointed Clintonite-Wall Street shills into all the top economic policy positions, and Clinton's and Bush's architects of prolonged imperial wars (Secretary of State Hillary Clinton and Secretary of Defense Robert Gates), the 'progressive true believers' found reasons to dog along with the charade. Many progressives argued that Obama's appointments of warmongers and swindlers was a 'ploy' to gain time now in order to move 'left' later.

Never ones to publicly admit their 'historic' errors, the same progressives then turned to writing 'open letters to the President' pleading the 'cause of the people'. Their epistles, of course, may only succeed in passing through the shredder in the Office of the White House Chief of Staff, Rahm Emanuel.

The conjurer who spoke of 'change' now extols the virtues of 'experience' in appointing to every key and minor position the same political hacks who rotate seamlessly between Wall Street and Washington, the Fed and Academia. Instead of 'change' there is the utmost continuity of policymakers, policies and above all, ever deepening ties between militarists, Wall Street and the Obama appointments. Even the neo-cons, whom it might have been thought were inseverably committed to the Republican Party (witness John McCain's constant accompaniment by Senator Joseph Leiberman) moved effortless across party lines to praise Obama's decision to send troops to Afghanistan at what one writer termed the "Neocons for Obama" neoconservative Foreign Policy Initiative Conference.[1]

True-believer progressives, facing their total debacle, grasp for any straw. Forced to admit that the great majority of Obama's appointments represent the dregs of the bloody and corrupt past, they hope and pray that 'current dire circumstances' may force these unrepentant warmongers and lifelong supporters of finance capital to turn volte face and become supporters and advocates of a revived Keynesian welfare state.

On the contrary, Obama and each and every one of his foreign policy appointments to the Pentagon, State and Justice Departments,

Intelligence and Security agencies are calling for vast increases in military spending, troop commitments and domestic militarization to recover the lost fortunes of a declining empire. Obama and his Cabinet have already begun to vigorously pursue Clinton-Bush's global war against national resistance movements in the Middle East and elsewhere. His most intimate and trusted 'Israel-First' advisers have targeted Iran, Syria, Afghanistan, Pakistan,North Korea, Somalia, Sudan, Palestine and Iraq.

Obama's Economic Con Game

Then there is the contrast between the trillions Obama has already and will continue to shower on the financial swindlers (and any other 'too big to fail' private capitalist enterprise) and his zero compensation for the 100 million heads of families swindled of $5 trillion dollars in savings and pensions by his cohort appointees and bailout beneficiaries. Not a cent is allocated for the *long term* unemployed, despite the campaign pledge titled "Barack Obama's Plan to Stimulate the Economy".[2] The issue of evictions didn't even make it on the aforementioned plan. Needless to say, not a single household threatened with eviction will be bailed out.

"Obama" might be viewed as the trademark name of a network of confidence people. They are a well-organized gang of prominent political operatives, money raisers, mass media hustlers, real estate moguls and academic pimps. They are joined and abetted by the elected officials and hacks of the Democratic Party. Like a virtuoso performer, Obama projected the image and followed the script. But the funding and the entire 'populist' show was constructed by the hard-nosed, hard-line free marketeers, Jewish and Gentile 'Israel Firsters', Washington warmongers and a host of multi-millionaire 'trade union' bureaucrats.

The electoral scam served several purposes above and beyond merely propelling a dozen strategic con artists into high office and the White House. First and foremost, the Obama con-gang *deflected* the rage and anger of tens of millions of economically- skewered and war-drained Americans from turning their hostility against a discredited presidency, congress and our grotesque one-party/two factions political system and into direct action on the streets, or at least toward launching a new political movement or coalescing behind those already on offer by Ralph Nader and by Cynthia McKinney at the head of the Green Party.

Secondly the Obama image provided a *temporary* cover for the return and continuity of all that was so detested by the American people and indeed, the world at large—the arrogant untouchable swindlers, growing unemployment and economic uncertainty, the loss of life savings and homes, and the endless, ever-expanding imperial wars.

Featuring Paul Volker, 'Larry' Summers, Robert Gates, the Clintons,

Geithner, Holder and General ('You drink your kool-aid while I sit on Boeings' Board of Directors') Jim Jones USMC, Obama treats the American public to a re-run of military surges and war crimes, Wall Street banditry, impunity for Abu Ghraib-style human rights torturers, AIPAC hustlers and all the sundry old crap. Our Harvard-minted *Gunga Din* purports to *speak* for all the colonial subjects but acts *in the interest of* the empire, its financial vampires, its war criminals and its Middle East leaches from the Land of the Chosen.

The Two Faces of Obama

Like the Janus face found on the coins of the early Roman Republic, Obama and his intimate cronies cynically joked about 'which is the real face of Barack', conscious of the con-job they were perpetrating during the campaign. In reality, there is only one face—a very committed, very consequential and very up-front Obama, who demonstrated in every single one of his appointments the face of an empire builder.

Obama is an open militarist, intent by every means possible to re-construct a tattered US empire. The President-Elect is an unabashed Wall Street Firster—one who has placed the recuperation of the biggest banks and investment houses as his highest priority. Obama's Cabinet members for all the top economic positions (Treasury, Chief White House economic advisers) are eminently qualified, (with long-term service to the financial oligarchy), to pursue Obama's pro-Wall Street agenda. There is not a single member of his economic team, down to the lowest level of appointees, who represents or has defended the interests of the wage or salaried classes (or for that matter the large and small manufacturers from the devastated 'productive' industrial economy). Secretary of Labor, Hilda Solis, acclaimed by the AFL-CIO and *Mother Jones,* raised no objections when Obama's economic task force on the auto industry demanded massive firings and wage reductions at General Motors.

The Obama propagandists claim his appointments reflect his preference for 'experience'—which is true: his team members have plenty of 'experience' through their long and lucrative careers in maximizing profits, buyouts and speculation favoring the financial sector. Obama does not want to have any young, untested appointees who have no long established records of serving Big Finance, whose interests are too central to Obama's deepest and most strongly held core beliefs.

Even if experience were recognized to be a requisite ingredient of office in such crisis-laden times, Obama still might have made progressive choices. What about Joseph Stiglitz, Nobel prize winner and former chief economist of the World Bank (who, in an interview with *Deutsch Welle,* declared that "Nationalized banks are the only answer"[3]), or even another liberal and Nobel prize winner, Paul Krugman? But what he really wanted was *reliable* economic functionaries who recognized that re-financing the out-of-pocket billionaire financiers is the central task of his regime. The appointments of Summers, Rubin, Geithner and Volker fit perfectly with that ideology: They are the best choices to pursue his underlying economic intentions.

Critics of these nominations write of the 'failures' of these economists and their role in 'bringing about the collapse of the financial system'. These critics fail to recognize that it is not their 'failures', which are the relevant criteria for these officials' appointment to office, but their unwavering commitment to the interests of Wall Street and their willingness to demand trillions of dollars more from US taxpayers to bolster their colleagues on Wall Street.

Under Clinton and Bush, in the run up to the financial collapse, they facilitated ('deregulated') the practice of swindling millions of Americans of trillions in private savings and pension funds. In the current crisis period with Obama they are *just* the right people to swindle the US Treasury of trillions of dollars in bailout funds to refinance their fellow oligarchs. The White President (Bush) leaves steaming financial turds all over the White House rugs and Wall Street summons the 'historic' 'African American' President Obama to organize the cleanup crew to scoop them out of public view.

Obama, the Militarist, Outdoes His Predecessor

What makes Obama a much more audacious militarist and Wall Streeter than Bush is that he intends to pursue military policies, which have *already greatly harmed* the US people with appointed officials who have *already been discredited* in the *context* of failed imperial wars and with a domestic economy in collapse. While Bush launched his wars after the US public had their accustomed peace shattered by an orchestrated fear-mongering after 9/11, Obama has launched his military escalation in Afghanistan in the context of a generalized public disenchantment with the ongoing wars, with monumental fiscal deficits, bloated military budgets and after 100,000 US soldiers have been killed, wounded or psychologically destroyed. He did so, not with the innocence that Bush might have claimed, thinking, as his CIA Director Tenet advised, that it would be a "cake-walk", but rather even after key officials among America's NATO allies had publicly advised that the war was "unwinnable".[4]

Obama's appointments of Clinton, General Jim Jones, former dual Israeli citizen Rahm Emanuel and super-Zionist Dennis Ross, among others, fit perfectly with his imperial-militarist agenda of escalating military aggression. His short list of intelligence candidates, likewise, fits perfectly with his all-out effort to "regain US world leadership" (reconstruct US imperial networks). If, as Obama claims, the (failed) nomination of seasoned

America-First diplomat, Charles Freeman as Director of the National Intelligence Council (the body that prepares the National Intelligence Estimates, whose findings on Iran's lack of nuclear development proved so devastating to Israeli efforts to promote war against that country), was made without his knowledge by Dennis Blair, then this potentially positive nomination should not redound to his credit.

All the media blather about Obama's efforts at 'bipartisanship', 'experience' and 'competence' obscures the most fundamental questions: The specific nominees chosen from both parties are totally committed to military-driven empire-building. All are in favor of "a *new effort to renew* America's standing in the world" (read 'America's imperial dominance in the world'), as Obama's Secretary of State-to-be, Hillary Clinton, declared. General James Jones, Obama's choice for National Security Advisor, presided over US military operations during the entire Abu Ghraib/ Guantanemo period. He was a fervent supporter of the 'troop surge' in Iraq and is a powerful advocate for a huge increase in military spending, the expansion of the military by over 100,000 troops, and the expanded militarization of American domestic society (not to mention his personal financial ties to the military industrial complex). Robert Gates, continuing as Obama's Secretary of Defense, is a staunch supporter of unilateral, and universal imperial warfare. As the number of US-allied countries with troops in Iraq declines from 35 to only 5 on January 1, 2009 and even the Iraqi puppet regime calls for a withdrawal of all US troops by 2012, Gates, the intransigent, insists on a permanent military presence. Having promised a graduated withdrawal of 100,000 by 2010 (which some commentators have advised will mostly take place at the end of that period)[5], Obama advised that 50,000 would remain, for the purposes of "training, civilian protection and counter-terrorism"... This of course does not include private contractors. Moreover even the minimal withdrawal of troops is contingent on a decline of armed opposition. In late April, with a resurgence of armed attacks, Clinton suggested that the US might be "forced" to prolong its presence.

The issue of 'experience' revolves around two questions: (a) experience related to whch past political practices? (b) experience relevant to pursue which future policies? All the nominoes' past experiences are related to imperial wars, colonial conquests and the construction of client states. Hillary Clinton's 'experience' was through her support for the bombing of Yugoslavia and the NATO invasion of Kosova, her promotion of the Kosovo Liberation Army (KLA), an internationally recognized terrorist-criminal organization, as well as the unrelenting bombings of Iraq in the 1990s, Bush's criminal invasion of Iraq in 2003, Israel's murderous bombing of civilian centers in Lebanon...and now full-throated threats that any Iranian attack on Israel would result in the 'total obliteration of Iran'. Gates and Jones have never in their mature political careers proposed the peaceful settlement of disputes with any adversary of the US or Israel. In other words, their vaunted 'experience' is based solely on their one-dimensional militarist approach to foreign relations.

Obama's overtures to Iran were a sham and were not taken seriously by the Iranians and most non-western experts because they were in fact accompanied by the pursuit of new and harsher economic sanctions, and demands that Teheran break relations with major political allies, Hamas and Hezbollah. Holbrook's attempt to rope Iran into aiding US war efforts in Afghanistan came to naught, as they were not accompanied by any reciprocal concession or gesture. Public relations gestures are no substitute for substantive negotiations in which universal legal public policies, like uranium enrichment, are not called into question or further demonized.

'Competence', as an attribute again depends on the issue of 'competence to do what'? In general terms, 'The Three' (Clinton, Gates and Jones), have demonstrated the *greatest incompetence* in extricating the US from prolonged, costly and lost colonial wars. They lack the minimum capacity to recognize that military-driven empire-building in the context of independent states is no longer feasible, that its costs can ruin an imperial economy and that prolonged wars erode their legitimacy in the eyes of their citizens.

Even within the framework of imperial geo-political strategic thinking, their positions exhibit the most dense incompetence: They blindly back a small, highly militarized and ideologically fanatical colonial state (Israel) against 1.5 billion Muslims living in oil and mineral resource-rich nations with lucrative markets and investment potential and situated in the strategic center of the world. They promote total wars against whole populations, as is occurring in Afghanistan, Iraq and Somalia and, which, by all historical experience, cannot be won. They are truly 'Masters of Defeat'.

The point of the matter is that Obama appointed the 'Big Three' for their experience, competence and bipartisan support in the pursuit of imperial wars. He overlooked their glaring failures, their gross violations of the basic norms of civilians (of the human rights of tens of millions civilians in sovereign nations) because of their willingness to pursue the illusions of a US-dominated new world order.

Conclusion

Nothing speaks to Obama's deep and abiding commitment to become the savior of the US empire as clearly as his willingness to appoint to the highest positions of policy making the most mediocre failed politicians and generals merely because of their demonstrated willingness to pursue the course of military-driven empire building even in the midst of a collapsing domestic economy and ever more impoverished and drained citizenry.

Just as Obama's electoral campaign and subsequent victory will go into the annals as the political con-job of the new millennium, his economic and political appointments will mark another 'historic' moment: the nomination of corrupt and failed speculators to heal the economy that they themselves broke, and warmongers to win wars that they themselves have already lost. Let us join the inaugural celebration of our 'First African-American' Imperial President, who wins by con and rules by guns!

Endnotes

1   David Weigel, "Neocons for Obama", *The Washington Independent*, March 31, 2009, <http://washingtonindependent.com/36467/neocons-for-obama>

2   The policy, carried on BarackObama.com, asserted that "Barack Obama believes we must extend and strengthen the Unemployment Insurance (UI) program to address the needs of the long-term unemployed, who currently make up nearly one-fifth of the unemployed and are often older workers who have lost their jobs in manufacturing or other industries and have a difficult time finding new employment." See <http://obama.3cdn.net/8335008b3be0e6391e_foi8mve29.pdf>

3   See *Deutsch Welle*, "Nationalized Banks Are 'Only Answer,' Economist Stiglitz Says", February 6, 2009, <http://www.dw-world.de/dw/article/0,,4005355,00.htm>

4   Such advice came, inter alia, from Brigadier Mark Carleton-Smith, Britain's top military commander in Afghanistan, and Canadian Prime Minister Stephen Harper, whose countries provided NATO forces that were most strongly engaged in the fighting in Afghanistan.

5   Ben Feller, "Obama details Iraq withdrawal schedule", Associated Press, 28 Feb 2009.

CHAPTER 4

LESSONS FROM
THE COLLAPSE OF
WALL STREET

The ongoing collapse of the stock market and the loss of hundreds of billions of dollars managed by Wall Street investment banks illustrate the pitfalls and danger of free market capitalism facing the entire working population of the United States, and through the United States, the world.

1. *The near bankruptcy of Social Security.* The attempt by the White House and leading Republican and Democrat congressmen as recently as three years ago to 'privatize' Social Security—essentially to turn over the management and investment of trillions of dollars in Social Security funds to Wall Street—with the argument that private investors would earn more for retirees, would have led to the bankruptcy of the entire Social Security fund. Privatization would have provided yet another income stream to the major private investment banks on top of that already forced into the market by the Federal Reserve's enforcement of low interest rates, enabling them to prolong their binge of highly-leveraged speculation and invention of even riskier financial instruments leading to an even greater calamity than the disastrous results we are witnessing today. While private pension funds go belly up—Social Security continues. It is the private pensions, which have gone bankrupt—not the publicly managed Social Security fund, contrary to the experts and critics of Social Security. Clearly the current private debacle argues for public control and management of pension programs.

2. *The insecurity of private pension funds.* All the major private

pension funds for public and private employees, including TIAA CREF, CALPERS and labor union pensions have lost anywhere between 23% to 30% since January and have shown negative growth over the past 5 years. Clearly linking pension funds to the stock market has severely reduced the living standards of retirees, forcing many to remain in the labor force into their seventies and beyond or to sink into poverty. Pensions linked to publicly funded productive activity would avoid the losses and risks embedded in investing in the stock market for old age security.

3. *The loss of a real economy manufacturing base.* The bipartisan strategic decisions to convert the US into a 'service' economy as opposed to an advanced and diversified manufacturing economy is the root cause of the collapse of the US financial system and the emerging long-term recession. From the 1960s onward, the political elite adopted policies that promoted finance, real estate and insurance, the so-called FIRE sectors, which raised rents, redirected subsidies, provided tax concessions and subsidies, and destroyed and displaced industry. The re-conversion of the FIRE economy back to a balanced manufacturing economy and welfare state, essential for reversing the collapse of the US economy, will require a major political upheaval.

4. *Corporate flight.* The massive flight of capital from productive sectors to FIRE was accompanied by the huge surge of capital overseas, as competition forced corporations to seek out the multitude of advantages of production in third world countries (cheap labor, tax concessions, lax regulation), leaving the domestic economy overly dependent on 'services' (sold to Americans as the knowledge economy), particularly volatile and risky 'financial services' and debt-based rather than wage-based sales to domestic consumers. The conversion of the US from a diversified economy to a 'FIRE' monoculture increased the vulnerability of a general collapse if and when the financial/real estate market went under. Recovery and sustained growth can only occur with the return to a diversified economy, and the retention of capital from overseas flight. This is not happening and will not happen because of higher rates of profit abroad and the deep structure *of the economy*—namely the dominant position of finance capital. Only with a new political leadership which breaks with Wall Street can we envision the kind of large-scale, long-term public investment and incentives for the

productive and social service sectors.

5. *The pursuit of military-driven empire building* at the expense of joint ventures and reciprocal trade agreements with countries with expanding markets, strategic energy sources and large populations and markets, created enormous budget and trade deficits and alienated potential sources of markets and strategic commodities. Trillion dollar military expenditures in pursuit of prolonged, costly colonial wars (still without end under Obama), diverted funds from the application of technological advances and high-end manufacturing, which would have lowered costs and increased market competition. Equally important, by shifting from market-driven domestic expansion to overseas military-driven expansion, the entire axis of economic power shifted from industrial to financial capital. Finance capital, which was essential to funding government budget deficits incurred through military expenditures, grew in influence—Wall Street replaced the steel-belt as the axis of power in Washington.

6. *The ascendance of militarism and financial capital* facilitated the increase in influence of a virulent power configuration promoting the regional hegemonic interests of a colonial-militarist state— specifically, a previously comparatively marginal political lobby—the pro-Israel-Zionist power configuration (ZPC). The military-driven empire builders saw in the ZPC a strategic ally in pursuit of their global conquests; the ZPC in turn saw an open door to high office and multiple opportunities to promote Israel's expansionist agenda through its influence in Congressional Committees, electoral campaigns and direct White House appointments. The ZPC surge to the top echelon of power was aided and abetted by an increase in financial support from members in strategic positions in the most lucrative financial institutions, particularly its leading investment banks, such as Goldman Sachs, whose former employees went on to hold high political and executive offices in the Clinton, Bush, then Obama administrations. The ZPC was a major economic beneficiary of the speculative bubble and it was the massive infusion of financial contributions that allowed the ZPC to vastly expand the number of full-time functionaries, influence peddlers and electoral contributors that magnified their power—especially in promoting US Middle East wars, lopsided free trade agreements (in favor of Israel) between the US-Israel[1] and unquestioned backing of Israeli aggression against Lebanon,

Syria and Palestine. Restoration of the banking system by plunging as yet untold trillions of dollars, even were it to restore banks' function of providing liquidity to the global economies, would not be sufficient to restore the US economy itself. *US economic recovery is contingent on ending budget-busting military imperialism.* That will not happen *unless* there is a wholesale restriction and replacement of the political elite nurtured on military metaphysics of military-based global power and cobbled to safeguarding the interests of Israel.

No economic recovery is possible now or in the foreseeable future as long as the US Congress and executives provide trillion dollar bailouts to Wall Street's insolvent speculators, bankroll trillions of dollars to the budgets of never ending wars called for by Zionist power brokers dictating US Mideast policies, and the US economy itself remains based on US consumer debt and the speculative issuances of finance capital. Indeed, as seems increasingly clear: none of this can continue—whether the political and financial elite like it or not.

The lessons of the past tell us a great deal about what paths we should and shouldn't take.

Social Security still exists precisely because the US public rebelled and defeated the proposed handover to Wall Street and it remained a publicly run program. The financial system collapsed because the US economy 'specialized' in a single crop—finance—at the expanse of a diversified productive economy. The political system is totally discredited because it is run by a failed political elite which blatantly represents and acts on behalf of a few thousand financial oligarchs; several hundred militarist oligarchs and a few thousand Zionist zealots.

The 'power elite' is only as powerful as it is able to manipulate, intimidate and beguile the more than three hundred million US citizens into thinking that they are indispensable to running the American economy—rather than complicit, in a class sense, to milking it for private gain:

> According to the man who may be the leading expert on banking fraud, there is also no innocent explanation for the events leading to the current economic crisis. Last week on his PBS show, Bill Moyers interviewed William K. Black, the senior regulator during the savings and loan scandal in the late 1980s. Mr. Black, who wrote a book based on his experiences and called it *The Best Way to Rob a Bank is to Own One*, said the fraud and deceit that resulted in the world banking system's dire distress makes Bernie Madoff look like a piker. In fact, says Mr.

Black, who is the former director of the Institute for Fraud Prevention, what we have experienced was caused by "calculated dishonesty" on the part of corporate CEOs, aided and abetted by politicians and regulators who tore down the barriers to financial shenanigans—perhaps the most important example being the repeal of the Great Depression-inspired Glass-Steagall Act that separated commercial banking from investment banking. This cleared the stage for the fraudulent investments that made a lot of people very, very rich in what we can now see was an immense Ponzi scheme, many times the size and scope of the scam pulled off by Mr. Madoff...

When asked by Mr. Moyers whether he was alleging that Timothy F. Geithner and others in the administration, and the banks, are engaged in a cover-up to keep us from knowing what went wrong, Mr. Black said, "Absolutely." The rulers are frightened to admit that many of the large banks are insolvent. They have ignored the proven methods for dealing with bank fraud and have instead adopted what they used to laugh at when the Japanese did it: covering up bank losses by lying about them and injecting money into failed institutions. Even though it's working exactly as one would expect—just as it did in setting Japan into a long, deep recession—they don't know what else to do.[2]

While the overwhelming initial popular rejection of the Wall Street bailout suggests that the ruling oligarchy is not invincible, what must next become a popular conviction is that they are *not competent* to do other than maximize their own private interests.

The world's future is not safe in their hands.

Endnotes

1   Further, as pointed out by Mitchell Bard, "as one of only three countries (Jordan and Mexico are the others) with free trade agreements with both the United States and the European Community, Israel can act as a bridge for international trade between America and Europe." See <http://www.jewishvirtuallibrary.org/jsource/US-Israel/FTA.html> IRMep argues the US has a $62.8 Billion deficit in trade with Israel, see < http://irmep.org/US-Israel_Trade.htm>. The US government predicts a $7 billion deficit for 2007. <http://www.ustr.gov/assets/Document_Library/Reports_Publications/2008/2008_NTE_Report/asset_upload_file184_14623.pdf>

2   Ron Smith, "A Fraud That Makes Madoff Look Small Time", *The Baltimore Sun*, April 12, 2009.

CHAPTER 5

LATIN AMERICA: PERSPECTIVES FOR SOCIALISM IN A TIME OF WORLD CAPITALIST RECESSION/DEPRESSION

Introduction

A serious discussion of the perspectives for socialism in Latin America today requires several levels of analysis, moving from world economic conditions, to US-Latin American relations, to their specific impact on Latin America. The analysis must focus on how the economic recession/ depression impacts on the changing political-economic systems and the class structures. Finally, within this framework, it becomes necessary to examine the development of the class struggle and anti-imperialist movement in specific countries and under different regimes.

While there are broad similarities to previous 'recessions' and economic cycles, there are many good reasons to think that what matters most in the present world conjuncture is the specific world historical conditions, which mark the present economic recession as very distinctive or 'unique'.

Specificities of the Current Recession/Depression

We refer to the present crisis as 'recession-depression' because the negative growth of capitalism is a current ongoing process that is still in its opening phase: The current recession is still spreading and likely will deepen into a depression as early as mid-2009, lasting onward for a prolonged period. Secondly, the recession/depression is spreading unevenly in terms of depth and timing, with some countries and regions in more 'advanced' states of crisis (US-EU-Japan) than others (India and China).

A serious analysis of the current RD must take account of the massive structural changes in the composition of capital which have taken place over the last 50 years, which preclude any attempt to theorize about 'long waves' of capitalist cycles, and to make comparisons with previous recessions/depressions between 1929-1939 and later.

Any attempt to theorize about the length, duration, possible collapse of capitalism and emerging anti-capitalist forces begins with recognition of the new economic configurations of capitalism and the resultant new class formations.

The Uniqueness of the 'New Capitalism' in the Contemporary World

There are several unique features that define the current RD of world capitalism. These include:

1. The entire world with minor exceptions is now incorporated into the world capitalist market under private capitalist owners who control the principal means of production and distribution, and employ wage labor. There are no longer communist economies run on the basis of state ownership and planning. The USSR, China and their allies and ex-clients in Eastern Europe, Asia and Africa have been converted into capitalist countries subject to the capitalist market. As a result, the entire world economy is now, for the first time in modern history, subject to the effects of world RD.
2. The level of integration between 'national' capitalist economies is deeper and more widespread than ever before in history, increasing the speed with which recessions in one major country or region are transmitted to the next.
3. The concentration and centralization of capital and their interlock, in particular in the financial sector, has reached levels unprecedented in the past, thus facilitating growth of credit, financial power, wealth and the paper economy in periods of expansion, and multiple crises in all economic sectors (manufacturing, agriculture, public finance) in time of collapse.
4. Today the size and extension of wage and salaried workers is qualitatively greater than any other period in world capitalist history: The working class, in all its variants (employed and unemployed, seasonal, contract or subcontracted, formal and informal) is the principle source of capitalist revenue and income (directly through profits or indirectly via interest, taxes, royalties and rents).
5. The composition of capitalism is vastly different from any previous period in history—in particular the relationship between finance and productive capital. In the United States and the

United Kingdom, finance capital is the nerve center for the concentration of capital; capital is transferred from all other economic centers and invested in speculative economic activities throughout the world economy. The centrality of finance capital explains the subsequent boom in commodity speculation, the real estate and housing bubble, and the conversion of the US economy from an export-manufacturing center to a 'FIRE' (finance, insurance and real estate) and consumer import economy. The rise of finance-consumer capitalism in the US and UK and to a lesser degree on the continent created a new world division of labor in which Asia, especially China, South Korea and Taiwan, became the manufacturing export workshops of the world, South America the agro-mineral and oil exporter, the Middle East the oil financial sub-center, and Africa the target of agro-mineral colonization subject to resource exploitation by the new Asian and older Euro-American imperial powers.

6. Latin America's 'restructured' capitalist economy emerged from the recession and financial crisis of the 1990s with its axis of growth anchored in agro-mineral exports. Between 2003-2008 all Latin American economies, regardless whether they were center-left or rightist, based their strategy on the 're-primarization' of their economies. The driving force of capitalist growth was centered on agro-business and mineral exporters. Export capitalism re-defined the class structure and increased dependence on overseas markets and diversified trading partners in Asia.

7. Primarization in Latin America led to the strengthening of neo-liberalism and the reconfiguration of state policy to favor agro-mineral exporters and accommodate the poorest section through vast clientelistic 'poverty programs'. Social movements and trade union leaders were co-opted. Surplus labor was 'exported' (overseas migration) and vast sums of overseas remittances were 'imported'.

8. The centerpiece of this 'new world order' was the United States financial system with its global networks penetrating the world economy. US financial dominance led to:

- de-capitalization of manufacturing;
- the massive expansion of real estate speculation;
- debt-financed consumer-based growth;
- the stimulation of Asian manufacturing growth and exports; and
- the boom in commodity production, exports and prices in Latin America.

The link between the rise of US finance capital, the growth of Asian export industries and Latin American commodity boom was responsible for the high growth period up to 2007 and the subsequent collapse and deep recession beginning in 2008.

9.   The emergence of Chinese financial power. As pointed out in *The New York Times* in April, 2009:

> "China's trade with Latin America has grown quickly this decade, making it the region's second largest trading partner after the United States. But the size and scope of these loans point to a deeper engagement with Latin America at a time when the Obama administration is starting to address the erosion of Washington's influence in the hemisphere...
>
> "This is how the balance of power shifts quietly during times of crisis," said David Rothkopf, a former Commerce Department official in the Clinton administration. "The loans are an example of the checkbook power in the world moving to new places, with the Chinese becoming more active."... China is rapidly increasing its lending in Latin America as it pursues not only long-term access to commodities like soybeans and iron ore, but also an alternative to investing in United States Treasury notes.
>
> Just one of China's planned loans, the $10 billion for Brazil's national oil company, is almost as much as the $11.2 billion in all approved financing by the Inter-American Bank in 2008.[1]

US Recession/Depression: The Domestic Consequences

The US economy is rapidly descending from a recession into a depression. Hundreds of thousands of workers are losing their jobs each month. One out of five workers are out of work or working part time. One out of every ten homeowners cannot meet their mortgage payments and faces eviction. The GNP will be receding at a rate between minus two percent (–0.2%) to minus five percent (–0.5%) for 2009. Manufacturing is declining to minus six percent (–0.6%). Consumer spending is down 25%. Bankruptcy rates are at depression levels. Credit is drying up. Major banks survive only because of the trillion dollar government bailouts. Unemployment, bankruptcy, credit freeze, corporate losses and debt—a general depression—has devastated the domestic US economy, severely damaged the 'real economy' and the stock market as well. Massive state spending and subsidies to banks have failed to stimulate the financial system and to encourage lending to the productive sectors and to finance household consumption. In fact, some have argued this is because the derivatives-based debt is in the hundreds of trillions of dollars, and that financial recuperation would not be feasible even with government assistance, without the cancellation of these contracts.[2] Others have argued, not only that the recipient banks are using the funds to take over other banks, but to make non-banking-related purchases elsewhere in the real economy.[3] US Treasury bonds are now paying negative interest rates (1%), far below the rate of inflation. The multi-billion-dollar Wall Street swindles have destroyed confidence between banks and investors, lenders and borrowers, government and industrial firms. The capitalist system has broken down. As an economic system it no longer performs its most basic functions at a minimum level of efficiency—to produce, lend, employ, consume, trade and house.

The US depression/recession has a profound impact on all the world's economies. Contrary to the 'decoupling theories', which argued that countries in Asia, Latin America or Europe had achieved autonomy, the US recession has led to a precipitous decline in European, Asian and Latin American exports to the US. The US financial crash has profoundly affected banks in Europe, Asia and Latin America—leading to the drying up of credit and massive capital flight as investors and speculators withdraw capital to cover losses in the US. The US-European-Asian recession is rapidly moving toward a depression and with it, massive numbers of bankruptcies, unemployment, pension loss, home foreclosures, poverty and the further concentration of capital in a few state-financed private banks.

The traditional 'monetary stimulus' of central banks—interest rate reductions—has clearly failed. Even though US interest rates are reduced to 0.25% (almost zero), the Federal Reserve admits these measures have not even slowed the descent into a deeper recession. The US capitalist state has resorted to unprecedented printing of money to finance its gaping 2 trillion dollar deficit for fiscal year 2009 and to avoid the collapse of basic federal, state and local government services. However the bulk of this unprecedented printing is going to loans and other commitments made by the Fed to banks, whose names and the quantities involved the Fed has refused to name… Major firings of public employees and the closure of social services have multiplied as social services have been slashed.

What is striking about the US political-economy in this deepening recession is the divergence in performance between the stock market and the real economy; the vast reduction in public spending in the civilian economy even as there is an increase in military spending; the reduction of civilian employees and the escalation of troops sent to war. In other words, the capitalist state is allocating its scarce resources to rebuild the empire and engage in multiple wars even as it starves the civilian administration of resources at a time when it verges on bankruptcy and the productive domestic economy collapses in a deepening recession.

A similar divergence in state policy is evident with relation to the vast sums allocated to support the financial sector and the total neglect of the productive economy. As the number of big banks appear to have been pulled back from the brink of collapse they still face outstanding derivatives which are scheduled to come due in the near future, while thousands of major manufacturing, mining, construction and transport enterprises have gone bankrupt or are on the verge of failure with virtually no state support.

This peculiar and specific character of the US capitalist crisis leads to several tentative observations:

1. Military-driven empire building is the primary priority driving state policy over and above the domestic (and even export) productive economy. While the military budget and personnel grow, private investment funds and employment in productive sectors shrink.

2. The military-imperial complex is relatively and perhaps temporarily independent or 'autonomous' from the domestic productive economy. Its growth and overseas expansion takes place despite the contraction of the economy. In fact, there seems to be an inverse relation: As the domestic economic crisis deepens, the military-imperial complex expands. Those who believed that the economic recession would undermine military-driven empire building and wars and force the government to concede defeat, withdraw or 'negotiate' with adversaries, submit to multilateral coordinated decisions have been proved wrong. One might concede that a prolonged recession/depression may ultimately force the government to retrench military empire building in the face of mass unemployment and even mass hunger. However, even that is uncertain given the lack of any mass protests and the reduction of the bureaucratized private trade union sector to below 5% of the labor force. There is no protest even with the massive layoffs of unionized automobile, steel and other industrial workers.

There is no pre-determined point at which sufficient political pressure might arise to reverse the predominance of military imperial priorities over the civilian domestic economy. How many imperial wars, of what duration, will be counterposed to what percentage of unemployed and underemployed workers to set in motion a political shift to confronting the domestic recession/depression? Will it be 2 or 3 wars versus 20-30% unemployment and underemployment? What is certain is that there is absolutely no pressure from within the Obama Presidency or among the Democratic and Republican members of Congress to reverse the supremacy of empire building over the domestic economy. The Imperial Wars will go on; the domestic economy will continue to decline. In current circumstances no planners can believe the lesson of the Great Depression—that only WWII brought an end to it. There are no economic benefits to be derived from the current wars similar to those that resulted from WWII (where America faced no significant costs, but rather reaped huge benefits from exports and reconstruction, etc.) These new wars are fought for military objectives. There are no economic benefits in fighting wars in Afghanistan and Pakistan. US efforts to encircle China have failed in the face of the lucrative trade and investment agreements signed with its neighbors and the tremendous debt dependency of the US on China.

The State's highest priority is placed on the military-imperial and financial sectors despite the breakdown of the domestic economy and the drain from the prolonged and failing imperial wars in the Middle East. This suggests that we are dealing with *deep politico-economic structural relations within the US*, which cannot be changed or reversed by one or another elected political official. Deep structures cannot be uprooted in the current context; new 'economic stimuli' can only activate short-term projects, whose scope and depth is limited by the voracious demands of the imperial wars and the dysfunctional financial system.

In conclusion, under present political conditions in the US, despite the deepening recession, the continued imperial military losses and the transition to an economic depression, the perspective is for the US to continue to drive toward political (and military) confrontation with nationalist, anti-Zionist, populist and socialist governments and movements. They will act unilaterally when necessary or with clients and collaborator states where possible.

The World Recession Hits Latin America

Latin America's economies are feeling the full brunt of the world recession: Every country in the region, without exception, is experiencing a major decline in trade, domestic production, investment, employment, state revenues and income. Latin America's GDP projected growth for 2009 has declined from 3.6% in September 2008, to 1.4% in December 2008.[4] More recent projections estimate Latin America's GDP per capita falling to minus two percent (-0.2%). As a result bankruptcies will proliferate and state spending on social services will decline. State credit and subsidies to big banks and businesses will increase. Unemployment will expand, especially in the agro-mineral and transport (automobile) export sectors. Public employees will be discharged and those still employed will experience a sharp decline in salaries. Latin America's external financial flows will suffer the loss of billions of dollars and Euros from declining remittances from overseas workers. Foreign speculators are withdrawing tens of billions of investment dollars to cover their losses in the US and Europe. Foreign disinvestment replaces 'new foreign investment', eliminating a major source of financing for any major 'joint ventures'. The precipitous decline in commodity prices, reflecting an abrupt drop in world demand, is sharply reducing government revenues dependent on export taxes. Foreign reserves in Latin America can only 'cushion' the fall in export revenues for a limited time and extent.

The recession means the entire socio-economic class configuration, around which Latin America's 'growth model' is based, is headed for a long-term, large-scale transformation. The entire spectrum of political parties, which dominated the electoral process, and are linked to the primary commodity export model will be adversely affected. The trade unions and social movements oriented toward increasing wages, reforms and greater social spending within the primary commodity export model will be forced to take direct action or lose relevance.

The initial response of the 'center-left' political regimes to the deepening recession/depression has largely focused on:

1. financial support for the banking sector (Lula) and lower taxes for the agro-mineral export elite (Kirchner/Lula);
2. cheap credit for consumers to stimulate car purchases (Kirchner); and
3. temporary unemployment benefits for workers laid off from closed small and medium size mines (Morales). The main response of the Latin American regimes up to the beginning of 2009 was, at first, self-delusion—the belief that their economy would not be affected. This was followed by an attempt to minimize the crisis, claiming that the recession would not be severe and that they would experience a rapid recovery in 'late 2009'. They argue that the existing foreign reserves would protect their country from a more severe decline.

According to the IMF, 40% of Latin America's financial wealth ($2.200 billion dollars) was lost in 2008 because of the decline of the stock market and other asset markets and currency depreciation. This decline will reduce domestic spending by 5% in 2009. Latin America's terms of trade have deteriorated sharply as commodity prices have fallen sharply, making imports more expensive and raising the specter of growing trade deficits.[5]

The onset of the recession in Latin America is evident in the 6.2% fall in Brazil's industrial output in November 2008 and its accelerating negative momentum.[6]

As a result, Latin America enters into a period of profound, prolonged recession without any serious plan or program to counteract its destructive impact.

The recession is transforming the Latin American class structure. The size and influence of all classes, from the top to the bottom, are deeply affected.

First of all the big fall in demand and price of primary commodities results in a sharp decline in income, power and solvency of agro-mineral exporters. Much of their expansion during the 'boom years' was debt-financed, in some cases with dollar- and Euro-denominated loans. Many of the highly indebted 'export elite' face bankruptcy and are pressuring their governments to relieve them of immediate debt obligations. In the course of the recession/depression there will be a further concentration and centralization of agro-mineral capital as many medium-sized and large miners and capitalist farmers are foreclosed or forced to sell. The relative decline of the contribution of the agro-mineral sector to the GDP and state revenues means they will have less leverage over the government and economic decision making. The collapse of their overseas markets and their dependence on the state to subsidize their debts and intervene in the market means that the so-called 'neo-liberal' free market ideology is dead—for the duration of the recession. Weakened economically, the agro-mineral elite will turn to the expanding role of the state as its instrument of survival, recovery and refinancing.

The New Statism

The 'new statism' has absolutely nothing 'progressive' about it, let alone any claim to 'socialism'. The state under the influence of the primary sector elites assumes the task of imposing the entire burden of the recession on the backs of the workers, employees, small farmers and businesspeople. In other words the state will be charged (once again) with indebting the masses of people in order to subsidize the debts of the elite export sector and provide zero cost loans to capital. Massive cuts in social services (health, pensions and education) and salaries will be backed by state repression. In the final analysis the increased role of the state will be primarily directed to financing the debt and subsidizing loans to the ruling class.

The economic decline of the agro-export elites makes them politically vulnerable because they will no longer function as the 'engine of growth'. Under conditions of 'neo-statism' one of the axes of the class struggle shifts to a confrontation over who controls the state, its budget, its expenditures and 'intervention'. Because of the central role of the state in the economy during a recession/depression, all class relations and class struggles pass directly into political confrontation with the state over whether the state will save capitalist ownership of the means of production or expropriate it.

The financial and industrial sectors, linked to overseas markets and financial sectors face serious deterioration in market shares, capital financing and credit. A serious process of 'de-capitalization' will result as the recession/depression deepens in North America, Europe, Central and South America. The worst affected sectors are those with the greatest 'integration in the world market'. The greater the globalization, the more rapid has been the spread of the financial crisis in the banking, automobile manufacturing and communications industries. Those financial and manufacturing sectors mostly linked to the domestic economy will partly escape the downturn in the early phases of the crisis.

No Reprieve in Sight

The idea that somehow because Latin America went through an earlier regional crisis (1998-2002) it can escape the full effects of the current recession/depression is not credible. Latin America cannot 'build capitalism on one continent.' Latin America's delay in feeling the full blast of the 'first wave of the recession' (2008) only means that as the second wave hits in 2009, there will be major plant closures of subsidiaries of multinationals and bankruptcies of all the 'satellite industries'. This will be accompanied by massive lay-offs of industrial workers and wage reductions. Because of the socio-political importance of industrial workers concentrated in urban centers and the dependence of service employment on the industrial sectors, the state will be forced to intervene with some compensatory unemployment programs with public works at subsistence wages. In so far as the trade unions cannot or choose not to transcend the collective bargaining framework, *new forms of mass organizations of the semi-employed and unemployed workers* will likely emerge, using the tactics of direct actions— paralyzing the roadways and transport networks, and occupying closed plants and public buildings, similar to what occurred in Argentina between 2000-2003.

The informal sector will multiply, as millions of unemployed crowd the streets, competing fiercely in a shrinking labor market. In the face of recession/depression and border controls, overseas emigration as an escape valve will no longer be available. Internal and inter-country migration will offer no relief. The lack of savings, unemployment benefits, and the decline of overseas remittances, combined with meager public works programs used for 'political patronage', will raise the 'political temperature' in the urban centers and slum settlements surrounding the capital cities.

Nevertheless, there will not be any 'automatic radicalization'. The specter of 'hunger' may just as well encourage a turn to rightwing populist demagogues or even an increase in urban gangs and the growth of the underworld economy, as well as leftist-led unemployed and informal worker organizations and anti-capitalist factory occupations. There are examples of vibrant unemployed workers organizations from the recent past, especially in Argentina. Nevertheless, the new circumstances require adapting and developing new forms of struggle, not merely repeating experience from the past, which were embedded in different historical contexts.

The abruptness, depth and extent of the capitalist recession will make most electoral institutions and formal legislative bodies irrelevant: The massive spread of unemployment, bankruptcies and revenue losses cannot be dealt with through the lengthy negotiations and inconclusive debates of parliaments. Executive and extra-parliamentary direct action will become the order of the day.

The Recession's Potential for the Left: Big Gains or Big Losses?

The capitalist recession/depression, by itself, does not guarantee that the Left will be the principle beneficiary of the ensuing popular discontent. Several contingencies will be crucial in determining the initial political character of the response—most of all that of the incumbent regime in power as the recession unfolds. Where the self-styled 'center-left' regimes are in power, as in Argentina, Bolivia, Ecuador, Uruguay, Paraguay, Chile and Brazil or the nationalist left as in Venezuela, and where state-funded 'stimulus packages' fail to counteract the recession-depression, political conditions will favor the return of the right. The right will rely on state intervention to finance capitalist recovery and to harshly repress mass protest. In Venezuela, Ecuador and Bolivia, the Right can only return to power through a coup. Where the Neo-liberal right rules as in Mexico, Peru and Colombia, the mass popular movements will find political expression through leftist political organizations.

In the absence of any strong nationally-organized revolutionary force, the recession/depression, by itself and even with mass protest, will not lead to a social transformation. At least in the initial phase of the crisis in 2009, most 'mass pressure and struggles' will be directed to conserve jobs, block mass layoffs and even some 'defensive' factory/enterprise occupations. This may be accompanied by demands for greater state involvement, either through subsidies to failed enterprises or selective nationalizations. The total demise of neo-liberal ideology is inevitable; but its initial replacement will most likely take the form of 'state capitalism'. The most radical responses and popular demands will occur in those countries most dependent on primary product exports and world demand, and in those countries most integrated to the depressed markets of the US and EU. These countries include, in particular, Mexico, Central America, Ecuador,

Peru, Venezuela and Bolivia. Chile, Argentina, Brazil and Colombia, with more diversified exports and a larger internal market, will also be impacted by world and regional recession but 'not as severely or abruptly'.

The recession will proceed in phases, cushioned initially by large foreign reserves. By mid 2009, the recession will accelerate as capital flight, the loss of credit, investment markets and remittances intensifies. Local producers and capital markets will be hit hard. By the beginning of 2010 Latin America will be deep in recession.

Leftwing radicalization will really take hold, once the large-scale economic stimulus and public works programs fail to stimulate the economy and as the recession deepens and becomes prolonged. The key to the growth of revolutionary movements will depend on their location in the socio-economic centers of the crisis with organized cadre and 'local opinion' leaders capable of articulating and linking local discontent with a national plan of struggle, informed by a clearly anti-imperialist, socialist program.

Given present circumstances the recession/depression opens a door of opportunity for the re-emergence of mass movements, which in turn provide an active audience for the revival and renewal of socialist movements. The renewal of socialist mass movements will reflect the recent limitations of 'leftist fragmentation', 'spontaneism' and its lack of deep implantation in factories and neighborhoods. The world recession not only undermines the legitimacy of neo-liberalism but of the entire capitalist class configuration. The collapse raises the specter of 'statist nationalism' as a prelude to a publicly directed economy. In the context of capitalism, which is unable to operate through market mechanisms, bankrupt and weakened export strategies and growing protectionism, severe strains in US-Latin American relations are inevitable and promising for the success of a socialist project.

US-Latin American Relations, 1998-2008

To understand the current and immediate future of US-Latin American relations, it is necessary to identify four clearly demarcated periods: 1) The 'Golden Age of Imperial Pillage (1990-1999); 2) Crisis and Political Challenge (2000-2003), 3) the 'relative autonomy' of the commodity boom period (2004-2008) and 4) world recession/depression and declining power of imperial capital (2009 onwards).

The 'Golden Age' of Euro-US imperial pillage of Latin America was characterized by relations of intense exploitation (what Giudo DiTella, Argentine President Menem's Foreign Minister dubbed a 'carnal relation'). This period was defined by unlimited pillage and the transfer of profits, resources, rents, royalties and interest payments. Euro-US capital acquired—at below market prices—banks, mines and vast expanses of land, which, in its totality, scope and durations, was unprecedented in modern imperial history (post WWII). Over three thousand lucrative public enterprises were 'privatized' and de-nationalized at a fraction of their market value. Loans were contracted at exorbitant interest rates, most of which rarely entered the country and rarely served any productive purpose. In all the international and regional forums, Washington could count on the votes, diplomatic support and even the provision of mercenaries to back Bush and Clinton's imperial military conquests (Yugoslavia, Kosovo and Somalia) and maintain embargoes (Cuba, Iraq and Iran).

The US economic domination of Latin America exceeded even that of the preceding decade under some of the dictatorial military regimes: The neo-liberal electoral regimes proceeded to privatize even military-run industrial enterprises.

The 'Golden Age' of Euro-US pillage and absolute dominance was based on close collaboration with corrupt rightwing electoral regimes. The latter were dubbed 'democratic' or 'in transition to democracy' by Euro-US and Latin American academics funded by the major imperial foundations (Adenauer, Ebert, Ford, Rockefeller, the Fulbright Scholarship, National Endowment for Democracy). US imperial rule operated through electoral collaborators, business elites and security officials at the top and an army of Euro-US-funded 'NGOs' in the countryside, cities and poor communities at the bottom. With World Bank funds, the NGOs acted to undermine independent class movements by focusing on 'local' micro-projects rather than national structural transformations'.

For US officials, relations with Latin America established in the 'Golden Age' were taken as the norm and the basis of all future relations. They were oblivious to the fact that: 1) pillage was leading to mass exploitation, unemployment, internal crisis and financial disintegrations; 2) independent extra-parliamentary movements were gaining influence and hegemony among the majority and the power to overthrow not only military dictatorships but especially corrupt imperial electoral clients; and 3) that US 'hegemony' did not penetrate below the top elites. Generalized opposition to US dominance was extending to broad sectors of the downwardly mobile middle class, especially in the public sector adversely affected by neo liberal 'privatizations'.

The Demise of US Dominance: The Popular Uprisings of 2000-2003

Just as US power stood virtually unchallenged during the 'Golden Decade'. The period between 2000 and 2003 witnessed mass popular urban uprisings, massive rural movements and the emergence of Indian-based takeovers of regional and local governments. As a result, US dominance evaporated along with the demise of its hegemonized collaborator elites.

Between 2000-2003, Latin American politics took a decidedly 'left turn' as the US' most prominent supporters were defeated, ousted and/ or fled from office. Badly hit by a combination of financial and economic crises, the pillage of resources, enterprises, bank accounts and the emptying of public treasuries, angry majorities took to the streets. The fallen US clients (or would-be clients), included the presidents of several countries of the region: De la Rua in Argentina, Sanchez de Losado in Bolivia, Noboa in Ecuador, Cardoso in Brazil, and the 48-hour civil military coup-plotters in Venezuela (2002).

The driving force behind these political revolutions were powerful social movements, in particular those representing the urban poor, Indians, peasants, unemployed workers and downwardly mobile public employees. In contrast to the past, organized urban trade unions and students played a secondary role. As in all empires, US dominance depended on the capacity of the local ruling class to maintain political control either through force, fraud or corrupt electoral procedures. Once the client ruling electoral class was ousted, US influence over the countries sharply diminished.

The political result of the period of mass mobilization was the emergence of 'center-left' regimes, a hybrid reflecting some of the priorities of the mass movements as well as the continuities of the clientele politics of the past. The period of mass mobilizations challenged many of the fundamental features of 'Golden Age' of US imperial rule. The movements called into question the privatizations and de-nationalization of the economy, the massive illicit foreign debt, the advance toward a highly prejudicial 'free trade—free market' agreement with the US and a banking system subordinated to and plundered by local and foreign speculators linked through overseas subsidiaries.

Even as the movements were not able to enforce any fundamental changes in property or class relations, they were able to force through a number of other important secondary changes, including banking regulations to limit pillage and foreign-dictated monetary policy, and the re-nationalization of a few enterprises that were taken over by workers or were considered of national importance.

In the case of Venezuela, the Chavez government carried out large-scale nationalization of the state petroleum company, which had been run by executives who subordinated the industry to US MNCs and foreign banks.

The most important mass movements initially imposed a rough framework of national autonomy, which allowed the emerging center-left regimes to adopt a more flexible and autonomous posture in pursuing national interests independent of the US.

The Period of 'Relative Autonomy': 2005-2008

If the US suffered a severe loss of influence in the first half decade of the early 2000s due to mass mobilizations and popular movements ousting its clients, during the subsequent four years the US retained political influence among the most reactionary regimes in the region, especially Mexico, Peru and Colombia. Despite the decline of mass mobilizations after 2004, the after-effects continued to ripple through regional relations and blocked efforts by Washington to return to the kind of relations that had existed during the Golden Decade of pillage (1990-1999).

While internal political dynamics put the brakes on any return to the 1990s, several other factors undermined Washington's assertion of full-scale dominance:

1.   The US turned all of its attention, resources and military efforts toward multiple wars in South Asia (Afghanistan), Iraq and Somalia and to war preparations against Iran while backing Israel's aggressions against Palestine, Lebanon and Syria. Because of the prolonged and losing character of these wars, Washington remained relatively immobilized as far as South America was concerned. Equally important Washington's declaration of an intensified worldwide counterinsurgency offensive (the 'War on Terror') diverted resources toward other regions. With the US empire builders occupied elsewhere, Latin America was relatively free to pursue a more autonomous political agenda, including greater regional integrations, to the point of rejecting the US-proposed 'Free Trade Agreement'.

2.   Washington's heavy emphasis on military-driven empire building drained state resources from bolstering its economic empire in Latin America and contributed to the relative decline of the US as the dominant market and source for Latin American exports and imports (except for Mexico). The result was that Asia, Europe, the Middle East, Russia and neighboring Latin American countries became increasingly important trading partners. With the declining importance of US markets, the US lost some of its leverage and influence, especially with regard to 'political issues'. Latin America rejected the US embargo of Cuba and its pressures to isolate Venezuela.

3.   The boom in commodity prices of primary exports from Latin America increased the region's trade surplus. The size of its foreign reserves reached record levels and eliminated the influence of the US via the IMF in particular, and the international lending agencies in general. With world demand high for energy, metals and agro-exports, Latin America diversi-

fied its markets, suppliers and sources of external financing. Paradoxically, while the center-left regimes gained relative autonomy in relation to the US via their agro-mineral exports, they strengthened the position of their primary product exporting elites, which historically have been the most pro-Washington sector of the class system.

In summary, the combination of failed US geo-military commitments, favorable world market conditions and the legacy of mass mobilizations, provided the center-left regimes with a degree of political autonomy from the US—a midpoint between the crass subservience of the 1990's and the rebellious spirit of national liberation of the earlier half of the first decade of 2000.

From Economic Boom to Bust: 2008

The advance of the center-left regimes during the first half of 2008, the continued increase in world agro-mineral prices, the abundance of world liquidity, the growing foreign reserves and the incremental social changes ended by mid-year. With the onset of the world recession/depression, Latin America's exports, growth and reserves stagnated. The decline of world trade and the collapse of commodity prices starting in September eroded the high growth expectations of the center-left regimes, particularly of Brazil, Argentina, Venezuela as well as other countries in the region.

The current world capitalist crisis has several features that require analysis in order to understand the political and economic dynamics of US-Latin American relations in 2009/2010.

Unlike in the past, the recession hit the US and Europe first and more severely before it spread to Latin America. In part this was the result of Latin America's most recent crisis (1999-2002), which had already 'destroyed' many of the toxic assets in the system and lessened the links to the speculative heartland. Secondly, the commodity boom reduced overseas dollar-denominated public debt and increased foreign reserves and stabilization funds, allowing Latin American regimes to 'cushion' the initial shocks of the world recession, at least from October 2008 to March 2009.

Because Latin American diversified its markets and because its new Asian markets retained their resiliency for a longer spell, the recession entered Latin America 'later' than in Europe and the US beginning around November-December 2008 and deepening in February-March 2009. Finally because Latin America's speculative sector was still weak after the crash of 2000-2001, it was not as 'integrated' into the Anglo-American housing bubble and therefore not as damaged by the bursting of the bubble in 2007-2008.

While recognizing these specificities of the Latin American economies and the differential impact of the world recession on Latin America, the fact of the matter remains that Latin America has been hit and with considerable force by the spread of the world recession throughout 2009 and beyond. The belief, stated by Brazil's President Lula da Silva in 2008, that Brazil can 'avoid' the worst effects of the recession, is pure fantasy.

The recession will spread and deepen in Latin America and it will undermine precisely the 'engines' of growth—the primary export sector—and spread throughout the economy. The budget surpluses are temporary stopgaps to finance some stimulus packages—but they are totally insufficient to reverse the fall in all export sectors, the drying up of private credit and the drying up of new local/foreign investment. In fact the first sign and substance of growing recessionary tendencies is the large outflows of capital by investors anticipating the crisis. The other sign of the deepening recession is the decline of exports (both in quantitative and value terms). The decline in government revenues especially derived from export earnings is eroding public spending. The decline of the twin dynamics of trade and state investment and earnings is precipitating a sharp fall in the services (finance, real estate, commerce and transport) and local consumption and production (manufacturing, automobiles, textiles and so on).

Latin America's growth over the past five years was heavily dependent on public and private debt financing. Over $150 billion dollars of Brazil's $600 billion dollar public debt falls due in 2009. With the US borrowing over $1 trillion dollars this year, it will be impossible for even the most 'neo-liberal' regimes in Latin America to raise sufficient financing in the international market. Large-scale private corporate debt in Latin America, especially dollar-denominated debt, will cause a serious liquidity problem and large-scale bankruptcies. Even countries with large foreign reserves, like Chile and Brazil, will see those reserves evaporate as the recession extends beyond 2009-2010. Latin America will need $250 billion dollars just to pay off maturing debt; these funds are just not available internally or externally. Clearly the 11.2 billion approved by the Inter-American Bank for 2008 was just a drop in the bucket. Not even China's new spate of loans to the region will be able to fill the gap. The IMF, however, is being taken out of the closet and revamped with a promised recapitalization to $1 trillion at the April 2009 Group of 20 summit. Despite promises for change due to trenchant critiques of its earlier disastrous enforcement of structural adjustment policies, IMF future will likely be a rerun of IMF past:

> The Fund's loans since September 2008 to countries rocked
> by the financial crisis almost uniformly require budget cuts,
> wage freezes, and interest rates hikes...And, the Fund con-
> tinues to counsel against capital controls, which could limit
> the ability of foreign funds to enter and flee a country easily.[7]

So once again, as has happened throughout Latin America before, the debt trap—and its closure on independent domestic policy initiatives—awaits.

That Latin America enters 'later' into the global recession does not mean that it will leave sooner or suffer less. There are several reasons to assume the opposite: The center-left regimes did little or nothing to deepen the internal market, nor did they diversify their export products. On the contrary, they created a new emphasis on primary products for export in order to take advantage of the temporary high prices of 2003-2008. The center-left retained the privatized, foreign-owned strategic sectors inherited from the previous neo-liberal regimes, and failed to diversify their economies, severely weakening the economic levers through which it could revitalize the economy. With the banks remaining under private foreign control, loans to the productive sector are restricted. The privately owned industrial sector is not willing to risk new investments especially in the face of the growing recession in the US. The state only intervenes via channeling state loans and investment to the private sectors and depends on their willingness to make the 'appropriate' productive employment-generating investments. At best, this is a hit or miss proposition; at worst, it leads to 'slippage' or loss of investment funds. Under these conditions the center-left has to re-nationalize in order to invest for recovery, focus on new public projects in infrastructure (with its limited effects on employment), impose capital controls, suspend debt payments and run large-scale fiscal deficits to avoid a depression.

Latin America, contrary to the illusions of some presidents and economists, cannot sustain regional growth or even stabilize capitalism in one region—not in an ocean of depressed advanced capitalist countries.

Taking Stock of Present Conditions

A discussion of immediate and future prospects for revolutionary politics must start with a realistic analysis of the anti-capitalist, socio-political forces, as they exist today, and their potential for growth in the near future.

A realistic assessment of the proximate period begins by taking account of the striking contrast between the extraordinarily favorable 'objective conditions' (the prolonged and deepening world capitalist recession/depression) and the weak and uneven development of the 'subjective' conditions (organized mass anti-capitalist movements or parties). In other words we are in an unstable period where both capitalism and socialism are weak. The question becomes which side will be able to intervene, reorganize and recompose its forces to take advantage of the other.

This requires an 'inventory' of advantages (and disadvantages), reserves and resources of each side in order to evaluate the possible outcome of future conflicts and confrontations in a time of deepening world recession.

The 'Left', as it is known in broad terms, includes the Chavez government, the independent rural and urban class social organizations, peasant and Indian movements, and the guerrilla movements of Colombia, militant independent trade unions and nationalist and Marxist political parties throughout the region.

Over the past 20 years the left has suffered several tactical defeats. At times it has been in retreat, and some organizations have declined or disappeared. Nevertheless, in the past two decades, the Left has not suffered any strategic historic defeats—such as the military seizures in Brazil (1964), Bolivia (1971), Uruguay (1972), Chile (1973) and Argentina (1976)—which destroyed the mass organizations, decimated the cadres and leadership, and atomized the rank and file. Rather, the left has experienced over 20 years of continuity, accumulating experiences, educating its supporters and recreating its organizations, at a minimum to defend the immediate interests of its supporters.

In the case of Venezuela—the pivotal center for the advance of the Latin American Left—the Left has moved from opposition to government (1999), has overcome coups, imperialist destabilization campaigns, employers' lockouts and sabotage. The Chavez government has financed a dynamic mixed economy, advanced welfare programs and created a mass socialist party (PSUV).

The left movements have demonstrated their capacity to effectively mobilize large masses of supporters on numerous crucial occasions to overthrow pro-imperial electoral client presidents, mobilized to defend left and center-left presidents (Venezuela and Bolivia) and engaged in street demonstrations and organized the unorganized in prolonged street warfare. The latter include the unemployed workers in Argentina (1999-2003), the Brazilian Landless Rural Workers Movement (MST) (1985-2002 with a decline under Lula from 2003-2008) and the Bolivian workers-peasant/Indian engaged in urban insurrections (2000, 2003 and 2005).

The trajectory of the mass movements however has not always been upward—the bulk of the most successful movement mobilizations took place between 2000-2005, followed by a relative decline in the three years predating the current world recession. The Left was weakened by the primary commodity boom. The brief but intense capitalist recovery of 2004-2008 (until September) gave rise to both the reformist and 'center-left' regimes of Correa, Morales, Kirchner/Fernandez/ Vazquez and Lula, as well as the rightist regimes.

The 'weak side' of the Left going into the world recession is the fragmentation, dispersion and internal conflict among the Leftist parties in Latin America, limiting their capacity to compete for state power.

The mass movements and trade unions have been weakened and divided, and sectors of their leadership have been co-opted by the center-left regimes. The latter used the movements to neutralize and depoliticize mass mobilizations.   Lula co-opted the majority of the trade union leadership of the CUT (its General Secretary became Minister of Labor), and weakened the MST through limited financial aid to its co-ops, broken promises, repression, and above all by channeling billions of Brazilian reales toward the agro-business export elite. As the recession deepens, agro-exports decline and unemployment rises, mass discontent will intensify and Lula's control will be severely 'tested'. .

The left movements under the rightwing and center-right regimes of Uribe in Colombia, Garcia in Peru, Bachelet in Chile and those of Central America and the Caribbean, have regained social and, in some cases, political space. The electoral and extra-parliamentary struggles challenge neo-liberal hegemony. Particularly in Colombia and Peru, the entire 'interior' (provincial capitals, towns and countryside) has produced mass peasant and urban regional movements. These movements have challenged the central state over the distribution of public wealth and the destruction of local habitat and economies by multinational corporations. The collapse of commodity prices and growing unemployment may create 'dual power situations' based on regional power blocs.

In the period immediately preceding the recession (2007-2008), mass mobilizations took place in countries and among classes, which were different from those of the earlier decade. For example, militant mass mobilizations in Colombia, Peru and Costa Rica exceeded those in Argentina or even Bolivia in the period 2005-2008. Within Colombia, while the guerrillas were regrouping and in tactical retreat, mass marches of Indians, students and trade unionists took the foreground in the struggle against the murderous Uribe regime.

The major weakness of the social movements is obvious: They have a largely 'sectoral' leadership and base, and do not have national structures. Even as they embrace a more general society-wide program, their leadership lacks independent sources of financial and material resources to provide for a national cadre structure. Above all, they lack a practice and program for taking political power—state power. As they gain influence and mass support, they tend to turn toward or ally with the 'center-left' political leaders who have demonstrated repeatedly that: 'Out of power they are with the Left, but in power with the Right'.

The end of the commodity boom means there will be a rise in unemployment among miners, petroleum workers, and the agricultural proletariat concentrated in homogeneous communities, with their traditions of class struggle, organizations and 'consciousness'. Isolated, localized protests are inevitable and, in fact, were already occurring by the end of 2008. The sharp fall in the exports and domestic consumer market will provoke an increase in unemployment among industrial workers, especially in the automobile and related manufacturing industries, opening the door for a renewal of the organization of 'unemployed workers' for direct action. The decline of state revenues, dependent on taxes from agro-mineral exports, will result in the firing of state employees and the freezing of new hires. This means that tens of thousands of young graduates of universities, teachers colleges, preparatory, technical and secretarial schools will be out of work, creating a potential vast army of young people with no future and available for organization and action.

The recession/depression (general crisis) will discourage international migration and will cause a return of migrants. There will be a huge loss of remittances from overseas relatives and workers, intensifying local hardships, tensions and the necessity to struggle 'at home'. The 'world' nature of the recession eliminates out-migration as the 'escape valve', as it had functioned over the past several decades. The sectors of the population, who in the past emigrated, are of the same age and ambition as those who stay and organize class organization. Blocked from overseas emigration, these young workers are likely recruits to reinforce and radicalize the movement of the under- and unemployed.

There is no question that the pressures 'from below' will intensify. But in the absence of concrete organizations of struggle rooted among the young in the neighborhoods, among the vocational students in the major plazas, and in the streets 'employed' as 'informal workers', the anger and discontent can take many apolitical or even reactionary forms. Crime will increase astronomically, especially contraband, drugs, prostitution, assaults and kidnapping. New recruits for rightwing paramilitary and 'security agencies' can be found among the chronically unemployed or those on the edge of subsistence. Millenarian cults, charlatans and spiritualists can mystify the least political and those socially isolated in household economies.

In other words, the same objective circumstances of economic desperation, the same subjective frustration can lead to divergent social and political/apolitical responses. The emergence of anti-capitalist consciousness is contingent on the active presence and close links of socialist organization to everyday struggles.

Perspectives on Latin American Relations to the US Empire

US foreign policy, especially 'everyday' decisions are made by the permanent officials of the state (Pentagon, State Department, CIA and Treasury). Permanent staff members make over ninety percent of the foreign policy decisions. They form the vast majority of functionaries engaged in collecting information, preparing policy papers and designing options. This means that there is great continuity in policies, methods of operation, strategy, alliances and, above all, interests to be pursued and adversaries to be attacked.

The continuities in US policy toward Latin America are exclusively defined by the need to defend its political, economic and military empire (and if possible extend and deepen its reach), defeat and destroy its enemies and out-compete its imperial rivals. Defense and expansion of the empire involves (1) retaining dominant economic positions, (2) maximizing economic linkages, profits, interest, royalties and capital transfers, and indebtedness, (3) maintaining control over strategic economic sectors and trading partners. Military supremacy is pursued by establishing military treaties, bases and joint military maneuvers with 'local military commanders'. Political supremacy is achieved by securing political officeholders willing to extend or consolidate US economic and military power.

The key to the success of US 'neo-colonial' empire building is the recruitment and control over collaborator/ client regimes. They perform all the 'colonial state functions' facilitating economic exploitation, putting down resistance and providing military force for imperial interventions. Without collaborator regimes and their ruling class supporters, Washington's imperial power is severely diminished, its regional influence over economic policy declines and the US must either resort to costly and risky direct military intervention or play a marginal role.

US-Latin American relations are profoundly influenced by political-economic-military contingencies, such as: war and peace, economic booms and recessions, economic crises, revolutions, uprisings and reactionary coups. An understanding of US-Latin American relations today is dependent on understanding both the structure (imperial) and the contemporary contingencies (world recession/multiple wars).

The economic boom in Latin America between 2003-2008 was led by Latin American exports, which increased its revenues and reserves and, most importantly, lessened its dependency on US-Euro controlled international financial agencies, like the IMF. Greater 'domestic financial resources' and greater diversification of trading partners provided the basis for Latin American governments exercising greater political flexibility and permitted the creation of a more 'nationalist' foreign policy. In some cases like Venezuela, it strengthened overt opposition to US imperial institutions, policies and interests.

US imperialism's prolonged and costly military efforts at empire building elsewhere, beginning in 2001 and continuing to the present, further weakened US imperial relations in Latin America. Most political-military resources were concentrated in the Middle East, especially Iraq and Afghanistan, which lessened US pressure on Latin America. Prolonged wars weakened domestic political support for new military interventions in Latin America. The hundreds of billions of dollars spent on military driven empire building in the Middle East, diverted funds from investments directed toward enlarging and consolidating the empire in Latin America.

The simultaneous abrupt overthrow of the collaborator regimes of the 1990s occurred when Washington was not in a position to engage in a reactionary restoration: At best it backed the emergent 'center-left' as the lesser evil forestalling any more radical socialist alternatives, which might emerge. The combined weight of the loss of collaborator regimes, the growth of social movements, center-left victories, imperial wars and economic boom set in motion a process of realignment in US-Latin American relations. The result was a wide spectrum of relations.

The spectrum of relations runs from independent (Venezuela), autonomous competitive capitalist (Brazil), autonomous and critical (Bolivia) to selective collaborator (Chile) to the deep collaborators (Mexico, Peru and Colombia).

Venezuela constructed its leadership of the alternative nationalist pole in Latin America in reaction to US intervention. Chavez sustained its independent position through nationalist social welfare measures, which expanded mass support. Venezuelan independence was financed by the commodity boom and the jump in oil prices. The 'dialectic' of the US-Venezuelan conflict evolved in the context of US economic weakness and over-extended warfare in the Middle East on the one hand and economic prosperity in Venezuela, which allowed it to gain regional and even international allies.

The US suffered major losses. Washington's proposed Latin America Free Trade Agreement was defeated. Its efforts to finance the overthrow of Chavez were defeated. The State Department's policy of isolating Venezuela was a failure. Regions and countries historically under imperial domination, like Central America and the Caribbean, joined Venezuela's 'Petrocaribe' organization, receiving subsidized oil as part of new trade and aid agreements. Venezuela initiated a new regional integration organization, ALBA, with plans for large-scale joint ventures.

The autonomous-competitive tendency in Latin America was embodied in Brazil. Aided by the huge agro-mineral export boom, Brazil projected itself on the world trade and investment scene, while deepening its economic expansion among its smaller and weaker neighbors like Paraguay, Bolivia, Uruguay and Ecuador. Brazil, like the other BRIC countries, which includes Russia, India and China, forms part of newly emerging expansionist powers intent on competing and sharing with the US control of the resources and land of the smaller countries in Latin America. Brazil under Lula shares Washington's economic imperial vision (backed by its armed forces) at the same time as it competes with the US for supremacy. Brazil seeks extra-regional imperial allies in Europe (mainly France) and it uses the 'regional' forums and bilateral agreements with the nationalist regimes to 'balance' its powerful economic links with Euro-US financial and multi-national capital.

At the opposite end of the spectrum are the 'imperial collaborator' regimes of Colombia, Mexico and Peru, which remain steadfast in their pro-imperial loyalties. They are Washington's reliable enemies against the nationalist Chavez government and staunch backers of bilateral free trade agreements with the US.

The rest of the countries in the region, including Chile and Argentina, oscillate and improvise their policies between these three blocs.

What should be absolutely clear, however, is that all the counties, from radical nationalist to imperial collaborators operate within a capitalist economy and class system, in which market relations and the capitalist classes are still central players.

The Impact of the Capitalist Crisis of 2009 on US-Latin American Relations

The election of Obama has not brought about any change in the structure of the US empire, its political-military apparatus and especially its economic interests. What has changed are the resources and capacities available to the US in pursuit of its imperial policies, given the depth of the US recession and the escalation of US wars in the Middle East, Afghanistan and elsewhere.

US policy to Latin America is determined by a militarist cabinet, intent on pursuing a global strategy of military driven empire-building. The key foreign policy positions in the Obama regime are occupied by notorious and well-known militarists: The National Security Adviser, the heads of the CIA and the Defense Department, the Secretary of State, and the US Ambassador to the United Nations have been closely identified with the militarist empire-building policies of the Bush and Clinton regimes.

Nevertheless unlike the regimes of Bush and Clinton, Obama's regime comes to power under severe material limitations in its capacity to enforce its will in the southern hemisphere:

1. The US is relatively isolated in terms of 'collaborator regimes', unlike Clinton, who ruled during the 'Era of 20 Clients', and unlike Bush, who, for a brief period after 9/11, was able to 'mobilize' Latin American presidents (except Venezuela's Chavez) behind the 'War on Terror'.

2. Obama comes to power after five years of rapid growth in Latin America, a time of relative autonomy in which an alternative anti-imperialist pole, led by President Chavez, has been established.

3. Obama faces a severe domestic recession while promising an escalation of the war in Afghanistan and more military confrontations in the Middle East (Iraq, Palestine, Lebanon and,

especially Iran).

4. Obama is facing 'protectionist pressure' as the economic crisis deepens, weakening any attempt to revive 'free trade' agreements.

5. US capital is in flight out of Latin America.

In contrast, the pressure of more plant closures is forcing Latin American governments to intervene and 'nationalize' bankrupt firms. Even 'bilateral free trade agreements' will be of minor significance if the US Congress refuses to approve the pact with Colombia. NAFTA, the US-Mexican free trade agreement has led to US- subsidized food imports flooding into Mexico while the Mexican-based manufacture of car parts sold in the US is leading to calls on both sides of the border for its modification.

The 'reactionary anchor' of Obama's imperial policy for Latin America will be Plan Colombia to counter Venezuelan influence. Free trade agreements with Chile and Peru in the Andean region will be used to counter Bolivia. New diplomatic initiatives with Brazil will include the likely recognition of the Lula regime as a regional imperial power.

Overall, Latin America represents a fifth level priority in the Obama imperial agenda: The first priority is to reconstruct the deteriorating domestic foundations of empire; the second is to launch a new imperial offensive in South Asia and the Middle East. The third level of priorities is to attempt to coordinate economic and military policies with Europe and Japan to counter the world recession and secure collective imperial-military interventions. The fourth is to negotiate with China over the severe trade imbalances and debt financing.

In the end, Latin America will receive 'residual' attention and resources. Whatever funding, military intelligence and diplomatic personnel are left over from Washington's higher priority areas will be assigned to Latin America.

Having noted the limitations of the US empire and Latin America's low priority, nevertheless, relative to its power potential in Latin America, Washington still has formidable instruments and assets of power. First and foremost, Obama has a formidable array of strongly entrenched political allies at the pinnacle of the class structure throughout Latin America. They include private bankers, industrialists, agro-mineral exporters and multi-national executives who dominate the economies, influence most governments (even the 'center-left') and control numerous major regions and cities (Guayaquil, Buenos Aires, Sao Paolo, Caracas and Santa Cruz in Bolivia).

Washington, given its own limitations, will operate through local clients/allies in the economic system to undermine adversaries and finance political assets. While the US is militarily over-extended in its empire, it still has assets in the Latin American military, which it can move under propitious circumstances. The key strategy in this period will be to operate through clandestine and legal civilian structures. The US will rely on NGOs, electoral parties, 'civic movements' and right-wing 'trade unions' to undermine nationalist parties, governments and popular movements. Washington will, by necessity, make major diplomatic overtures to Brazil, especially toward Lula. To be successful, Washington will be obligated to recognize Brazil's emerging imperial/regional ambitions.

Recession/depression and military spending undermines any large-scale US 'economic offensive' toward Latin America in the form of investments and loans. The US will have to rely on much weaker political and diplomatic inducements or joint political-civic-military interventions, which however will occur under the most constraining economic circumstances.

The Latin American Left has unusual political advantages: The over-extension of the US outside of Latin America weakens the strength of its ruling class allies in Latin America. The defeat of its clients in the earlier half of the decade and the 'relative distancing' of the center-left has legitimated anti-US/anti-imperialist politics. The spread of the world recession/depression to Latin America will erode support for the capitalist system among the better-paid private workers and the lower middle class, trade unions and public employees. The demise of the 'free market' ideology will weaken the 'hard right', at least temporarily, before it regroups as a more eclectic and repressive 'state capitalist right'.

Latin America: What Is To Be Done

The panorama of new conditions facing the left in Latin America as a whole requires that it sharpen its focus on:

1. The central role that the domestic ruling class plays in sustaining the imperial edifice.
2. The diversification of substitutes for the US—especially among the old and new economic empires of Europe and Asia (The Lula-Sarkozy Pact is one example.)
3. The rise of Brazil as an emerging regional imperial empire (with overseas ambitions) and how it influences the national and class struggles. In Paraguay, Bolivia, Ecuador and Uruguay nationalist struggles pass through a confrontation with Brazil over unequal and exploitative gas, oil and hydropower treaties and the colonial exploitation of vast tracts of land and resources.
4. The unification of previously fragmented economic demands and their formulation into a socialist political program in the face of a system-wide economic crisis and class-wide unemployment.

The strategic strength of the US (and Brazilian) imperialists is not found in their own resources but in the fragmented organizations, dispersed actions and ideological cacophonies of the left political formations, competing social movements and spontaneous mass mobilizations.

There is no easy answer or readily available, easily discernible political leadership on the current horizon, even as the dark clouds of recession/depression obliterate the hopes of sustaining the capitalist expansion of 2005-2008. While Venezuelan President Hugo Chavez offers some political direction, with his program pointing toward social mobilization and the nationalization of privatized strategic enterprises, the economic crisis will hit Venezuela hard. Venezuela has tied its fortunes with weak countries, like Cuba, Bolivia and Nicaragua and with center regimes, like Brazil and Argentina who themselves are part of the obstacles to developing a socialist alternative to recession-prone crises of capitalism.

The strategic advances of the Left in Latin America are found in its heritage of recent class victories over neo-liberalism, the relative weakness of the US Empire and, above all, the deepening world recession.

The current gap between favorable objective economic conditions and the under-development of (subjective) revolutionary socialist consciousness is probably a temporary phenomena: The 'lag' can be overcome by the direct intervention of conscious socialist political formations deeply inserted in everyday struggles capable of linking economic conditions to political action.

Endnotes

1   See *The New York Times*, April 16, 2009, <http://www.nytimes.com/2009/04/16/world/16chinaloan.html?_r=1&hp>

2   James Lieber, "Who Cooked the World's Economy," *The Village Voice*, January 27, 2009 at <http://www.villagevoice.com/2009-01-28/news/what-cooked-the-world-s-economy>

3   Michel Chossudovsky, "Taxpayers, Where is Your Money Going?", GlobalResearch.ca, April 20, 2009.

4   *Financial Times*, January 9, 2009.

5   *Financial Times*, January 9, 2009 p. 7.

6   *Financial Times*, January 7, 2009 p. 5.

7   *Financial Times*, January 9, 2009 p.7.

CHAPTER 6

OBAMA'S
LATIN AMERICAN
POLICY

To decipher the real content of the Obama regime's policy to Latin America one needs to look at the foreign policy priorities, the allocations of financial resources and public policy commitments, and ignore its inconsequential diplomatic rhetoric. The first major pronouncement, in line with its global military policies, was to militarize the US-Mexican frontier, allocating nearly one-half billion dollars in military and related aid to the right wing Calderon regime. The entire focus of White House policy toward the Mexican and Colombian regimes over the problem of narcotics and narco-violence is military—ignoring its socio-economic structural roots: millions of young Mexican peasants and small farmers driven into bankruptcy, unemployment and poverty by the North American Free Trade Agreement NAFTA) created a large pool of recruits for the narco traffickers.

The expulsion of hundreds of thousands of Mexican immigrant workers from the US and the new militarized borders has closed off a major escape for Mexican peasants fleeing destitution and crime. In contrast to the formation of the European Union, which provided tens of billions to the less competitive countries like Spain, Greece, Portugal and Poland on entering, the US has provided Mexico with no compensatory funds to upgrade its productive competitiveness and provide needed employment for its people.

The highly militarized Colombian regime, notorious for its violation of human rights, is currently the biggest recipient of US military aid in Latin America. Under Plan Colombia, the US-financed counterinsurgency program, Bogota has received over five billion dollars, the most advanced military technology, and thousands of American military advisers and sub-contracted mercenaries. Obama's support for the right-wing Colombian regime is his response to the emergence of democratically elected populist and radical governments in Ecuador and Venezuela.

Obama's policies toward Latin America are driven by his extension of the military priorities of the Bush Administration, including the economic embargo of Cuba and its virulent hostility toward Venezuelan nationalism. While he may have relaxed travel restrictions and limitations on remittances from Cuban Americans, there are no new economic initiatives or plans to lift the embargo. Despite the rhetorical support for free trade, Obama upholds past quotas and tariffs on more competitive imports from Brazil, and has even added new protectionist measures against Mexican trucks and truck drivers.

Obama's relentless pursuit of military-driven empire building while in the United States is in the midst of an ongoing and deepening domestic economic depression forms the basis for understanding Washington's contemporary relations with Latin America today. His regime's military approach to Latin America is reflected in his inability or unwillingness to allocate economic resources and underscores his concern to sustain two major US clients, Colombia and Mexico, through military aid programs. Obama's limited interest in and sparse commitment of economic resources to Latin America reflects the very low foreign policy priority it has in the current White House. Latin America is a fifth level priority after the US domestic economic depression, the Middle East and South Asian wars, coordinating economic policies with the European Union, and formulating economic and military strategies in relation to Russia and China. With these priorities, the Obama regime has little time, interest, or programmatic offerings to help Latin America cope with the onset of the economic recession.

At the most basic level the Obama regime is following a three-fold strategy of (1) retaining support from rightist regimes (Colombia, Mexico and Peru); (2) increasing influence on 'centrist regimes' (Brazil, Argentina, Chile, Uruguay and Paraguay); and (3) isolating and weakening leftists and populist governments (Cuba, Venezuela, Ecuador, Bolivia and Nicaragua).

What is most striking about the supposedly "progressive" Obama regime's policy for Latin America are the continuities with the previous reactionary Bush administration in almost all strategic areas. These include:

1. Latin America's very low priority in US global policy;
2. The US emphasis on military ("security") drug enforcement collaboration over any long term socio-economic poverty alleviation and drug addiction treatment programs;
3. Its close collaboration with the most rightwing regimes in the region (Mexico and Colombia);
4. The continuation of the US economic embargo of Cuba, despite the loss of its last two Latin American backers;
5. Obama's double discourse of talking free markets while practicing protectionism;

6.   The US financing and strengthening the role of the IMF as an instrument of imperial expansion;
7.   The US policy of driving a wedge between 'centrist regimes' (Lula in Brazil, Fernandez in Argentina, Vasquez in Uruguay and Bachelet in Chile) and 'left and center-left nationalist regimes', (Chavez in Venezuela, Morales in Bolivia, Correa in Ecuador and Ortega in Nicaragua) and
8.   Its support for separatist regional elites' actions to destabilize center-left governments operating from their traditional far right-wing bases in Santa Cruz (Bolivia), Guayaquil (Ecuador) and Maracaibo (Venezuela).

In other words the Obama regime has embraced overall the strategic agenda of the Bush Administration, leaving it essentially intact, while making several secondary changes having to do with adaptations based on the decline of US power. While reiterating the anachronistic demands for Cuba to convert to capitalism (dubbed a "democratic transition") as a condition for ending the US embargo, Obama has slightly eased restrictions for US-based Cuban families to visit relatives in Cuba and to send them money. The State Department relies less on confrontational diplomatic language and has made overt gestures to centrist regimes, including White House meetings with Lula Da Silva (March 2009) and Vice President Biden's attendance at a meeting with centrist Presidents (March 27-28, 2009) in Chile. Obama's resort to "soft power", which is not backed by any new economic initiatives and which continues the basic policies of his predecessor, has not gained him new allies.

Obama has facilitated a few major negative changes, which go further than the Bush administration in harming Latin America's financial and trading position.

One set of 'changes' results directly and indirectly from the US depression and Obama's gigantic deficit financing, which has a very negative impact on Latin America's economic recovery. The Obama regime is absorbing most of the hemisphere's credit to aid the financial bailout. This policy makes it difficult for Latin American exporters to finance their sales. Moreover, the Obama regime's demands on the financial sector to expand its capital reserves and to direct its lending to the American domestic market has led banks to repatriate capital from their Latin American subsidiaries at the expense of Latin American borrowers—extending and deepening the recession in Latin America.

The second change is to introduce a new and more virulent financial protectionism, while continuing the double discourse of talking up "free trade". The Obama regime's diplomatic and linguistic changes and affirmation of free trade have little substance.In addition to the twenty billion dollar subsidies to agricultural exporters, the Democrats have pushed the "Buy American" provisions in Federal procurement policy and multi billion dollar subsidies to the auto industry.

Latin America faces a rising tide of US protectionism as the Obama regime reacts to the domestic economic depression by forcing Latin America to seek new trading partners, to protect their internal markets and to seek new sources for trade and credit.

The Export-Driven Model Breaks Down

Throughout Latin America, the economic depression is wrecking havoc on the economy, the labor market, trade, credit and investment. All the major countries in the region are headed toward negative growth, and experiencing double-digit unemployment, rising levels of poverty, and mass protests. In Brazil in late March and early April, a coalition of trade unions, urban social movements and the rural landless workers movement convoked large scale demonstrations—including participation from the union confederation, CUT, which is usually allied with Lula's Workers Party.

Unemployment rates in Brazil have risen sharply, exceeding 10%, as massive lay-offs hit the auto and other metallurgical industries. In Argentina, Colombia, Peru and Ecuador, strikes and protests have begun to spread in protest over rising unemployment. There is an increase in bankruptcies among exporters, who are unable to secure financing, and are facing worldwide decline in demand.

The more industrialized Latin American countries, whose economies are more integrated into world markets and have followed an export growth strategy, are the ones most adversely affected by the world depression. This includes Brazil, Argentina, Colombia and Mexico. In addition, countries with 'open' economies and dependent on overseas remittances and tourism like Ecuador, the Central American and Caribbean countries, and even Mexico, are badly hit by world recession.

While the US financial collapse itself did not have a major and immediate impact on Latin America—largely because the earlier financial crashes in Argentina, Mexico, Ecuador and Chile led their governments to impose limits on speculation—the indirect results of the US crash, especially with regard to the credit freeze and the decline of world trade, has brought down productive sectors across the board. By mid-2009, manufacturing, mining, services and agriculture, in the private and public sector were firmly in the grip of a recession.

The vulnerability of Latin America to world crises is a direct result of the structure of production and the development strategies adopted the region. Following the 'neo-liberal' or empire-centered 'restructuring' of the economies which took place between the mid-1970s through the 1990s, the economic profile of Latin America was characterized by a weak state sector due to privatization of all key productive sectors. The de-nationalization of strategic financial, credit, trading and mining sectors increased vulnerability as did the highly concentrated income and property ownership held mainly by small foreign and domestic elite. These characteristics were further exacerbated by the primary commodity boom between early 2003 until the middle of 2008. The regimes' further shift toward an export strategy relying on primary products set the stage for a crash. As a result of its economic structure, Latin America was extremely vulnerable to the decisions taken by US and EU policy makers in charge of key economic sectors. De-nationalization denied the state the necessary levers to meet the crisis by reversing the direction of the economy.

Structural changes imposed by the IMF/World Bank and its domestic 'neo-liberal' ruling class partners 'opened' the countries to the full blast of the world depression while dismantling the very state institutions which could have protected the economy or at least avoided the worst effects of the crisis.

Privatization led to the concentration of income, lessened local demand and heightened dependence on export markets while depriving the state of levers to control investment and savings, which could counteract the decline of overseas inflows of capital and the collapse of its overseas markets.

Denationalization facilitated the outflow of capital especially in the financial sector, deepened the credit crises and adversely affected the balance of payments. Foreign ownership made Latin American countries subject to strategic economic decisions made by overseas economic elites looking at the costs and benefits to their economic empires. For example, in Brazil the closing of US-owned auto factories and the mass firings of workers are based on 'global market' cost calculations, totally divorced from the needs of the Brazilian labor market.

The 'export strategy' was dependent on the state subsidizing the expansion of agro-business plantations producing staples for export markets. This came at the expense of small farmers, landless peasants and rural workers, weakening the domestic market which might have afforded an alternative to collapsing overseas markets, increasing dependence on food imports and undermining food security.

Export strategies depend on holding down labor costs, wages and salaries, thus weakening domestic demand and making employment dependent on the fluctuations of overseas demand. Specialized production in a vast complex international division of labor is central to the multinational corporations. This has dramatically reduced the national diversification of industry and integral manufacturing where all components of a product are produced within a single geographic region. Under the current division of labor, a Brazilian manufacturer of car brakes is totally dependent on external demand determined by the MNC. The strategic disadvantages of this 'specialization' in a global capitalist chain of production have become strikingly evident in this depression.

Despite these deep structural weaknesses inherited from previous regimes, the current center-left regimes in Latin American have not moved toward any structural changes to decrease their economic vulnerabilities, with the partial exception of Chavez's Venezuela.

The March 2009 summit of self-styled 'third way' regimes (plus the Obama-Biden and British Labor governments) met in Santiago, Chile where participants studiously avoided even mentioning the flawed internal structures which have brought on the economic crises and promise to deepen it.

The consensus proposals of the "third way" regimes repeated anachronistic appeals for greater capital flows, appeals which are divorced from the reality of the current crises. They called on the US, EU and Japan to resurrect collapsing markets and to promote trade. Specifically the Santiago meeting called for increased funding for the Inter American Development Bank (IDB, BID in Spanish), and encouraged the G20 leaders to promote stimulus packages and to pledge against protectionism. They called on Latin American regimes to increase spending and liquidity, to lower interest rates and prop up financial institutions, and to promote exporters.

The center-left regimes meeting in Santiago made no mention of plans to increase domestic demand through intervention in the labor market by preventing industrialists from firing workers. They did not mention increasing the minimum wage. They avoided any discussion on increasing demand in the rural areas through income generating agrarian reforms. They did not consider establishing publicly funded import substitution industrialization, which could generate employment for workers dismissed from export sectors.

In the face of rising food prices, no provisions were proposed to subsidize low income families, the unemployed, children and pensioners on fixed income. The center-left regimes' proposals demonstrated high structural rigidity and their incapacity to break with failed strategies tied to the powerful agro-mineral export ruling class. Instead their proposals reaffirmed their dependence on the 'expansionary' stimulus programs of the ruling classes in the US and Europe. Their repeated calls for 'free trade' and appeals to avoid 'protectionism' fell on deaf ears as all the imperial countries follow a dual policy of promoting free trade for their dynamic overseas multinationals and protectionism for their financial and troubled manufacturing sectors at home.

While eschewing any structural domestic changes that would favor unemployed workers, peasants, public employees and small businesses, they persist in following policies favoring the bankers, export elites and multi-national corporations. The main economic focus of Latin America's center-left regimes is not internal reform; it is the pursuit of new overseas markets and investors.

In early April, Latin American leaders and their business elite met with their Arab counterparts in Qatar to expand investments and trade through joint ventures. Similar missions to China, Russia and Japan have led to investments almost exclusively in capital intensive extractive industries (petroleum and minerals) and mechanized export agriculture. Inter-regional trade via MERCOSUR has been highly asymmetrical as evidenced by Argentina's $4 billion dollar trade deficit with Brazil. The center-left is structurally incapable of recognizing that the world depression has in large part undermined the 'export strategy'; that the elites cannot overcome their internal contradictions and class constraints by 'exporting' their way to economic recovery. The search for new markets and investors in Asia and Middle East may provide a limited boost to the export enclaves but they will have little or no impact on the industry, service and related sectors, which employ the mass of workers and employees. Moreover, the Middle East and Asian countries are in serious crises as trade (both imports and exports), manufacturing and employment decline. Moreover China has opted for a vast economic stimulus plan based on increasing domestic demand. Asia can provide Latin American regimes with little relief from the crisis.

The one country absent from the Santiago meeting of the center-left regimes was Venezuela, in part because President Chavez has pursued an alternative economic strategy to the world depression.

Chavez' strategy includes the nationalization of key economic sectors like oil and gas, which increases state revenue; protection of strategic social sectors/food processing and distribution sectors; and the expansion of agrarian reform to increase local production of food. The government has a program of subsidized food prices, has passed a 20% increase in the minimum wage to cushion the effects of inflation and public spending on labor-intensive infrastructure projects, which has resulted in a drop in unemployment with the creation of 280,000 new jobs in Jan-Feb 2009.

Chavez is pursuing a radical Keynesian program, which depends on large-scale public investments to expand the domestic market and social subsidies targeting a large swath of the lower classes. His state investment policy relies on the 'cooperation' of the still-dominant private sector, especially finance, construction, agro-mining and manufacturing, either via financial incentives and state contracts or through threats of intervention or nationalization.

Chavez' domestic structural reforms are complemented by his promotion of regional political-economic pacts, like PETROCARIBE and

ALBA, with Bolivia, Cuba, Nicaragua and several Caribbean and Central American states. He is counting on the growing financial and investment agreements with China, the Middle East, especially Iran, and Russia, particularly in joint ventures in the petroleum and mining sectors.

While Chavez' strategy represents a clear break with and alternative to the center-left 'export-elite' centered approach, it still confronts a series of serious contradictions. Venezuela is over-dependent on a single export (petroleum) for 75% of its foreign exchange earnings and a single market (the US). Secondly it is rapidly depleting its foreign reserves. Thirdly, its efforts to promote regional integration have not prospered as the principal countries in Latin America look toward the G20 for salvation. State intervention and nationalization have increased national leverage over the economy but has not confronted the mal-distribution of income, property and power.

As a result, a wave of worker/employee strikes in education, mining, smelting and manufacturing have hit the Venezuelan economy. Equally serious, a 30% rate of inflation has eroded buying power for those with fixed incomes and salaries, undermining recent increases in the minimum wage. Increases in the price of foodstuffs, over 90% of which are imported, adversely affects the balance of payments. The immediate future could pose a threat to the social stability of the Venezuela.

G20 Adopts Protectionism, Promotes Return of the IMF

The participation of several major Latin American countries in the G20 meeting in London on April 2, 2009, and the subsequent agreements reveal the political bankruptcy of their current political leadership. The declaration of a major new "stimulus" package was belied by the fact that most of the funds cited ($1.1 trillion dollars) were already allocated before the meeting and would have no effect. The actual amount of 'new money' was only a "fraction" ($250 billion dollars) and mostly geared to rescuing the financial sector.

The G20 solemn agreement to oppose protectionist legislation was belied by an OCED report that 17 of the 20 countries have recently adopted measures protecting local industries and restricting overseas financing. The biggest winner at the G20 was the IMF, which was promised an additional $500 billion dollars to provide credit lines and financing. Given the US-EU dominance of the IMF and given its past history of imposing restrictive conditions favoring the imperial countries, the strengthening of the IMF poses a major obstacle to any progressive Latin American recovery. The high expectations of Latin America's center/left and rightist regimes that the G20 would provide a meaningful stimulus were dashed.

On the left, Fidel Castro and like-minded allies in Latin America cite China as an alternative market and investment partner. Yet China's overseas investments are almost always directed to the extractive export sectors (minerals, petrol) and, to a lesser degree, agriculture. As a result, Chinese investment in Latin America has created few jobs while favoring sectors that pollute the environment. Latin America's export profile with China is reduced to a primary goods monoculture, highly vulnerable to the fluctuations of world prices. Moreover, China's trade agreements with Latin America include the import of Chinese manufactured goods produced by non-union, super-exploited workers which undermines any recovery of Latin America's manufacturing sector.

Latin American leaders, who look to China or any other country to pull them out of the depression, are committed to a neo-colonial style recovery based on a raw material export model. Likewise, the turn to Russia as a new market and stimulus is a highly dubious proposition, given Russia's petrol-gas dependent economy, its lack of competitive industries and above all its deepening depression with an economic decline of over 7% for 2009.

The Latin American leaders' search for a new stimulus package from the US and EU or new trade alternatives with China and Russia are desperate efforts to save the failing elite export model. The idea promoted by Brazil that since the imperial countries caused the world depression, they should provide the solution, is a non-sequitor, especially in light of their incapacity to stimulate their own economies. The US promotion of the IMF is directed toward undermining any progressive Latin American policies and independent regimes, and not helping them recover from the crisis.

Facing Up to De-Globalization—or Not

Because of the Obama regime's profound and costly commitment to military-driven empire building and the multi-trillion dollar refinancing of its banking sector (while backing credit-financing protectionism), Latin America's ruling classes cannot expect any "stimulus package" from the US.

The deep political divisions between the US and Latin America (and between the classes within Latin America), and divergent national and class strategies preclude any 'regional strategy'. Even among the left nationalist regimes, apart from some limited complementary initiatives among the ALBA countries, no regional plan exists. In this regard it is a serious mistake to write or speak about a "Latin American" problem, or initiative. What we can observe today is a generalized breakdown of the export-driven model and divergent social responses, between income protecting policies of Venezuela and export subsidy policies of Brazil, Argentina and Chile, Peru and Colombia. Throughout the recession, these center-left regimes have demonstrated a high degree of structural rigidity, making no effort to deepen and expand the domestic market and public investment, let alone nationalize bankrupt enterprises. The crisis highlights the process of *de-globalization* and the increasing importance of the nation state.

The deepening economic crisis adversely affects incumbent regimes, whether they are center-left or right, and strengthens their opposition. In Argentina the right and far-right have dominated the streets, with a growing power base in the 'interior' among the Argentine agrarian elite and the middle class in Buenos Aires. The progressive trade union, CTA, which has organized strikes and protests, is not connected with any new left alternative political organization.

Brazil has witnessed similar protests by social movements and trade unions against rising unemployment of over 10% and the decline in export-oriented industries. But again the principal political beneficiary of the declining popularity of Lula's self-styled "Worker's Party" is the Right.

In contrast, the center-left will benefit where rightist regimes are currently in power—namely Mexico, Colombia and Peru. But as is the case elsewhere, the mass movements lack an organized political response to a collapsing capitalism.

Moreover neither Cuba nor Venezuela offers a 'model' for the rest of Latin America. The former is highly dependent on a vulnerable tourist economy while the latter is a petrol economy. Given the systemic collapse of capitalism, these countries will need to move beyond 'piecemeal reforms'(such as Chavez food subsidies) and piecemeal nationalizations and toward the socialization of the financial, trade and manufacturing sectors.

Mass protests, general strikes, and other forms of social unrest are beginning to manifest themselves throughout the continent. No doubt the US will intensify its support for rightist movements in opposition and its existing rightist clients in power. US 'hegemony' over the Latin American *elite* is still strong even as it is virtually non-existent among the mass organizations in civil society. Given the overall militarist-protectionist posture of the Obama regime, we can expect intervention in the form of covert operations as class struggle escalates and moves toward a socialist transformation.

CHAPTER 7

ADDRESSING ECONOMIC NEEDS VIA ELECTORAL PROCESSES: THE CASE OF VENEZUELA

Electoral Systems and Democracy: Substance and Structure

A democratic political system involves at a minimum: (1) Free and equal competition for political office and (2) access to the means of communication and (3) competing ideas and freedom to speak and act without physical or psychological coercion. Procedures and conditions leading up to elections that violate these norms are incompatible with the notion of democracy, or the possibility of its being exercised. The most obvious case is Colombia where state terror against opposition groups has been practiced in every recent election.

However, while electoral processes are necessary, they are not sufficient conditions to define a democratic system. In other words there are numerous examples where electoral processes are embedded in institutional structures (oligarchy-controlled mass media or political parties) and preceded by political conditions (threats, patronage and corruption), which violate the basic norms of democracy. In other words, we can have non-democratic (authoritarian) as well as democratic electoral systems.

The most common authoritarian features of electoral systems, which deny its democratic character include:

1. Restricted access to the mass media because of monopoly ownership denying freedom of expression and undermining equality of competition.
2. The failure to regulate or limit spending on electoral campaigns, thereby favoring the moneyed classes' capacity to monopolize electoral campaign spending and biasing the competition to

favor candidates who amass the greatest funds.
3. State violence and repression of opposition parties, candidates and electoral constituencies during the electoral campaign. This nullifies any claims to a legitimate outcome based on 'an honest vote count' on election day.
4. Large scale financing by external foreign powers of the internal electoral process, drastically undermining internal competition and distorting free and equal electoral competition. Important organizational and financial links between foreign multinational corporations, intelligence agencies and foundations to domestic parties, personalities and NGOs introduce non-democratic, non-elected actors to the political process.

Taking account of these possible structural constraints, we see that there are numerous non-democratic variants of electoral systems. These include:

1. *Death-squad electoral systems* in which long-term, large-scale state violence against dissident civil society organizations (trade unions, peasant movements and human rights groups) is practiced prior to election day. Colombia is the prime example, where over the past decade, the military and paramilitary groups have murdered over 2500 trade unionists and 4 million, mostly peasants, were driven from their homes and communities.
2. *Imperial-collaborator electoral regimes* in which there is a mass infusion of political financing by European/US state entities to incumbent regimes and parties to counter growing mass popular opposition. Nicaragua, El Salvador and Dominican Republic are prime examples of electoral regimes, which have experienced 'externally controlled political processes'.
3. *Oligarchic electoral systems* are the most common type of authoritarian systems, many emerging from the crises of military dictatorships of the 1970-80s. They resulted from a political pact between economic oligarchs, political party elites and the military. The usual pattern is a two-party or modified three-party political system or coalition where the parties compete electorally for the opportunity to represent competing ruling class interests. Mexico, Chile, Uruguay and Brazil represent this type of oligarchic electoral system.

The Role of the Mass Media in Influencing Mass Politics

The role of the mass media (MSM) in influencing mass and class behavior has been a central concern among critical writers, especially since the turn of the Twentieth century. Debates and studies on the MSM have focused on its political bias, ownership and links to big business, relationships and ties to the state, relative openness and diversity, promotion of wars and corporate interests among other major issues affecting the relations of power, wealth and empire. Of particular interest to writers opposing and supporting the role of the MSM is the impact of the MSM in influencing mass outlook, opinions and behaviors. Essays, monographs and empirical studies have been published as to the extent of MM influence, the time frame during which it retains control, the 'depth' of loyalty to MM-inculcated opinions, and the 'place' in which MSM messages have the greatest influence in inducing mass opinion in conformity with ruling class interests.

There are three paradigms on the role, power and relation of the mass media on mass opinion and action: the conservative, liberal and Marxist.

The conservative, or 'pluralist' paradigm, propagated largely by US and European social scientists, emphasizes the multiple voices, competing networks and outlets and diversity of opinions. The conservative—'pluralists'—contend that even if the ownership of the mass media is concentrated and its message biased in favor of the status quo, the mass media are simply one 'resource' in favor of the status quo, countered by other 'resources' such as 'large numbers' of low income voters, who are presumed to be able to exercise their vote effectively to produce change. Though conceding the unequal access to the mass media between labor and capital, or a pro-war regimes and anti-war opposition, they argue the opposition does have some outlets, numerous writers and publicists: control over the mass media is 'unequal by disperses'. Moreover, they argue that with the growth of the internet, there are multiple sources of information, and the mass media monopoly has been severely diluted, in effect 'democratizing' the 'communication system'. The more astute pluralist ideologues cite empirical studies, which show that, in any event, most individuals' views are shaped by their family, friends and neighbors—by face-to-face relations—much more so than by the 'impersonal media'. In summary, the conservative argue, there *is* no all-powerful mass media elite, but to the extent that it exists, it is counterbalanced by alternative media, local opinion and its own tolerance of diverse and competing opinions.

The liberal paradigm describes the MM as the key instrument of ruling class domination in a liberal democracy. Beginning with a historical account of the concentration of ownership in the hands of a small number of corporations interlocked with business and the state, the MM is seen as an essential component in the 'system of control' which perpetuates the ruling class and empire-building by its control and indoctrination of mass opinion. The majority are converted into a malleable mass, induced to conformity to the interests and policies of the ruling class, thus preventing change and perpetuating the rule by the corporate elite.

For the liberals, the top-down control by the mass media explains the 'paradox' of a highly unequal, military-driven empire in the context of a free and democratic political system. The principal role of the academics is to convince other academics to *unmask* the media, to expose its fabrications, deceptions and hypocrisy, by emphasizing the 'contradictions' between 'our' democratic values and the lies of the powerful. The more radical version of the 'liberal' view of the mass media attributes the high degree of consensus between elite and masses in the United States to the omnipresence and omniscience of the mass media.

The Marxist approach to the mass media begins necessarily with a critique of the conservative and liberal perspectives. Against the conservative critique, it points out that 'power' is not a disembodied resource but a relationship in which the owners of wealth and power can multiply and accumulate political and economic assets. The presumption that 'everyone' or all groups can have some influence overlooks the fact that ownership of the means of communication is linked to other powerful economic groups, which wield power over banks, investment, trust funds, and these, in turn, influence political leaders and parties controlling legislation, candidate selection and government spending and agendas: this undermines the foundations and validity of the pluralist paradigm. On all the major events of our time, the mass media loyally echoed the political line of the capitalist state, justifying the invasion of Iraq, the demonizing of Iran and echoing the state line on Iran's nuclear program, Israel's blockade of Palestine and invasion of Lebanon and the bailout of Wall Street. In all the major events, a unified mass media played a leading role in propagating the message of the ruling class among the masses, with varying degrees of success.

The liberal paradigm of 'mass media determinism' appears to have more credibility than that of conservative 'pluralism' as its diagnosis of the structure of power and ownership of the MM corresponds to reality, as does its analysis of the MSM role in providing supportive propaganda for the lies of the state on war and the economy. However, when we turn to the liberals' image of the extent of MSM control over mass opinion and attitudes, its assertions of an all-powerful, all-controlling mass media successfully manipulating the public, these assumptions are questionable.

Historically, monopoly-oligopoly control of the mass media has been unsuccessful in shaping mass attitudes and action in a number of important political contexts. This is true even in the United States. For example, despite unanimous MSM support for the privatization of the Federal Social Security Program, the continuation of the military occupation of Iraq and military escalation in Afghanistan and the current private for profit health system, the great majority of the US public is strongly opposed to the MSM line, in fact so strongly as it relates to the huge public bailout of Wall Street, that the MSM has had to abandon that position or become completely discredited. Despite the fact that the leaders and the majorities of both ruling political parties do not reflect mass opinion, a majority of Americans have consistently backed a national, universal public health care, and the withdrawal of US troops, and they have vehemently opposed the Congressional support for Wall Street and the big finance industry.

An analysis reveals that the MSM are influential in shaping mass opinion in line with ruling class and state policies on foreign policies, particularly the war policy, at the start of a war, aggression or militarist posture before the economic and human costs are brought home to US citizens in their everyday lives. The MSM is relatively ineffective when it supports domestic measures, which adversely affect the everyday socio-economic life of the masses of the American people. The MSM operate most successfully when they dominate the flow and access of information, as in foreign policy, where they can fabricate, distort and emotionally charge what is heard and seen by the public. In contrast, MSM ruling class propaganda is severely weakened in the realm of domestic policy by the empirical experience of Americans in relation to their health, pensions, wages and employment. Marxists would argue that particular economic conditions create a class awareness, which counterbalance the power of the MM. The same is true re foreign policy/wars, where it is the military/ families (or 9-11 families) who are the primary forces sustaining the peace or protest movements. Again, experience conditions perceptions of reality in a manner that cannot be erased by the MSM.

The weakness of the liberal view of the dominance of the mass media fails to take account of the impact of *class contexts*, the constraints of economic crises, the costs of war, the impact of downward mobility and the importance of basic social security in measuring or describing public perception of the operations of the mass media. Most liberal theory of the mass media is based on a *selective* view of contexts, issues, time and places to back their theory. For example, the notion of mass conformity with mass media 'fits' with the period of an expanding economy, upward social mobility, relative peace or less costly military interventions, particularly with regard to foreign policy issues. The MSM's long term backing for capitalism or the 'free market' dominates mass opinion up to the collapse of capitalism. However, with the crises and breakdown of the financial system and especially the loss by millions of people of their pensions, and the realization by some of the MSM that their position is indefensible and that they must appear to question the policies of the capitalist state, the liberal view of MSM omnipotence and dominance of mass opinion is revealed as deeply flawed. It fails to account for political-economic and indeed MSM changes resulting from mass opinion which strongly deviates from earlier state-policy-supporting MSM propaganda.

The Marxist perspective relativizes the influence of the MSM, making its power over the masses contingent on the degree to which the working and allied classes depend exclusively on the MM for information and for defining their political interests and social action. Marxists argue that the MM exercises maximum influence where there is little or no class organization or class struggle (like in the US). In contrast, where there is or was class organization, as in Venezuela or Bolivia, Chile in the 1970s, and Central America in the 1980s, the mass media have a far weaker impact on mass public opinion. Marxists argue that where there is a history and culture of working class, peasant, Indian or other class-based movements and class solidarity, the ruling class/state propaganda promoted by the MM has only a weak effect. The masses have a preexistent framework, communication network and local opinion leaders, which filter out messages/propaganda that violate social/class/ethnic/national solidarity.

For example, in Chile during the Presidency of Salvador Allende (1970-73), the vast majority of the print and broadcast media were violently opposed to the Democratic Socialist President—yet President Allende won the election, and the left increased its vote in subsequent municipal and congressional elections based on overwhelming support from the workers, poor peasants, Indians and unemployed shanty town residents.

More recently in Venezuela, the vast majority of the MM has opposed President Chavez (1998-2008) in every congressional and municipal election, yet he has won massive electoral victories. In both cases, socio-economic programs (vast increases in health and education programs, land distribution, increased opportunities for and real instances of upward mobility, progressive income programs, nationalization of basic resources), strong class-based organized support and mass mobilizations creating class consciousness undermined the effectiveness of the mass media.

Throughout Latin America during the first decade of the new millennium, powerful popular movements grew in membership and organization despite their intense demonizing by all the major MSM. In Brazil, the Landless Rural Workers expanded its membership and support for land occupation despite the criminalization of its activity by the MSM. The same was true of the miners, workers, peasant and Indian movements in Bolivia—leading to the overthrow of MSM-backed neo-liberal presidents. Similar mass uprisings overthrowing MSM-backed Presidents took place in Argentina (2001) and Ecuador (2000 and 2005).

These cases illustrate the contingent and circumstantial conditions that influence MSM dominance of mass opinion. There are several common conditions in all these cases:

1. History, cultural, community and family linkages, which create a 'block' or 'filter' on MSM propaganda, especially on socio-economic issues affecting workplace, neighborhood and living standards.

2. Class struggle creates horizontal class bonds, especially in response to state and ruling class repression, declining living standards, concentration of wealth and mass evictions and displacement. Class struggle creates positive reciprocity to messages reinforcing the struggle and a negative response or closure to messages from publicly-identified media taking the side of the ruling class.

3. Class-based advocacy organizations provide alternative frameworks for understanding events, define mass interests in class terms that resonate with their everyday experience, and provide information and interpretation that counters the MSM. The higher the degree of class organization, the greater the class solidarity and struggle, the weaker the MSM impact on mass opinion. The converse is also true. In the US, those trade unions that still exist are run by officials drawing salaries of $300,000 dollars or more a year, who emphasize collaboration with the bosses (and publicly reject class struggle politics), while the trade union movement overall has failed to organize 93% of the private workforce, leaving the masses vulnerable to the onslaught of the MSM.

4. The stronger the alternative class networks of opinion formation, the weaker the influence of the MM. Where social movements develop local cadre, opinion leaders and community rooted activists, the less likely the masses will take their 'cues' on events from the formal, distant MM. In many cases the masses *selectively* tune into the MM for entertainment (sports, soap operas, comedies) while rejecting their news reports and editorials. Multi-generational families living in close proximity, located in homogenous occupational neighborhoods, and with strong histories of construction of class-based communities generate class solidarity and social messages which come in conflict with the ruling class messages whether in its disguised manipulative form of 'private initiative' and 'successful micro-capitalism' or in its overt form of criminalization of collective class action. Both liberal and conservative views of the MM fail to account for the *class context* of media reciprocity and power; the pluralists understate its capacity to *dominate* in times of weak class organization; the liberals overstate the power of the MM by ignoring the countervailing power of class-

based organization, class struggle, culture, history and family traditions and solidarity that link individuals to their class and undermine receptivity to the ruling class message of the MM.

Navigating the Barriers to Change Through Democratic Process

Even authoritarian electoral systems are not static. Old oligarchic parties collapse and new ones emerge. Some oligarchic parties begin by adopting populist postures to gain office and then, post-election, pursue and deepen oligarchic ties, co-opting and corrupting the emerging insurgent social leaders and aborting the democratic realization of their political agenda. Authoritarian electoral systems are subject to the pressure of non-electoral parties and movements to modify or reform repressive practices and the privileging of economic inequalities.

Major economic crises and political uprisings are equally significant in challenging oligarchic electoral systems, capable of displacing oligarchic regimes and leading to the emergence of plebian-based democratic movements. Regimes can emerge which attempt to 'mediate' or 'balance' between the mass democratic movements and oligarchic ruling classes. In recent years, mass popular movements and uprisings have led to the overthrow of a number of oligarchic electoral regimes. Such events have taken place in Bolivia, Argentina and Ecuador. In addition, established oligarchic electoral regimes have been defeated because of mass mobilizations in Venezuela, Brazil, Uruguay and Paraguay. As a result, some of the authoritarian political constraints have been temporarily reformed, while the economic ruling classes remain intact. The inequalities in economic resources and access to the mass media remain in place or are, at best, merely modified.

In other words, in recent years a process of democratizing the Latin American electoral system has been underway. Over the past eight years the democratization of electoral politics advanced with the breakdown of the neo-liberal political-economic system, the rise of popular mass movements and the defeat of abortive oligarchic uprisings designed to restore strict authorization rule. However this process is not linear, homogenous or irreversible. Democratic reformers frequently retain the repressive state apparatus, limiting changes in authoritarian structures and repressive practices. In summary, usually electoral politics, and not democracy, has resulted from the transition between military to civilian rule.

Over the past eight years, however, the democratization of electoral politics advanced with the breakdown of the neo-liberal political-economic system, the rise of popular mass movements and the defeat of abortive oligarchic uprisings designed to restore strict authorization rule.

Venezuela represents the most exemplary case of a sustained

effort to democratize electoral politics. Venezuela, during the Chavez Presidency (1999-2008), represents a unique case of an effort to *combine the democratization of electoral politics with the socialization of the economy*, deepening and extending democratic politics into the sphere of the economy.

The Transition to Democracy

Venezuela is the country in Latin America that best exemplifies the transition from oligarchic electoral politics to democracy. During the preceding 40 years (1959-1998) the country was ruled by a two-party elite (Democratic Action and Social Christian—COPEI), which competed to represent the petrol-rentier oligarchy, powerful importers, and the real estate-financial speculative elite. The two parties were dominated by a predator political class, which pillaged the public treasury. The economic collapse during the infamous decade of 1989-1998 resulted in a 10-fold increase in poverty, which led to the mass uprising and state massacre of 1989 known as the 'Caracazo'. This, in turn, paved the way for the election of President Chavez in 1999.

President Chavez took the first steps toward reforming the authoritarian electoral system through a referendum and subsequent new constitution. Chavez's opposition to Washington's imperial 'War on Terror' was part of a foreign policy designed to end US tutelage and affirm Venezuela's national sovereignty. The colonial oligarchy sought to regain power, propagandizing constantly against Chavez through its dominant control of the local media. In an effort to return the country to its authoritarian past, it initiated a US-backed civil-military coup in April 2002. The coup was defeated. Chavez was restored to power by a popular uprising backed by loyalist military officials. The President dismissed the coup participants within the government and arrested their civilian collaborators. As a result, the political elite's ability to exercise social control through authoritarian organizations in civil society and the state was weakened. A subsequent lockout was led by an elite group of petroleum executives who sought thereby to sabotage the economy and overthrow the elected president. They were defeated by a joint effort of the Government and the petrol workers. This victory further weakened the colonial oligarchs in the strategic oil industry. The defeat of the strategic pillars of authoritarian electoral power led to the effective nationalization of the petroleum industry. Through these victories President Chavez strengthened the process of democratization of the state and civil society.

Under the leadership of President Chavez, the petroleum industry became more responsive to the social needs of the majority of its citizens. Under democratic leadership the PDVSA (the national oil company) financed a vast number of citizen educational programs which in turn further enhanced citizen capacity to function effectively in relation to Venezuelan democracy. With a powerful electoral mandate after his re-election and vast increases in public revenues through public ownership and high world oil prices, President Chavez pursued policies that encouraged citizen participation through elected community councils, thereby providing a new dimension to the process of democratization.

Vital Steps Towards Deepening Venezuelan Democracy

Democratizing the electoral process and dismantling the oligarchic electoral system took several directions:

1. The encouragement, promotion and financing of a vast array of neighborhood cooperatives, peasant organizations and trade unions, which increased the power and political influence of the working class and informal workers. Freed from upper class patronage and control, the new social organizations equalized the effective role of the poor in the political process. Greater freedom and equality were essential ingredients in the strengthening of democratic politics.

2. The weakening of the linkages between the oligarchic political and economic elites and the military/Pentagon diminished the power of the authoritarian state over civil society. Electoral outcomes were less subject to the intervention of undemocratic imperial agencies. Conversely the new mass organizations increased the importance of internal democratic processes. While the US and EU continued to channel funds into opposition oligarchic NGOs, this was countered by domestic mass social movements and social programs funded by these democratically elected public institutions.

3. Publicly financed television stations and the proliferation of popularly controlled community radio stations have broken the oligarchy's media monopoly. The result is more pluralistic, balanced and diverse sources of information. Better-informed citizens can make more rational political decisions.

4. Freedom of speech has been greatly enhanced by the proliferation of political forums not controlled by the oligarchy. A greater number of more diverse opinion leaders have greater access to more organized groups and media outlets than ever before.

5. Civil society has been enriched by the growth of multiple trade unions and community-based groups. Competing voter lists in

social movements have greatly increased internal democracy in civil society organizations. Electoral competition within civil society has been greatly enhanced. Civil society has been strengthened in relation to the state. The democratization of civil society movements has strengthened public debate and the electoral processes.

Victory for Venezuelan Socialists in Crucial Elections: November 2008

The pro-Chavez United Socialist Party of Venezuela (PSUV) won 72% of the governorships in the November 23, 2008 elections and 58% of the popular vote, dumbfounding the predictions of most of the pro-capitalist pollsters and the vast majority of the mass media who favored the opposition.

PSUV candidates defeated incumbent opposition governors in three states (Guaro, Sucre, Aragua) and lost two states (Miranda and Tachira). The opposition retained the governorship in a tourist center (Nueva Esparta) and won in Tachira, a state bordering Colombia, Carabobo and the oil state of Zulia, as well as scoring an upset victory in the populous state of Miranda and taking the mayoralty district of the capital, Caracas. The socialist victory was especially significant because the voter turnout of 65% exceeded all previous non-presidential elections. The prediction by the propaganda pollsters that a high turnout would favor the opposition reflected their wishful thinking.

The significance of the socialist victory is clear if we put it in a comparative historical context:

1. Few if any government parties in Europe, North or South American have retained such high levels of popular support in free and open elections.
2. The PSUV retained its high level of support in the context of several radical economic measures, including the nationalization of major cement, steel, financial and other private capitalist monopolies.
3. The Socialists won despite the 70% decline in oil prices (from $140 to $52 dollars a barrel), Venezuela's principle source of export earnings, and largely because the government maintained most of its funding for its social programs.
4. The electorate was more selective in its voting decisions regarding Chavista candidates—rewarding candidates who performed adequately in providing government services and punishing those who ignored or were unresponsive to popular demands. While President Chavez campaigned for all the Socialist candidates, voters did not uniformly follow his lead

where they had strong grievances against local Chavista incumbents, as was the case with outgoing Governor Disdado Cabello of Miranda and the Mayor of the Capital District of Caracas. Socialist victories were mostly the result of a deliberate, class-interest based vote and not simply a reflex identification with President Chavez.

5. The decisive victory of the PSUV provides the basis for confronting the deepening collapse of world capitalism with socialist measures, instead of pouring out state funds to rescue bankrupt capitalist banks, commercial and manufacturing enterprises. The collapse of capitalism facilitates the socialization of most of the key economic sectors. Most Venezuelan firms are heavily indebted to the state and local banks. The Chavez government can ask the firms to repay their debts or handover the keys—in effect bringing about a painless and eminently legal transition to socialism.

The election results point to deepening polarization between the hard right and the socialist left. The centrist social-democratic ex-Chavista governors were practically wiped from the political map. The rightist winner in Miranda State, Henrique Capriles Radonsky, had tried to burn down the Cuban embassy during the failed military coup of April 2002 and the newly elected Governor of Zulia, Pablo Perez, was the hand picked candidate of the former hard-line rightwinger, Governor Rosales.

While the opposition-controlled state governorships and municipal mayoralties can provide an institutional basis to attack the national government, the economic crisis will sharply limit the amount of resources available to maintain services and will increase their dependence on the federal government. A frontal assault on the Chavez Government spending state and local funds on partisan warfare could lead to a decline of federal welfare transfers and would provoke grassroots discontent. The right wing won on the basis of promising to improve state and city services and end corruption and favoritism. Resorting to their past practices of crony politics and extreme obstructionism could quickly cost them popular support and undermine their hopes of transforming local gains into national power. The newly elected opposition governors and mayors need the cooperation and support of the Federal Government, especially in the context of the deepening crisis, or they will lose popular support and credibility.

Democratic Socialism and the February 2009 Vote on the Re-Election Amendment

On February 15, 2009 Venezuelans voted to pass a constitutional amendment, which will permit the electorate to re-elect an incumbent President without term limits. In the past, many democratic analysts were opposed to 'presidential re-election' for several reasons. According to their critique: 1. Re-election was a method used by dictators to provide pseudo-legitimacy to regimes, which repressed democratic freedoms of speech, assembly, and access to mass media. 2. Re-election allowed incumbent regimes to utilize the state apparatus to engage in fraud and violence, perpetuating authoritarian oligarchic rule and undermining free and equal competition. 3. Re-election allowed the incumbent president to monopolize the mass media and deny the opposition equal access to campaign resources. 4. Repeatedly re-elected presidents concentrated and accumulated state power while weakening popular social organizations in civil society and strengthening the links between the state and the oligarchic civic and economic organizations.

These were legitimate criticisms of presidential re-election in past historical contexts, but were not applicable to the case of Venezuela under Chavez.

The historical record of the past decade and the present realities in Venezuela today demonstrate that democratic principles and practices have deepened and extended following each election and re-election of Hugo Chavez. For example:

1. The mass media are now much more diverse; access is more equal and there is a greater variety of competing socio-economic paradigms under debate.

2. Civil society contains a greater number of free and independent competing and organized social classes than ever in the history of Venezuela. Over the period 1999-2009, competing neighborhood groups with diverse social perspectives have flourished.

3. Electoral campaigns and procedures are less subject state corruption, intervention and violent manipulation than ever before.

4. Citizen participation and defense of democratic freedoms was never more widespread and intense, as was witnessed by the massive popular mobilization defeating the US-oligarchy-military coup of April 2002, and the restoration of the elected President (Chavez), the Congress and the Venezuelan constitution.

5. The nationalization of foreign- and oligarchy-controlled strategic enterprises has made key economic enterprises subject to legislative and executive oversight by elected public representatives.

6. The re-election of President Chavez has resulted in politics which lowered socio-economic inequalities, and increased social expenditures for the poor, the working class and peasantry, thus increasing their stake in democratic institutions, their interest in

electoral campaigns and providing them with greater time and resources to participate in social and political organizations.

Contrary to previous historical experiences, in Venezuela under President Chavez, there is a positive correlation between his re-election and the extension and deepening of democratic institutions and practices as well as a richer civic culture. In the 40 years prior to the Chavez presidency (1959-1998) during which re-election was prohibited, the alternating presidents perpetuated a profoundly authoritarian oligarchic electoral system which effectively disenfranchised the masses of low-income voters, offering few choices and subjecting them to a corrupt party patronage system.

The key is to view re-election versus single-term presidencies in their historical context and in terms of the political practices and pragmatic consequences of each. For example, the 're-election' of Alvaro Uribe means the perpetuation of death squads and forced dispossession of millions of peasants. The limits on re-election of presidents in Mexico has not altered highly authoritarian rule, vast inequalities, foreign control of all strategic sectors of the economy and the power of the capitalist class to replace one oligarch for another.

Approval of the constitutional amendment allowing for the re-election of President Chavez was essential for the continuation of the democratic process and social welfare of Venezuelans. Because of President Chavez' audacious and courageous defense of world peace and humanitarian justice, his re-election was especially important in the face of imperial wars and genocidal colonial wars in Iraq, Afghanistan, Palestine and elsewhere.

Approval of the amendment will facilitate the continuation of vital socio-economic reforms, which provide free education, health and subsidized food for the vast majority of Venezuelans.

Particularly in a time of worldwide capitalist recession/depression, only a democratic-socialist government will give highest priority to protecting social welfare programs over and against bailing out bankers, industrialists and export elites. All alternative capitalist candidates in Venezuela would follow the practice of the North American, European and Asian rulers of cutting social programs to save the ruling class.

The re-election of President Chavez will facilitate the democratization of the economy through nationalization and socialization. The defeat of the re-election amendment would have aborted and reversed the process leading to the privatization of strategic economic sectors, which would lead the country back to foreign capitalists arbitrarily making all key economic decisions.

Continuing Obstacles to Democratization

In contrast to past oligarchic electoral regimes, Venezuela under

Chavez has moved decisively toward the consolidation of its democratic transition.

Nevertheless, numerous and serious authoritarian impediments to the full consolidation of democracy still exist. Principally, they are found in the continuation of vast concentrations of oligarchic wealth and ownership of strategic banking, mass media, real estate, agricultural lands, distribution networks and the manufacturing sectors. Concentrated private economic ownership and wealth results in vast social inequalities, which translate into the continuation of political inequalities in the form of unequal competition for political influence, despite the countervailing power of the government and an invigorated civil society.

The immediate and most pressing task facing the PSUV, President Chavez, the legislators and the newly elected Chavez officials is to formulate a comprehensive socio-economic strategic plan to confront the global collapse of capitalism. This is especially critical in dealing with the sharp fall in oil prices, federal revenues and the inevitable decline in government spending. Chavez has promised to maintain all social programs even if oil prices remain at or below $50 dollars a barrel. This is clearly a positive and defensible position if the government manages to reduce its huge subsidies to the private sector and doesn't embark on any bailout of bankrupt or nearly bankrupt private firms. While $40 billion dollars in reserves can serve as a temporary cushion, the fact remains that the government, with the backing of its majorities in the federal legislature and at the state levels, needs to make hard choices and not simply print money, run bigger deficits, devalue the currency and exacerbate the already high rates of annual inflation (31% as of November).

Conclusion

The consummation and completion of the process of democratization requires the equalization of socio-economic conditions in society and the introduction of democratic reforms in the state and within publicly owned enterprises.

The full realization of democracy requires the implementation of a socialist transformation in which elections take place in the work place and through a program of re-distribution of wealth, land and financial resources.

The only reasonable strategy is to take control of foreign trade and directly oversee the commanding heights of the productive and distributive sectors and set priorities that defend popular living standards. To counteract bureaucratic ineptness and neutralize lazy elected officials, effective power and control must be transferred to organized workers and autonomous consumer and neighborhood councils. The recent past reveals that merely electing socialist mayors or governors is not sufficient to ensure the implementation of progressive policies and the delivery of basic services. Liberal representative government (even with elected socialists) requires, at a minimum, mass popular control and mass pressure to implement the hard decisions and popular priorities in the midst of a deepening and prolonged economic crisis.

The challenge for the Left, especially for a socialist-aspiring regime that is holding the reins of government, is different from that faced by the Left, when it is out of power.

When the Left is unable to access the lawmaking powers and access to resources enjoyed by government, it must rely on mass organizations and face-to-face education to create counter-information. Political education is key to creating successful organizers and leaders of popular opinion. Education must be 'general' in terms of strategic conceptions and 'particular' with regard to focusing on specific class, gender, race, sectoral, occupational and historical conditions. Education should be integral, historical and focused on contemporary class struggle, development of productive forces and social relations of productions.

The Left in power commands greater material resources to deepen and extend face-to-face education and to develop the communication facilities for mass education to counter the established media power of the capitalist/imperialist ruling class. The first rule of a Left government is to protect the constitutional and democratic political order from MM political destabilization campaigns. The right of free speech should be protected from the violent media campaigns by the displaced ruling class. While dissent is legitimate free speech and should be protected, systematic propaganda by private media-owning elites designed to overthrow the government by force and violence and to incite political sabotage of the economy should feel the full weight of the democratic state. Competition between the socialist and capitalist media is inevitable in the transition to the new society.

The socialist media alternative requires a multi-pronged strategy, which includes:

1. Daily *mass newspapers* of quality carrying news and investigative reports, including independent, critical, or pro-revolution items or perspectives.

2. TV: information, reportage, not just 'state propaganda', entertainment, sports, original scripts, on-site coverage of the news, balances seminars or 'round tables', speeches with in depth investigatory reports, together with special movies, plays and music programs.

- TV and radio segments should be devoted to specific segments of mass movements (community councils, trade unions, peasant confederations, small business, progressive religious programs). They should include:

    a. children movements, summer programs of recreation and education.

    b. technical and ideological training schools for skill productive workers, rather than local co-ops', involved in construction, industry and services.

    c. sports, mass participatory and social solidarity: physical and moral training.

    d. Defense and security: technical and political training for multiple units of civil and military defense. Modern arms and political education.

3. Community radio with local news, testimonials, local debates, municipal politics and entertainment.

4. Cadre or leadership educational programs.

5. Social movement-developed social communication

6. Ideological theoretical clarification. Basic concepts of *Socialist Education*: class struggle, state and productive system, application of key concepts to national-historical-cultural realities (Concrete application to historical experience):

    a. history-materialist concept of development

    b. empirical-Marxist method: applied Marxism

    c. Comparative 'models' of political economy, neo-liberal vs. populism vs. nationalism vs. socialism

    d. Critical studies of society, class structures and ruling class

    e. State institutions and ideologies

    f. Transition from capitalism to socialism: comparative experience and contradictions

    g. Transition from socialist to communism: consequences

    h. Crises of post-socialist regimes

    i. Socialist models: advantages and contradictions

7. Politics, innovations, productive system, class structures.

PART II

REGIONAL WARS

CHAPTER 8

MASTERS OF DEFEAT: RETREATING EMPIRE AND BELLICOSE BLUSTER

"Washington is forced to watch other powers shape events"
Financial Times, August 25, 2008

Introduction

Everywhere one looks, US imperial policy has suffered major military and diplomatic defeats. With the backing of the Democratic Congress, the Republican White House's aggressive pursuit of a *military* approach to *empire-building* has led to a worldwide decline of US influence, the realignment of former client rulers toward imperial adversaries, the emergence of competing hegemons and the loss of crucial sources of strategic raw materials.

However, the defeats and losses have not dampened militaristic policies nor extinguished the drive for empire building. On the contrary, both the While House and the Congressional incumbents have embraced a hardening of military positions, reiterated a confrontational style of politics and an increased reliance on overseas, bellicose posturing to distract the domestic populace from its deteriorating economic conditions.

As the economic and political cost of sustaining the empire increases, as the Federal government allocates hundreds of billions to the crises-ridden financial sector and cuts tens of billions in corporate taxes, avoiding collapse and recession, the entire economic burden is borne by the wage and salaried class in the form of declining living standards, while 12 million immigrant workers are subject to savage police state repression.

The overseas failures and domestic crises however have not led to the emergence of progressive alternatives; the beneficiaries are overseas competitors and the domestic elite. In large part where public opinion majorities have expressed a desire or clamored for progressive alternatives, they have been thwarted by political representatives linked to militarist ideologues and the corporate elites.

Paradoxically the defeats and decline of US military-directed empire building has been accompanied by the retreat of the anti-war movements in North America and Western Europe and the sharp decline of political parties and regimes opposing US imperialism in all the advanced capitalist countries. In other words, the defeats suffered by the US Empire have not been products of the Western Left, nor have they led to a 'peace dividend' or improved living standards for the working classes or peasants, or any significant renunciation of US policy goals. To the extent that there are beneficiaries, these are found largely among the newly-aspiring economic imperial countries, like China, Russia and India, among the oil rich countries of the Middle East, and especially among a broad swath of large agro-mineral export countries like Brazil, South Africa and Iran, which have carved out important niches in their regions.

Prior to the financial crisis and the onset of recession, the growth and overseas expansion of the new economic empire building countries and their agro-mineral-financial ruling classes (with the possible exception of Venezuela) greatly benefited a tiny elite, comprising not more than twenty percent of the population. The relative decline of US military imperialism and the rise of new economic imperialist powers redistributed wealth and market share *between countries* but *not among classes* within the ascendant powers. While the militarists-Zionists-financial speculators ruled—and continue to rule—the US Empire, the new billionaire manufacturers, real estate speculators and agro-mineral exporters prospered in the emerging economic empires

The second paradox is found in the fact that the *political forces militarily defeating* the US military-centered empire are not the forces benefiting from the struggle. While the Iraqi and Afghan resistance have imposed almost a trillion dollar cost on the US Treasury and tied down over 2 million rotating US troops over the past six years, it is the Chinese, Indian, Russian, European, Gulf Oil and financial ruling classes which have reaped the benefits from massive US non-productive expenditures. While the new economic beneficiaries are, in large part, secular, imperial and elitist, the politico-military forces undermining and defeating the US military empire are religious (Islamic), nationalist and mass-based—but their evident military success has not yet led to the point where these movements could be said to have taken control over their respective territories, or over any implementation of socio-economic policy therein.

The contemporary defeats of US military empire building are not a product of Western, secular, mass leftist movements. Nor indeed have these military defeats as yet run their course to result in conclusive military withdrawal. Instead, to date they have resulted in repressive societies still ruled by US-planted proxies with slender public support, who are engaged in a fettered overseen management of fast-growing highly unequal economies, led by ruling classes promoting imposed 'national' versions of Western-promoted free market/neo-liberal strategies, which seek to maximize profits through economic exploitation of labor, resource extraction and pillage of the environment. Until the mass movements, intellectuals and activists of the West break from their passivity and blind allegiance to the existing major parties, the decline of US militarism will be a costly burden solely assumed by the masses of the Third World while the benefits will accrue to the rising new billionaire economic imperialists not resident in the countries where the wars are being fought.

The Geography of Imperial Failures

Iraq and Iran

The ascendancy of military-directed empire building in the US has once again demonstrated its utter incapability to impose a new imperial order. After years of war and occupation in Iraq, the US has suffered enormous military casualties and over half a trillion in economic losses, without securing any political, military or natural resource gains. The losses from the war have generated domestic opposition to US military intervention, undermining current and future imperial military capacity, but this opposition is unable to find any political expression, having gambled on the intentions of Obama and crew, and lost. While the US designated puppet ruler in Iraq, Al Maliki, may have demanded a set date for US withdrawal, and Obama may have indicated that 50,000 troops will be drawn down, it remains questionable whether this in fact will take place. US client Afghan President Karzai may have called for greater oversight over US military operations which have killed thousands of non-combatants and civilians, thus deepening and extending support for the national resistance which now operates throughout the country, but the Obama regime's response has been to send more troops into a conflict which many have already deemed cannot be won.

For those in the US, particularly on the 'Left' who mistakenly argued that the invasion of Iraq was a 'War for Oil' (rather than a war in support of Israeli hegemonic ambitions), Iraq's signing of a $3 billion dollar oil contract with the China National Petroleum Corporation in late August 2008[1] demonstrates the contrary, unless one wishes to revise the slogan to 'US War for Chinese Oil'. Since the 2003 US invasion of Iraq, US oil companies have still failed to secure major oil deals.

On October 4-5, 2008, Shell, one of the world's biggest petroleum multinationals and OMV, an Austrian energy corporation, sponsored a conference in Teheran under the auspices of the National Iranian Gas Export Company to promote 'gas export opportunities and potentials of the Islamic Republic of Iran'. This conference was simply one more example of the role of major petroleum companies attempting, through peaceful means, to build their overseas holdings ('economic empire'). The major opposition to this 'oil for peace' move on the part of Shell Oil came from the leading Jewish-Zionist promoter of US engaging in Middle East wars for Israel— the Anti-Defamation League, which criticized Big Oil. According to its two principle leaders, Glen Lewy and Abe Foxman, "...these two companies are co-sponsoring a conference with the state-owned energy company of the leading state-sponsor of terrorism and human rights violator. By promoting one of Iran's strategic industries, natural gas, OMV and Shell are hindering the effort of responsible states (sic) and corporations to isolate Iran."[2]

The conflict between Shell/OMV and a leading American Zionist-Jewish organization highlights the fundamental conflict between economic-centered empire building and military-centered empire building. The fact that Shell and OMV went ahead with the Iranian conference shows that at least some sectors of the oil industry are finally beginning to challenge the stranglehold that Zionist-militarists have over US Middle East policy. After having lost tens of billions of dollars in lucrative oil contracts thanks to Zionist-dictated policies, the oil companies are finally taking the first tentative steps toward formulating a new policy.

By pursuing the Israeli-US Zionist agenda of sequential wars and sanctions against oil-rich Muslim countries, Washington has lost access, control and profits to global economic competitors in a strategic region.

Africa

In the African nation of Somalia, Washington opted for military intervention via the proxy Ethiopian dictatorial regime of Meles Zenawi to bolster the discredited and defeated pro-US puppet regime of Abdullah Yusuf. After almost two years the Ethiopian and the puppet regime had only succeeded in controlling a few blocks of the capital, Mogadishu, while the rest of the country remained in the hands of the Somali resistance. In August 2008, the Ethiopian regime "expressed a desire to curtail its military engagement in Somalia",[3] and not long thereafter, it began its withdrawal. The US surrogate was militarily and politically defeated; the US failed to secure initial support for its proxy occupation from the African Union, and even now the situation remains chaotic, manifesting itself, inter alia, in episodes of piracy off the Somalia coast.

Throughout Africa, China, the EU, Japan, Russia and to a lesser degree India and Brazil all have made inroads in securing joint ventures in oil, raw materials export markets and large-scale, long-term infrastructure investments, while the US backs armed separatists in the Sudan, subsidizes the corrupt Mubarak regime in Egypt for over a billion dollars a year, and most lately, threatened to invade Eritrea! Not only has the US empire lost out economically to its global competitors, it has suffered a major military-diplomatic defeat in Somalia and severely politically and financially weakened its Ethiopian client.

South Asia

In South Asia, the US strategic puppet ruler, Pakistani dictator Musharraf was forced to resign—and the weak and divided electoral coalition which replaced him has not been able to match the military, diplomatic and intelligence support for the US war in Afghanistan which Musharraf provided. The Pakistan-Afghan border is virtually open territory for cross border attacks, recruitment and military supplies by Afghan resistance organizations. The empire's loss of Musharraf further undermines US efforts to impose an outpost in Afghanistan.

Through frequent ground and air attacks by unmanned drones on Pakistan regions bordering Afghanistan leading to civilian casualties, the US-NATO 'coalition' has multiplied, deepened and made massive civilian political and armed opposition throughout the country. The 'election' of the US client and convicted warlord and thug, Asif Ali Zadari, as President of Pakistan, will not in any way contribute to the recovery of US influence outside of very limited elite political and military circles. Washington's pursuit and extension of military imperialism from Afghanistan to Pakistan has led to even more severe political defeat among a much wider population in South Asia.

Top NATO generals and officials have recognized that the 'Taliban' has reorganized and extended its influence throughout the country, controlling most throughways to the major cities and even operating in and around the capital Kabul. Repeated US bombing and missile strikes on civilian housing, cultural events and markets have alienated vast numbers of Afghans and led to widespread opposition to US client ruler, Karzai. The promises of both US presidential candidates to vastly expand the US occupation forces in Afghanistan upon taking office was immediately implemented upon an Obama win with an Afghan "surge" of 21,000 troops, seemingly unmitigated by his call for an "exit strategy" that had so cheered the dwindling pro-Obama progressive flank when the surge was first announced. As Associated Press put it:

> The president, who declared last weekend an "exit strategy" was needed for Afghanistan, never used those words in announcing his plans on Friday. His strategy is built on an ambitious goal of boosting the Afghan army from 80,000

to 134,000 troops by 2011—and greatly increasing training by U.S. troops accompanying them—so the Afghan military can defeat Taliban insurgents and take control of the war.[4]

Caucasus

Washington's attempt to extend its sphere of influence in the Caucasus through a territorial grab by its authoritarian Georgian client, President Mikheil Saakashvili, led instead to a profound defeat of the local satrap's regional ambitions. The political break and integration with Russia of South Ossetia and Abkhazia represents the end of unrestricted expansion of the US and EU in the region—and a rollback in contested terrain. The rash adventurism and subsequent destruction of the Georgian economy by Saakashvili has provoked widespread internal unrest. Worse still, Georgia, the US and its Eastern European clients' call for 'sanctions' against Russia, threatened to undermine Western European strategic energy supply lines, as well as end Moscow's collaboration with US military policies in Afghanistan, Iran and the Middle East. If Washington escalates its military and economic threats to Russia, the latter can provide Iran, Syria and other US adversaries with powerful middle range ultra-modern anti-aircraft missiles. Equally important Russia can dump over $200 billion in US Treasury notes, further weaken the US dollar and set in motion a global run in the currency. Further, perhaps at Russia's instigation,[5] the Kyrgystan government announced its decision to close the US Manas Air Base, forcing the US to reroute its supply lines to Afghanistan. (In 2006, Uzbekistan took steps to rejoin the Russian-dominated Collective Security Treaty Organization (CSTO) and the Eurasian Economic Community (EurASEC), having closed its US base in 2005.) Russia also announced the formation of a rapid-reaction military force comprising post-Soviet nations, including Armenia, Uzbekistan, Kyrgystan, Belarus, Kazakhstan and Tajikistan.

In Georgia as elsewhere, US military-centered empire building gave priority to a failed marginal land grab by a third rate client over lucrative strategic economic and military relations with one of the world's global oil and gas powers and a crucial collaborator in its ongoing military operation in the Middle East. While US economic relations with Russia crumble in the wake of its aggressive military encirclement of Moscow—military bases in the Czech Republic, Poland, Georgia, Bulgaria, Romania— Western European empire builders resist making military threats in favor of harsh rhetoric and 'dialog' in order to sustain strategic energy ties.

Israel and the Arabs

In the Middle East, the US unconditional backing of Israeli military aggression in Lebanon, Palestine and Syria, and US backing of weak and ineffective Arab clients has led to a sharp decline in US influence. In

Lebanon, since the defeat of the Israeli invasion in 2006, Hezbollah literally rules the southern half of the country—and holds veto power within the national government, reversing US client rule.

In Gaza, US and Israeli military attempts to seize power and oust Hamas via its client Abbas and Dahlen were roundly defeated and the independent nationalist movement led by Hamas consolidated power.

Washington's effort to regain its influence and improve its image among conservative and moderate Arab rulers by 'mediating' a peace agreement between Israel and Palestine in Annapolis in November 2007 was utterly destroyed by Tel Aviv's open and total repudiation of all the basic conditions set forth by the Bush Administration. Washington has no influence on Israel's colonial expansion. On the contrary, the US Middle East policy is totally subject to the Israeli state through the Zionist Power Configuration and its control over Congress, Presidential selection, the mass media and major propaganda 'think tanks'. The Zionists demonstrated their power by even dictating who could or could not even speak at the Democratic National Convention with the unprecedented censoring of former President James Carter because of his humanitarian criticism of Israel's policies toward the Palestinians. Zionist-Israeli usurpation of US Middle East policy has led to strategic losses of investments, markets, profits and partnerships for the entire multi-national oil and gas industry.

The political fusion of imperialist militarists confronting Russia at the cost of strategic economic relations and Zionist-militarists pursuing Israeli regional power has led to multiple failed military adventures and tremendous global economic losses.

The Western Hemisphere

The application of the militarist strategy as well as the relative decline of economic hegemony has led to strategic defeats and failures in the Western Hemisphere. In late 2001, Washington challenged and threatened to take reprisals against President Chavez for refusing to submit to Bush's 'war on terror.' Chavez at the time informed a bellicose representative of the State Department (Grossman) that, "We don't fight terror with terror." Less than 6 months later in April 2003, Washington backed a failed military coup and between December 2002 to February 2003, a failed bosses' lockout. The failure of the US militarist strategy devastated Washington's military and ruling class clients, and radicalized the Chavez Government. As a consequence, the Venezuelan leader proceeded to nationalize oil and petrol sectors and develop strategic ties with countries that compete with or oppose the US Empire, such as, Cuba, Iran, China and Russia. Venezuela signed strategic economic agreements in Latin America with Argentina, Bolivia, Ecuador, Cuba and Nicaragua. While Washington poured over $6 billion dollars in *military* aid to Colombia, Venezuela signed petrol and gas investment and trade agreements with most of the Central American and Caribbean countries, severely challenging Washington's influence in the region.

High commodity prices, booming Asian markets, unacceptable US tariffs and subsidies led to the relative independence of Latin America's 'national capitalist' regimes, who embraced 'neo-liberalism' without the constraints of the IMF or the dictates of Washington. In these circumstances the US lost most of its leverage—except Colombia's military threats—to pressure Latin America to isolate Chavez—or even Cuba. Washington's military strategy led to its self-isolation.

Overseas Consequences of Failed Military Strategies

Isolation in Latin American cannot be overcome because Washington's pursuit of empire via prolonged military aggression—in the rest of the world and in Latin America—cannot compete with the profits, wealth, investment and trade opportunities offered to the ruling classes of Latin America by the new markets in Russia, the Middle East, Asia and by oil rich Venezuela.

Washington's militarist imperial strategy is evident in its dual policies: prioritizing the spending of $6 billion in military aid to repressive Colombia while sacrificing $10 billion in trade, investments and profits with oil rich Venezuela. Washington has spent over $500 billion in wars in Afghanistan and Iraq; billions are spent in war preparations against Iran; over $3 billion annually for Israel's military; all the time losing hundreds of billions of dollars in trade and investment with Latin America.

The most striking aspect of this historical contrast is that the military spending embedded in military-centered empire building has failed to achieve even its minimum goal of gaining political control, military outposts and strategic resources for war. In contrast, global market competitors have secured access and control over strategic economic resources, and signed lucrative political co-operation agreements without costly military commitments.

Domestic Consequences of Failed Military Empire Building

The cost of military-Zionist driven empire building to the domestic economy has been devastating. Competitiveness has declined, employment with stable living wages is disappearing, unemployment and loss of jobs is skyrocketing, the financial system is disconnected from the real economy and on the verge of collapse, home foreclosures are reaching catastrophic levels and taxpayers are being bled to death to bail out the trillion dollar home mortgage debt speculators. While the Obama campaign and election awakened the hopes of millions by its success in refurbishing the image of the American presidency, actual US policy remains entrapped in the worldview of officials from the previous Bush and Clinton administrations, and in the historically-evolved realities of the US situation. As recovery policies continue to fail, bankruptcies both personal, corporate and governmental[6] continue to rise, and the sheen wears off the Obama image, political malaise will be widespread.

In the midst of system-wide crisis, an emerging police state has taken hold: thousands of legal and undocumented immigrant workers have been seized at their factories and detained in military camps away from their children. Muslim and Arab associations have been raided and prosecuted on the bases of paid informers, including hooded Israeli 'witnesses'. The federal and local police practiced 'preventative detention' of activists and journalists prior to the Presidential conventions, seizing protestors before they could exercise their constitutional rights and systematically destroying the cameras and tapes of citizens attempting to document abuses.

Failed military imperialism brings in its wake a burgeoning police state—backed by both political parties—in the face of economic crises which threatens the political and social foundations of the empire. In August 2002, then Attorney General John Ashcroft called for American citizens who are deemed 'enemy combatants' to be detained indefinitely without charge and independently of the judiciary. A current estimate of the number of detainment camps is over 800 located in all regions of the United States with varying maximum capacities.[7] The 2006 Military Commissions Act permits individuals to be labeled as "enemy combatants" to be imprisoned indefinitely without charge.[8] The 2006 repeal of the Posse Comitatus Act by Public Law 109-364 has given the president the right to declare a "public emergency" and station troops anywhere in America and take control of state-based National Guard units without the consent of the governor or local authorities, in order to suppress public disorder—despite a letter from the governors of all 50 states protesting this increment in presidential power.[9]

Conclusion

The economic crisis has not led to the emergence of mass-based progressive alternatives. Both the Democratic and Republican parties remain committed to prolonging and extending the imperial wars and both submit to unprecedented Israeli-Zionist dictates with regard to Iran.

Crises and military defeats have not led to a re-thinking of global economic and military commitments. Instead we witness a right-wing radicalization, which seeks to escalate confrontations with China, Russia and Iran. With ever-increasing failure, the US seeks to draw in its wake the client regimes of Eastern Europe and the Caucasus and Baltic regions to counter Western Europe's emphasis on 'economic-centered' empire building.

The reality of a *multi-polarized economic* world however undermines US efforts to impose a bipolar military confrontation. China holds $1.2 trillion dollars in US debt, has already raised the issue internationally of an alternative global currency to the dollar, and is attempting to diversify its holdings out of Treasurys and into loans and investments elsewhere. Western Europe, in general, depends on over one-third of its energy for its homes, offices and factories from Russia. Germany relies on Russia for almost 60% of its gas. The economies of Asia: Japan, India, China, Vietnam and South Korea all depend on oil from the Middle East and not on the Middle East war plans of the Israeli-American militarists.

Brazil, Russia, India, China, South Africa, Venezuela and Iran are essential to the functioning of the world economy. The US-Israel-United Kingdom cannot support their empire on the bases of failed military strategies abroad and economic disaster and police state policies at home.

Endnotes

1   *Financial Times* August 28, 2008.

2   "ADL Criticizes Oil Companies for 'Hindering Effort to Isolate Iran'", Anti-Defamation League press release, August 29, 2008.

3   *Financial Times*, August 28, 2008.

4   Ben Feller, "Obama Widens Al-Qaida War, Making It His Own," Associated Press, March 28, 2009.

5   Huma Yussuf, "Kyrgystan Parliament delays vote on US Base Closing," *Christian Science Monitor*, February 5, 2009.

6   "States are facing a great fiscal crisis. At least 47 states faced or are facing shortfalls in their budgets for this and/or next year, and severe fiscal problems are highly likely to continue into the following year as well. Combined budget gaps for the remainder of this fiscal year and state fiscal years 2010 and 2011 are estimated to total more than $350 billion." See Iris J. Law and Elizabeth McNichol, "State Budget Troubles Worsen," Center on Budget and Policy Priorities, March 13, 2009, at <http://www.cbpp.org/cms/?fa=view&id=711>

7   Turley, Jonathan. "Camps for Citizens: Ashcroft's Hellish Vision" *Los Angeles Times*. 14 August 2002 <http://www.commondreams.org/views02/0814-05.htm>.cited in Geopolitical Monitor, "US Fema Camps" Globalresearch.ca at < http://www.globalresearch.ca/index.php?context=va&aid=7763>

8   It has yet to be decided how the repeal of the term "enemy combatants" will impact the Military Commissions Act; however the change in definition has been described by a spokesperson for the Center for Constitutional Rights as "old wine in new bottles". See Daniel Nasaw, "Obama Administration to Abandon the Term "Enemy Combatants", *The Guardian*, March 13, 2009 at <http://www.guardian.co.uk/world/2009/mar/13/enemy-combatant-guantanamo-detainees-obama>

9   See National Governors Association website at <http://www.nga.org/portal/site/nga/menuitem.cb6e7818b34088d18a278110501010a0/?vgnextoid=0a05e362c5f5d010VgnVCM1000001a01010aRCRD>

CHAPTER 9

THE OBAMA REGIME, THE ZIONIST POWER CONFIGURATION AND REGIONAL WARS

In the worst economic crisis since the 1930's 'Great Depression' and facing a *$1.7 Trillion Dollar budget deficit* and over 8.1 million unemployed workers in March 2009,[1] numbers which are expected to double by the end of the year, the Obama Administration has increased the open and hidden military expenditures to $800 billion-plus dollars, a 4% increase over the previous warmongering regime of George W. Bush. The key target of US military expansion is the Middle East and South Asia, with a population that includes hundreds of millions of mostly Muslims, who are pro-Palestinian, and oppose the colonial policies of Israel and the current US military occupation of Muslim countries in the region.

Zionist/Jewish officials and advisers occupying strategic government positions are the driving force behind US militarism in the Middle East. They are aided and encouraged by a multiplicity of major American Jewish political action and 'civic' organizations, an army of editors, academics, publishers, journalists and propagandists embedded in all the mass media who systematically promote the interests of the state of Israel.[2]

A careful analysis of the Obama regime demonstrates the high level of Zionist penetration and provides an empirical basis for understanding US military escalation in the Middle East, despite the catastrophic condition of the domestic economy. Fighting Israel's crusades against the Muslims takes precedence over the mass impoverishment of the US population. Nothing speaks to the overweening stranglehold of the Zionist Power Configuration (ZPC) more than their ability to escalate a war agenda in the Middle East over the needs and desires of 350 million Americans, the bankruptcy of United States' 500 Blue Chip corporations and its 5 leading banks, not to mention the over 50 million working Americans without access to health care.

Israeli policy in the Middle East has two vectors:

1. Leveraging its agents leading the 51 Major Jewish American Organizations to push US policy toward militarily destroying Israel's adversaries (like Iran), providing diplomatic and propaganda cover and military aid in its invasions and attacks on Syria, Lebanon and occupied Palestine (Gaza/West Bank), authoring and pursuing economic sanctions—amounting to deliberate acts of war—against Israel's targets including Iran, Hamas, Hezbollah, Sudan[3] and Somalia.
2. Dividing and conquering its adversaries via negotiations and diplomatic feints. In recent years Israel, with US backing, has successfully split the Lebanese (the Beirut elite versus Hezbollah), Palestinians (PLO/PA versus Hamas), Iraqis (Kurds versus Arabs), Sudanese (Darfur secessionists versus Khartoum) and, not least of all, Americans (Israel-Firster elites versus the American people).

Obama Acquiesces to Major Israeli Positions

The Israeli-Zionist stranglehold over Obama's foreign policy, especially with regard to Middle East issues affecting Israel's hegemonic ambitions, was evident in the run-up to his taking office and in the first months of power. An empirical survey of major Israeli positions and actions and the Obama regime's response demonstrates the power of the US Zionist power configuration:

The Israeli Invasion of Gaza

Israel's savage invasion of Gaza, slaughtering well over a thousand civilians, mostly women and children and destroying a large proportion of the civilian infrastructure, as well as the brutal starvation blockade of the entire imprisoned population of over 1.5 million and the US response is a case in point. Obama's regime and the entire Democratic Party leadership wholeheartedly endorsed the ongoing slaughter and refused to hold the military and civilian leadership of Israel to a minimal level of responsibility for its crimes—even as the question of whether Israel was committing war crimes in Gaza began to be raised in such mainstream media as the BBC.

Obama refused to call for an end to the murderous Israeli land and sea blockade, which prevented the entry of basic foodstuffs, like rice, and critical items for any reconstruction per se, but only after "a credible anti-smuggling and interdiction regime" had been put in place, and "as part of a lasting ceasefire".[4]

The Israeli leadership arrogantly dismissed US Secretary of State Clinton's suggestion for a minor easing up of the blockade, without the least response from Obama. Israel's continued military attacks on the people of Gaza have been supported by the Obama-Clinton-Gates regime.

Israeli Illegal Activities in Occupied Palestine

Israel's expansion of its illegal settlements in the occupied West Bank and the massive expropriation of homes and property in Arab East Jerusalem, as well as the ongoing destruction of Palestinian homes, is another instance. The US has merely reiterated its position in support of a 'two-state' solution.'

Clinton's earlier very mild questioning of the expansion of colonial settlements in Israeli-occupied land met with the same dismissal from the Jewish State with no consequences to US-Israeli relation.

Israeli Condemnation of the World Conference Against Racism

Israel condemned the international anti-racist conference in Durban, South Africa because of its critique of Israeli-Zionism as a brutal form of racism. When a sector of the Obama regime proposed sending an American delegation to the preparatory meeting to discuss the agenda, the ZPC immediately mobilized its activists and Obama capitulated.

The US and several other European states withdrew their participants and condemned the Durban meeting as 'anti-Semitic', all parroting the Israeli position.

The Appointment of Key Advisers and Policymakers in the Middle East

Israel and its American followers insisted that Obama appoint leading Zionists as his closest advisers and policymakers in strategic positions dealing with US negotiations with Syria and Iran, to ensure that the Israeli state's own position was pursued. To this end they scuppered the announced appointment of retired Marine General Anthony Zinni because of his known independence from Israeli dictates. The grotesque casting aside of General Zinni and the Administration's appointment of Israel's most 'loyal' US-Middle East agent, Dennis Ross, as US 'negotiator' with Iran, means that the Israeli war agenda of blockading and attacking Iran will dominate any decisions. Ross, also known as 'Israel's lawyer', is highly distrusted by the governments of the Middle East and Iran because of his past position as a blatant partisan of Israel under the previous Clinton administration. Even the fact that Ross had been working for an Israeli think-tank directed and funded by the Israeli government, and which made him an un-declared agent of the Jewish state, did not deter his appointment.

Among the group of Zionists who inhabit the foreign policy apparatus of the Obama regime, Secretary of State Clinton has appointed Jeffery Feltman, Acting Secretary of State for Near East Affairs and Daniel Shapiro of the White House's National Security Council to head up negotiations with Syria.[5] Appointments of Zionists to top negotiating positions will ensure that very few moves necessary for reciprocal exchanges and concessions, which might conflict with Israel's hegemonic regional ambitions, will ever happen under Obama. The Obama regime's appointment of prominent pro-Israel Zionists and well known non-Jewish Israel-Firsters to all major policy and analysis positions, with the fleeting exception of Charles Freeman to head the National Intelligence Council (see below)—guarantees that US Middle East policy will continue to be formulated in Tel Aviv.

The Charles Freeman Appointment

Seeking total control over all possible or potential appointees who can enhance Israel's positions, the Zionist Power Configuration successfully launched a massive, slanderous national campaign to block the appointment of veteran US diplomatic and intelligence official, Charles Freeman, one of the few non-Zionists (or Gentiles, for that matter) to hold key foreign policy-related positions, to the position of head of the National Intelligence Council.

From the first moment that Zionist 'insiders' *leaked* the proposed appointment of Freeman, the ZPC launched a frontal attack: scurrilous articles were written attacking Freeman, a veteran officer who had served in successive US Administrations dating back to Richard Nixon, which were published in the major newspapers and magazines and broadcast by the main TV and radio programs.

AIPAC approached its stable of Zionist Congress-people led by Congressman Eric Cantor to round up the usual herd of elected shills beholden to Zionist campaign financing. Ten US Representatives demanded that the Director of National Intelligence Inspector General, *"Fully investigate Mr. Freeman's past relationship with the Kingdom of Saudi Arabia and look into the contributors to the Middle East Policy Council* (a Washington think-tank headed by Freeman)".[6] The entire Republican leadership led by the House 'whip' Cantor carried the ball for the ZPC in trashing Freeman and his supporters, whom they also demanded be punished for their endorsement.

Obama, faced with the Zionist onslaught, crumbled without even a whimper. *"The White House made no comment."*[7] Zionist Power worked through both political parties. *"Steve Israel (appropriately named!), a Democrat on the House Select Intelligence Oversight Panel, wrote to Mr. Maguire (the Inspector General) about the seemingly prejudicial public statements made by the proposed NIC Chairman (Charles Freeman)".*[8]

The 'prejudicial public statement' in question was Freeman's criticism of Israel's savage bombing of Lebanon during the summer of 2007 and their unending repression of Palestinians under their occupation. Not a single area of government, not a single appointment, perhaps not even a single criticism by a public official, escapes the censorious eye of the Jewish pro-Israeli power structure in the US and its stable of compliant non-Jewish members of Congress.

The Zionist success in purging Freeman from the appointment to head the National Intelligence Council is an effort to avoid a repeat of the major intelligence setback to their anti-Iran propaganda in 2007. Back then, sixteen US intelligence agencies published their National Intelligence Estimate on Iran's nuclear weapons program, completely undermining Israeli and US-ZPC claims that Iran was producing weapon-grade nuclear material and was 'months' away from producing a nuclear weapon.

The NIE forced the ZPC to launch a furious assault on the findings and the professional intelligence agencies themselves in order to sustain Israel's campaign to push the US into a war with Iran. The central purpose of the Zionist-led Congressional campaign against Freeman was to use the 'investigation' to harass and undermine his independent, professional expertise and advocacy of an 'even-handed' approach to the Middle East. By labeling him as pro-Arab, pro-Hamas (with the implication of links to terrorism) they forced the withdrawal of his appointment in favor of an official willing to manipulate intelligence to fit Israeli objectives.

As is almost always the case when any issue or political appointment of interest to the state of Israel arises in the US, AIPAC seized the initiative. In the case of the Freeman Purge, once the Director of National Intelligence, Dennis Blair, announced his appointment of Charles Freeman, AIPAC circulated a 'dossier' of lies, slanders and fabrications about the man and his positions, centered on his criticism of specific Israeli actions, namely their brutality in Gaza and Lebanon and their violations of human rights. The Zionist-Jewish onslaught was led by (none-other-than) Steve Rosen, the long-time AIPAC hatchet man and indicted felon, currently on trial for espionage—handing over classified US documents related to Iran policy to Israeli government agents.

Under AIPAC's promotion, a tsunami of articles and commentaries attacking Freeman appeared in the major media, painting him as an 'Arab tool', 'anti-Israel' and worse. Parallel to the media campaign, the leading Jewish-Zionist Senators Schumer and Leiberman and Representative Cantor launched a virulent campaign in Congress, even though his nomination did not require Congressional approval. Schumer ensured White House complicity in the purge through direct communication with White House Chief of Staff and fellow Zionist, Rahm Emmanuel, who likely passed on the 'line' to fellow Zionist David Axelrod, Obama's chief adviser.

Not a single official in the entire Obama regime at any time voiced a single word in support of Blair's appointment of Freeman nor refuted the lies and character assassination harangues by the likes of Lieberman, Schumer and their fellow travelers. Where the Obama regime was not openly complicit, the Zionist purge machinery cowed it into silent acquiescence.

The deep and insidious authoritarian and partisan character of the Zionist congressional leadership evident in the purge of Charles Freeman is consistent with Schumer and Lieberman's support for Michael Hayden as Obama's CIA Director, the key agent in implementing Bush's illegal domestic espionage program and their support for the ultra-Zionist Michael Mukasey as Bush's Attorney General, who condoned the use by American agents of water-torture on 'suspects'.

What is striking about the Zionist-led Congressional purge of Freeman is the fact that its leaders openly stated that they killed his nomination in order to stifle any criticism of Israeli policy. New York Senator Schumer said: *"Charles Freeman was the wrong guy for this position. His statements against Israel were way over the top and severely out of step with the administration. I repeatedly urged the White House to reject him and I am glad they (sic) did the right thing."*[9]

The power and arrogance of the ZPC is such that Schumer openly boasted on how he brought the Director of National Intelligence, Dennis Blair to capitulate and force the resignation of his own appointee. In his widely published withdrawal statement, Freeman eloquently described the destructive power and operations of the Zionist Power Configuration:

> The libels on me and their easily traceable e-mail trails show conclusively that there is a powerful lobby determined to prevent any view other than its own from being aired....
>
> The tactics of the Israel lobby plumb the depths of dishonor and indecency and include character assassination, selective misquotation, the willful distortion of the record, the fabrication of falsehoods, and an utter disregard for the truth...
>
> The aim of this lobby is control of the policy process through the exercise of a veto over the appointment of people who dispute the wisdom of its views, the substitution of political correctness for analysis, and the exclusion of any and all options for decision by Americans and our government other than those that it favors.[10]

By purging Freeman, the ZPC is in a position to influence future US intelligence directors and ensure that their reports do not contradict

Israeli 'intelligence', especially its fabrications about Iran's nuclear program. Schumer, Lieberman, AIPAC and the Presidents of the Major American Jewish Organizations have gained another vital lever of power in forcing US policy into a military confrontation with Iran in line with the dictates of Israel.

The ZPC's successful blacklisting and purge of Charles Freeman from his appointment as chairman of the National Intelligence Council illustrates the stranglehold that it has on *all appointments* within the US Government. The Freeman purge reveals the ZPC tactics and methods, its web of power among different branches of government and their links with the leading Zionist Jewish American organization. The purge highlights the fact that *loyalty to the state of Israel* has become a condition for holding any significant office in the US government and that, conversely, any candidate for high office, no matter what their qualifications, who has criticized Israeli policy, is automatically banished. The application of the loyalty oath to Israel, which occurred in the purge of Charles Freeman, is a clear act of *intimidation* directed against the entire US political class: *Criticize* Israel, in any context, and write off your career forever! The purge of Freeman has vast present and future consequences for US politics, public debate and democratic freedom in America.

The Break-Up of the Syria-Iran Alliance

Unable to precipitate an American air strike against Iran or its collaboration with an Israeli first-strike, the Israeli government, directly and via its US supporters, has promoted a new policy, which involves a break-up of the Syria-Iran alliance.

The Obama-Clinton regime, following Israel's lead, has proceeded to talks with Damascus. The purpose of the US negotiators is to offer greater diplomatic recognition and economic concessions to Syria, in exchange for a Syrian break with Iran, Hezbollah and Hamas. To ensure that Israeli interests would be defended and no territorial concession (like Israel's illegal colonial occupation of Syrian territory in the Golan Heights) would be addressed, the Obama regime appointed two prominent US Zionists, Feltman and Shapiro, to conduct the US 'negotiations'.

The Syrian diplomatic gambit, intermittently pursued 'covertly' by Israel, and now taken up by its US protégé, Secretary Clinton, has thus far failed—because of Israel's unwillingness to make any territorial concessions in the face of its colonial settlers' political power and its inability to open Western trade and investment opportunities. The Obama regime will pursue Israel's goals of 'neutralizing' Syria as a political base of support for Hamas leaders and a logistical link between Iran and Hezbollah in Southern Lebanon.

The Weakening and Destruction of Iran

The centerpiece for the most sustained large-scale political, mass media and military campaign, involving all the major Jewish organizations, Zionist lobbies, front groups, legislators and top official in the government has been and continues to be the weakening and destruction of Iran. The opposition to the Zionist power configuration's confrontational policy is located in *sectors* of the government—including the intelligence services, the US military, career officials in the State Department and many former top officials.

The Zionists have succeeded beyond their wildest dreams. The right-wing Zionist David Frum, (who wrote the most bellicose speeches for the former President Bush and included Iran as a leading member of the 'Axis of Evil'), and fanatical Zionist Treasury official Stuart Levey have been and continue to be in the forefront of those enforcing and extending the economic sanctions and secondary boycotts against Iranian banking, trading and investment. Every aspect of US policy and legislation pertaining to Iran is closely overseen and often formulated by the Jewish pro-Israel lobby. As a result, efforts by US policymakers seeking to reach agreements with Iran on matters of strategic interest have been sabotaged exclusively by the Israel Firsters.

Ignoring Iranian Concessions and Assistance

Right after September 11, 2001, Iran supported the US attack on the Taliban and played an important role in stabilizing the eastern half of Afghanistan, especially Herat; it supported the overthrow of Saddam Hussein, even as it opposed any long-term US military occupation of Iraq. Influential Zionist agents, inside and outside the Bush regime, rejected and effectively blocked any consideration in Washington of Iran's offer for a mutual-security agreement. Despite statements from elements in the US military high command recognizing Iran's critical role in facilitating the US invasions of Afghanistan and Iraq, there was not a single reciprocal concession offered to Iran.

Instead, the entire Zionist 'state' within the US state launched a series of punitive measures, echoing Israeli hostility to Iran, including the setting up and training of cross-border death squads to murder Iranian officials on both the Iraqi and Afghan-Pakistani borders. Israel called for harsh sanctions: AIPAC authored legislation for severe sanctions, and their puppets in the Congress co-signed and secured Congressional approval. Zionists in the Treasury implemented the measures and Israel-First officials in the US State Department pressured European governments to do the same.

Punishing and Prohibiting Iranian Development of Nuclear Energy

The Israeli regime, through its worldwide network launched a successful campaign against Iran's entirely legal and closely monitored nuclear energy program. The hysterical Zionist propaganda campaign was pursued with an intensity, which surpassed even its earlier aggressive blitz against Iraq. The entire Jewish-Zionist apparatus was hell bent on putting the US on a path toward another Middle East war by conflating Iran's long-stated opposition to Israeli colonial massacres against the Palestinians and Lebanese with a threat to the very survival of the Jewish state and the security of US against an Iranian nuclear attack. However, as pointed out by Senator Kerry, "Iran's uranium enrichment program was legal and did not represent a threat to the US."

Sixteen US intelligence agencies published a report in November 2007—the National Intelligence Estimate on Iran, which carefully and systematically refuted Israeli and Zionist charges against Iran's nuclear power program. The report completely dismissed any allegation of ongoing, let alone advanced, Iranian nuclear weapon development. In response to this 'heresy' of the US intelligence establishment, the Zionist power configuration went into overdrive and, by the time of Obama's election, had managed to convince the incoming administration to accept Israeli fabrications on Iran's 'nuclear threat' and create their own 'revised' National Intelligence Estimate (NIE) to fit their policy goals.

The Obama regime, facing an unsuccessful counter insurgency war in Afghanistan has, once again had to turn to Iran for support. To ensure that no meaningful negotiations involving reciprocal concessions take place, the lobby secured the appointment of pro-Israel fanatic Dennis Ross to head the team. In the summer of 2007, Ross co-authored an extraordinary 'policy' report on Iran, which advocated the harshest sanctions, including a total naval blockade, escalating into a land and air embargo and inevitable military attack.

Under Zionist tutelage Obama extended severe economic sanctions against Iran on February 2009, ensuring that his highly publicized offer in March 2009 to open a new chapter in US-Iranian relations would not be taken seriously by Tehran.[11] Whatever takes place (if anything) pro-forma between the US and Iran will automatically be conveyed, filtered, censored and subject for final Israeli approval.

A Wider Campaign Against Arabs, Muslims, and Islam

Israel and its US policymakers and Congressional followers have been at the cutting edge of ferocious anti-Muslim and anti-Arab propaganda, 'diplomacy' and military aggression that has spanned decades. The

Obama regime reflects their pervasive influence. Despite the failed war in Afghanistan and increasing mass opposition in the region, despite a catastrophic domestic crisis, Obama has increased the military budget, increased the number of US troops in Afghanistan (without any European support), and extended the war into Pakistani territory, with daily bombing of anti-US Pashtun villages in Pakistan.

The ZPC and its Congressional delegation of fellow-travelers have blindsided millions of American citizens, especially Democrats, who voted for Obama as a 'peace candidate', and now face a prolonged large-scale presence of US troops in Iraq, an escalation in Afghanistan, US bombing inside Pakistan and US warships, aircraft carriers and nuclear submarines off the coast of Iran. Zionist power over-rode the entire US National Intelligence apparatus and the American voters on the issue of Iran and promises even greater confrontations with Dennis Ross in charge.

Implementing an Illegal Claim to Jerusalem

Israel is forcibly evicting thousands of Palestinians, generations-long residents, from Jerusalem in their drive to ethnically cleanse and annex the entire city, contrary to the demands of the European Union, world opinion, international law and any 'two-state solution' proposed by every US President, including Obama, in the last three decades.[12]

But in his electoral campaign speech to the AIPAC Convention, Obama went further than any US President had gone, in asserting that "Jerusalem will remain the capital of Israel, and it must remain undivided", then a day later, against the ensuing outrage, defended his remarks that Jerusalem should not be divided under any Israeli-Palestinian peace pact, by saying a divided city would be "very difficult to execute."[13] As an irate Mahmoud Abass responded, addressing Obama's support for the two-state solution, "The entire world knows perfectly well that we will never accept a state without (east) Jerusalem (as its capital)."

Jewish wrecking crews were actively bulldozing the homes of Palestinian families while Secretary of State Hilary Clinton pledged unconditional support for Israel and, in passing, commented that ethnic cleansing and evictions were 'not helpful'.[14] Obama/Clinton blatantly ignore the strong objections made by the leaders of Muslim and Christian religious congregations, representing many hundreds of millions of faithful. The major American Jewish organizations and the entire Congressional Zionist leadership, including the uber-Israel Firster Senator Joseph Lieberman, enthusiastically back the Obama regime's endorsement of Israeli ethnic cleansing.[15]

Zionist Control of US Foreign Policy: Some Consequences

The power of the ZPC over the Obama regime has major consequences for US foreign policy, especially war policy in the Middle East and throughout the world where countries, regions, movements and ordinary people reject Israel's militarist-colonialist state and racist Zionist ideology. The same politicians who 'stand with Israel' are also the ones who follow the line of military confrontation with Iran unless it capitulates to Israeli-US ultimatums to surrender its nuclear-energy policies and links to anti-colonial Muslim/Arab and other independent movements and governments.

'Negotiations' with Iran, Syria and Palestine, as proposed by Obama and with his Zionist appointees and the conditions, which they demand, are non-starters: They become automatic set-ups for failure and pretexts for resorting to a military confrontation, escalation of sanctions and for condoning Israeli land grabbing. They fail to achieve even a second's hesitation in the Obama regime's ongoing massive military build-up and expenditures for war in a time of catastrophic economic recession. The apparent irrationality of diverting scarce economic resources toward endless wars and military confrontations in which no US security interests are at stake can only be explained by the militarist interests of the state of Israel and the power of its US supporters to impose its definition of 'security' on the US government.

To empirically test our hypothesis about the scope and depth of the influence of the Zionist Power Configuration and its ability to subordinate Obama Administration's policies to Israeli interest, we examined above eight important issue areas. We stated Israeli positions and actions, particularly on vital issues of war and peace affecting US interests, key appointments and strategic relations. We have found that in almost all issue areas, the Israeli position was translated into US policy. This high level correlation in turn was explained by the intense activity of the Zionist Power Configuration and the high level of penetration of pro-Israeli functionaries of all relevant policy-making positions and their veto power over appointments exercised by the ZPC and its Congressional leaders.

Now They're Obama's Israel-Firsters

The 'coincidence' or correlation between Israel's illegal, militarist policies and the Obama regime's approval and compliance, even when it involves sacrificing electoral promises, national economic and security interests and world public opinion, can in large part be explained by the appointment of veteran Israel Firsters to decisive foreign policy and advisory positions.

At the very center of the Obama regime, in the most influential policy-making position, is David Axelrod, Senior Adviser to the president, who was recently described in *The New York Times* as: *"carrying more weight than most anyone else on the president's payroll…There are few words that come across the president's lips that have not been blessed Mr. Axelrod. He reviews every speech, studies every major policy position and works… to prepare responses to the crisis of the day."*[16] Axelrod's longtime friend, fellow Zionist, White House Chief of Staff, and former Israeli-American, Rahm Emmanuel, meet every morning to coordinate their agendas for the White House. The Zionist duet, the pizza-munching, herbal tea drinking Rasputins from Chicago, are the most direct and influential political Zionists ensuring the primacy of Israel's interests in setting US-Middle East policy— from starving Gaza to attacking Iran.

No doubt, Axelrod and Emmanuel had their 'input' on the Obama-Clinton appointment of fellow-Zionists Jeffery Feltman and Daniel Shapiro as chief negotiators with Syria.[17] Their agenda, Israel's priorities, is certain to preclude any comprehensive settlement. The Zionist White House duet was strikingly silent, as their fellow Zionists skewered Charles Freeman's appointment to lead Obama's National Intelligence Council and ignored Israel's humiliation of Secretary of State Clinton during her visit to Israel when the Jewish state bulldozed the homes of Palestinian families in Arab East Jerusalem on the very day of her arrival, repudiating Obama's 'two-state' solution.

With the advice and consent of Zionist chief economic adviser, Laurence Summers, the Obama regime appointed fellow Zionist and ex-Clintonite crony David Cohen to the top job of monitoring 'terrorist financing'.[18] Cohen will be in a position to pursue several crucial tasks for the Israeli state, including persecuting any and all Muslim charities and Palestinian humanitarian organizations, and pressuring US and overseas financial, export and investment funds to disinvest from Arab and Muslim countries critical of Israel. He can be expected to aggressively pressure European and Asian banks and exporters to cease trade and investment with Iran. While on paper a *'secondary appointment'*, in reality Cohen will play a key role in promoting the hard-line Israeli-Zionist economic sanctions against Iran and maintaining the blockade on Gaza.

The head of Obama's nuclear non-proliferation agency is Gary Samore, who clearly established his Israel-First credentials in a speech in Israel on December 18, 2008 when he declared that he favored bombing Iran if it failed to shut down its uranium enrichment program—a program, which is legal under the Nuclear Non-Proliferation Treaty.[19]

On February 24, 2009 the Obama regime appointed Dennis Ross as special adviser to Hilary Clinton for the Gulf Region. Ross is one of Israel's top operatives in the Washington political establishment with long-term working relations with Israeli and US policy institutes linked to the

Israeli military, intelligence and foreign policy establishment. In November 2008, Ross signed off on a document advocating a military assault on Iran.[20] Ross, as President Clinton's envoy to the Israel-Palestine negotiations, contributed to the breakdown by embracing Israel's non-negotiable positions and vilifying Yasser Arafat as the 'stumbling block'. First posted at the State Department, Ross has now been shifted to the National Security Council after Iran refused to negotiate with an Israeli mouthpiece openly advocating the military option.

The Zionist power configuration dominate all the key foreign policy committees in Congress, either directly through Jewish Zionists or elected representative who are in tow via financial contributions or threats of electoral retaliation and mass media smear campaigns. In the first weeks in office, the Zionist political machine has successfully blocked initiatives by some Obama advisers to attend the Durban anti-racism conference, and has deflected criticism of Israel's starvation blockade against Gaza by two Congressmen who visited Gaza to view the destruction themselves. The ZPC has slandered and forced the withdrawal of Charles Freeman's nomination as chief of the Intelligence Advisory Committee. It has openly endorsed Israel's massive land grab in the West Bank and East Jerusalem. The Obama regime, in line with Israel, has effectively buried any pretence of peace negotiations with the Palestinians by shifting focus to 'regional settlement/negotiations', in which Zionist envoys are directed to pressure Syria, Lebanon and Iran to isolate all Palestinian leaders who opposed Israel's annexation of their land and expulsion of their people.

The ZPC's deep and extensive penetration of the Obama regime represents the greatest national security threat by a foreign-directed power since the founding of the American Republic. The scope and destructive consequences will be further detailed in the text (see chapter "Israel Asserting Middle East Supremacy: From Gaza to Tehran.").

The ZPC's power is also manifested in the judicial branch and best illustrated in the spy trial of two prominent leaders of AIPAC—the principle pro-Israel 'lobby', Steve Rosen and Keith Weissman. Both were arrested and indicted after they admittedly took classified US documents relating to US policy toward Iran and handed them over to an Israeli Mossad Intelligence operative assigned to the Israeli Embassy in Washington, DC. The Federal Judge in the case, T.S. Ellis, has made several rulings in favor of the spies—strengthening their contention that the act of handing classified documents to a foreign power is a 'common practice' in Washington and not espionage. The ZPC has been successful in mobilizing its entire mass media apparatus, Congressional followers and a broad swath of Jewish and Gentile progressives in defense of Rosen and Weissman in the name of 'freedom of expression'—now perversely equating the stealing of official classified US documents relating to security matters and secretly passing them to an agent of a foreign government with investigative journalism's use of government sources. Since, Rosen and Weiss have been exonerated, and Larry Franklin, who was actually convicted, received a reprive to probation plus 10 months in "community confinement".

Ben-Ami Kadish, a Jewish nuclear spy, was convicted of having handed over to Israel highly confidential documents for a period of 6 years.

> From 23 August 1979 to 15 July 1985, Kadish provided Yagur with 50-100 classified documents from the library at the US Army, Armament Research, Development and Engineering Center, Picatinny Arsenal. The documents contained:
>
> Information concerning nuclear weaponry and atomic-related information (labeled Restricted Data Document)
>
> Information regarding a modified version of an F-15 fighter jet the US sold to another country (labeled NOFORN--"Not Releasable to Foreign Nationals"
>
> Information regarding the US Patriot missile air defense system (classified Secret).[21]

Kadish merely received a $50,000 fine and received no prison sentence, while supporters of Muslim charities helping Palestinians are sentenced to 60 years in jail.

The numerous FBI arrests and quiet deportations of scores of Israeli spies without charge or trials, and the frequent complaint of former US officials that 'orders from above' blocked their prosecution attests to the power of highly placed Zionists or authorities under their control in securing impunity to Israeli-Jewish operative committing illegal and hostile acts against the security and economic interest of the United States.[22] The presence of so many Zionists in positions of power in the Obama regime ensures that Israeli espionage operations in the US may now be superfluous, because Israel can obtain any documents or deliberations directly from officials in the Obama Administration. Even better, Israelis can co-author some White House and US intelligence position papers themselves!

With Zionists in power, the US empire will continue to energetically and aggressively pursue military confrontations and regional wars in the Middle East and further, on into Pakistan or Sudan—or wherever pronounced anti-Israel public sentiment may reside—at the behest of Israel. At no point has the Zionist-dominated White House or Congress questioned the exorbitant costs of serving Israeli interests—even in the midst of a major economic depression. Virtually the entire major media establishment and all 51 Major American Jewish Organizations, which are pressing for blockades, sanctions and preemptive war against Iran, are free to ignore the tremendous loss and suffering that this diversion of billions of US tax dollars from domestic investment to wars for Israel has caused to the American people.

Zionist control over White House Middle East policy ensures that the US will be mired in endless wars in the Persian Gulf and South Asia because Israel has an open-ended military agenda encompassing the entire region and an army of agents willing and able to impose this agenda on the American goverment.

Endnotes

1   *BBC News*, March 6, 2009.
2   See my books, *The Power of Israel in the United States*, and *Zionism, Militarism and the Decline of US Power*, Clarity Press, Inc., 2006 and 2008 respectively.
3   Israel itself undertook an air attack inside of Sudan.
4   Daniel Dombey and Tobias Buck, Obama urges Israel to open Gaza borders, *Financial Times*, January 22, 2009.
5   *BBC News*, March 7, 2009.
6   *Financial Times* (London), March 7, 2009, p. 3.
7   Ibid.
8   *Financial Times*, ibid
9   Quoted by Glen Greenwald in "Charles Freeman Fails the Loyalty Test", salon. com, March 10, 2009.
10   Quoted in *Aljazeera*, March 10, 2009.
11   *Financial Times*, March 23, 2009
12   *The Guardian* (London), March 7, 2009.
13   "Obama Defends Jerusalem Remarks," Agence France Presse, June 7, 2008.
14   *The Guardian*, March 7, 2009.
15   *Boston Globe*, March 9, 2009.
16   *The New York Times*, March 9, 2009.
17   *BBC*, March 7, 2009.
18   *Financial Times*, March 9, 2009, p.2.
19   *Financial Times*, February 24, 2009, p. 9.
20   See Robert Dreyfuss, "Dennis Ross's Iran Plan," *The Nation*, April 8, 2009, for an extensive review of Ross's anti-Iran undertakings, and their projected military dimen sions.
21   See < http://cicentre.com/spycase/ben_ami_kadish_case.html>
22   See Carl Cameron Investigates (Parts 1-4) Fox News Network, Dec. 17, 2001, available at <http://www.informationclearinghouse.info/articles5133.htm>

CHAPTER 10

ISRAEL MIDDLE EAST SUPREMACY FROM GAZA TO TEHRAN: IMPERIAL OVERSTRETCH?

"The Israeli Defense Force is the most moral army in the World!"
Israeli Prime Minister Ehud Olmert

Introduction

Fascist Italy and Nazi Germany bombed, invaded and annexed countries and territories as a prelude to their quest for World Empire. Israel's drive for regional dominance has followed in their footsteps, imitating their style: indiscriminate aerial bombings of civilian and military facilities, a savage blitzkrieg led by armored vehicles, disdain and repudiation of all criticism from international agencies, accompanied by an open, military buildup for a new and bigger war against Iran. Like the Nazi leadership who played on the 'Bolshevik threat', the Israeli high command has set in motion a vast worldwide propaganda campaign led by its world Zionist network, raising the specter of 'Islamic terror' to justify its preparations for a military assault on seventy-four million Iranians.

Just as Nazi Germany interpreted the passivity, sympathy and impotence of the West when confronted by 'facts on the ground' as license for aggression, the Israeli military machine receives a powerful impetus for new wars by the Western governments' inaction and flaccid response to its invasion of Lebanon, the bombing of Syria and most recently its Nazi style blitz and conquest of Gaza. For the Israeli high command, the impotence and complicity of the Western states marks the way to bigger and bloodier wars to establish Israel's supremacy and dominance of the Middle East, from the Red Sea to the Persian Gulf.

Gaza Blitz: Dress Rehearsal for an Assault on Iran

Israel's military victory in Gaza is a dress rehearsal for a full-scale military assault on Iran. In the course of their Gaza extermination campaign, Israeli political and military strategists gained a great deal of vital information about: (1) the levels of complicity and impotence of European, North American and Arab states; (2) the high degree and depth of material and political support obtainable from the United States government for pulverizing adversaries; (3) the high degree of internal support among the Jewish electorate for even the most brutal killing fields; (4) the massive unquestioning backing of an offensive war from all the biggest and most politically influential and wealthiest Jewish-Zionist organizations in the US and Western Europe; (5) the weakness and ineffectiveness of the United Nations and the incapacity of the entire range of humanitarian organizations to limit Israel's extermination campaign directed at destroying the very existence of an entire people; (6) the unconditional backing of the entire mass media and news agencies in the US and most of the mass media in Europe and the rest of the world; (7) the willingness of the liberal critics to equally blame the victims of extermination and the exterminators for the 'violence', thus neutralizing any effective consequential condemnation of the Israeli state; and (8) the adaptation of practically all the journalists, writers, academics and politicians to the entire euphemistic vocabulary of the Israeli propaganda office.

For example, sustained total war is called an 'incursion'. Ten thousand aerial assaults by hundreds of Israeli helicopters and fighter-bombers is equated with sporadic harmless homemade rocket attacks as 'violence'. Thousands of civilian homes, hospitals and basic infrastructure targeted by Israel are labeled 'terrorist' targets. Resistance fighters are labeled 'Hamas terrorists'. The bombing of the Red Cross, the United Nations relief facilities, hospitals, mosques are called 'mistakes' or justified by their having served as 'launching sites for Hamas terrorists'.

Israeli political leaders have drawn the lesson from their dirty little 'war' that they can totally destroy a nation, decimate a society and murder and maim 7000 civilians with *impunity*. Israeli leaders learned they can carry out an offensive genocidal war without suffering breaks in diplomatic relations (except with Mauritania, Qatar, Bolivia and Venezuela). The Israelis have successfully tested the loyalty and submissiveness of the major Arab regimes in the region and secured cooperation and acquiescence from Egypt, the 'Palestinian Authority', Jordan and Saudi Arabia. Israeli civilian-military leaders calculate that with this high degree of governmental complicity, combined with support from all the major Zionist leaders and mass media moguls, they can dismiss even large-scale street protests, repeated calls for boycotts and United Nations denunciations. Israeli leaders know that the criticism of major religious leaders and the growing number of Jewish dissidents, critical intellectuals and activists will have no consequential impact on Western governments nor lessen the fervor and loyalty of the major Jewish organizations.

Invisible Threats and Visible Impunity

The two potential threats to Israel's genocidal offensive wars, namely, economic boycotts by important trading and investing countries and a cut-off of military aid, did not materialize. In North America, the leading Zionist organizations ensured that the issue of a boycott was never even raised in the legislature and executive branches. In the US, AIPAC wrote resolutions and secured near unanimous passage (100% in the Senate, 90% in the Congress) of an AIPAC-dictated resolution endorsing Israel's invasion and slaughter. Moreover the Zionist-colonized Pentagon authorized massive new shipments of missiles and 1000 pound bombs to re-supply Israel in the midst of its massacres of the Palestinians. Israel's leaders gloated over the fact that Jewish Zionist lobbies control over US policy went uncontested by the anti-war protestors. Few, if any, of the demonstrators around the world identified and denounced the role of the Zionist organizations in their own countries in making US, Canadian and European policy toward the Middle East.

Nothing exemplifies the total and blind subordination of the 51 Major American Jewish Organizations[1] to Israeli foreign policy goals—and their belief in their own power to impact US and global Middle East policy—as two incidents during the Gaza Genocide. When the '51' got wind that Secretary of State Condoleezza Rice was working to come up with a Security Council resolution calling for a ceasefire in Gaza to stop Israeli genocide, every major Jewish organization mobilized their entire membership to oppose her. As the Jewish weekly magazine, *Forward*, reports:

> During a January 5 (2009) conference call with Jewish activists, Malcolm Hoenlein, executive vice chairman of the Conference of President of Major American Jewish Organizations, *gave special priority to blocking the international body from taking a stand* on the Gaza issue. 'We need to work hard to ensure the Security Council doesn't pass the resolution, Hoenlein said.'[2]

The resolution, of course, did not pass; Rice was even forced to endure the ignominy of voting against the resolution she herself had sponsored.

A second example demonstrating Zionist belief in Israeli supremacy over US Middle East policy and Presidential servility, occurred in response to Israeli Prime Minister Olmert's boast that he had successfully dictated and imposed White House policy in the United Nations. According to *Forward*:

> Israeli Prime Minister Ehud Olmert didn't do anything wrong but he should have kept his mouth shut. That was the reaction of several Jewish leaders...'I have no problem with what Olmert did', said Abraham Foxman, National Director of the Anti-Defamation League...[3]

Former AIPAC chief lobbyist Douglas Bloomfield, stated that he (an American citizen) had no problem with Israel dictating US policies but *'it is a mistake to talk about it.*[4] Talking about Israel's power in Washington exposes the role of the Zionist Power Configuration in deciding US policies.

These examples demonstrate once again the indivisible links between Israel and its US-Zionist Fifth Column and their power to make US policy—even when it is a question of supporting genocide. These cases also illustrate the fact that the major American Jewish organizations will not tolerate the smallest White House deviation from any Israeli policy, even if it involves mass murder. It wasn't enough that for eight years, President Bush slavishly followed and funded Israel's war machine. Israeli and US Jewish leaders required 100% subservience up to and including his last days in office, to the extent that Bush, while giving a speech in Philadelphia, was literally forced to leave the podium to take a call from Olmert. As *Forward* put it: Those tough words from Israel and the Jewish groups..."serve as a message to the incoming (Obama) administrations..."[5]

Gaza: Testing the Subservience of the US Congress and the White House

By savaging Gaza with extreme brutality, Israel is testing the waters of US support for more offensive wars. Gaza allowed the Jewish leaders to measure the depth and scope of US Zionist political influence and their willingness to 'go all the way' if and when Israel ultimately decides to bomb 74 million Iranians into the stone age. Or as the famous Israeli Zionist historian, Benny Morris, suggested in *The New York Times* on July 18, 2008, turn Iran "into a nuclear wasteland" if it doesn't drop its nuclear aspirations.

Prime Minister Olmert's public boasting that he pulled President Bush off the stage from an official public appearance and successfully ordered him to instruct the Secretary of State Condaleeza Rice to abstain from voting on her own authored resolution calling for a ceasefire in Gaza before the Security Council has many profound meanings. On the most obvious level Olmert's revelation confirms the power of Israeli leaders over the White House. Secondly, the public nature of that exercise of power, Olmert's subsequent public boasting of its usage, and the US administration's tepid denial that its chief executive had been so humiliated tells the world that Israel can *openly flaunt* its capacity to humiliate and ridicule the President of the United States and later brag before Israeli officials with no adverse consequences. It tells the world that even the US cannot stop it, that Israel has a greater say in US foreign policy than the American Secretary of State (or Foreign Minister), that how the US behaves, votes, vetoes and abstains in the Security Council, are all subject to Israeli approval.

Promoting Israel's Big Lie

In addition to capturing positions of political power, one of the highest priorities of all the major Zionist Jewish organizations in the US is to propagandize, apologize for and fabricate stories on behalf of Israel. Even in the face of Israel's most blatant violent crimes against Palestinians—which have been condemned by the UN General Assembly, the International Red Cross and every humanitarian group[6]—the principle American Jewish religious institutions and lobbies have demonstrated their loyalty to the state of Israel. The modus operandi as documented by their internal memos is to dominate the mass media through 'plants'—pro-Zionist journalist, academics, 'experts' and editors—who write and broadcast justifications and apologies for Israeli war crimes (parroting the line of the Israeli state) in the mass media. The Zionist propagandists then circulate the planted articles by their colleagues for further circulation or citation by others, giving the impression of broad public support when in fact they are reproducing prepared Israeli-Zionist propaganda.

The style and substance of the Zionist propaganda operation is evident in its defense of Israel's Gaza bloodbath, to be addressed in the following chapter.

Israel's Military Threat to Iran

Israel exercises power in the Middle East through its military weaponry. Its repeated threats and aerial and ground assaults on neighboring countries is a deliberate strategy to assert its regional supremacy. In recent years, Israel's regional power has been enhanced by the Zionist Power Configuration in the US and Canada, who use the armed forces in their own countries to destroy any country that contests Israeli military supremacy. The classic case was the run-up to the US invasion of Iraq and the follow-up occupation, in which it is now widely recognized that long-term Israel Firsters in the US Government played a deadly role in promoting the war.

From the late 1980s to the present, the US Zionist Power Configuration has been in the forefront of a campaign to promote a US military confrontation with Iran in collaboration with Israel. The Zionist military proposals gained tremendous momentum during the eight years of the Bush Administration. The ZPC mounted an unrelenting mass media propaganda campaign demonizing Iran, brazenly fabricating and disseminating falsified accounts of its nuclear programs despite IAEA reports and the 2007 National Intelligence Estimate (compiled by 16 US intelligence agencies) to the contrary. Infiltrating and occupying key positions in the US Treasury Department (led by Stuart Levey) it has aggressively bludgeoned other governments, industries, banks and investors to boycott Iran. Zionist Treasury Department officials hoped to strangle and weaken Iran's economy, just as had been done in Iraq, in order to soften it up for a military strike. No other single or combined force in North America, or, for that matter, any place in the world (except Israel) has played as big a role in promoting an offensive war against Iran as the Zionist politicians and officials in the US government. They were aided and abetted by Jewish lobbies, Zionist propaganda centers, multi-billionaires and hundreds of Jewish community organizations providing propaganda shock troops against wherever opposition reared its head: from the media to the universities to local bookstores and city councils.[7]

Israel, contrary to some leftist skeptics, had advanced operational plans to launch a massive aerial assault on Iran. On several occasions in the recent past, Israel has planned aerial attacks on Iran, only to be thwarted by the Bush White House. The Jewish state has publicly announced that it will unilaterally strike Iran if it continues its legal, internationally recognized, right to enrich uranium. The winner in February's national elections, Binyamin Netanyahu, has publicly stated that a military attack on Iran is at the top of his agenda—a message which has activated all the major Zionist-Jewish organizations in the US to redouble their efforts to secure US compliance, support and active collaboration. On January 7, 2009 *The London Sunday Times*, quoting several high level Israeli military sources, reported:

> Israel has drawn up secret plans to destroy Iran's uranium enrichment facilities with tactical nuclear weapons. Two Israeli Air Force squadrons are training to blow up an Iranian facility using low-yield nuclear 'bunker-buster'... Robert Gates, the new [*sic*] US Defense Secretary, has described military action against Iran as a 'last resort' leading Israeli officials to conclude that it will be left to them to strike. The preparations have been overseen by Major General Eliezar Shkedi, Commander of the Israeli Air Force.[8]

A subsequent article in the pro-Israel *New York Times* by David Sanger, a prominent Zionist sympathizer, reported:

> President Bush deflected a secret request by Israel last year (2008) for specialized bunker-busting bombs it wanted for an attack on Iran's main nuclear complex... the Bush administration was particularly alarmed by an Israeli request to fly over Iraq to reach Iran's major nuclear complex...The White House denied that request outright.[9]

(In point of fact, U.S. actually did approve the sale of 1,000 GBU-39, those "specialized bunker-busting bombs", and Israel went on to use them in Gaza.)[10] Sanger then went on to claim that the Israelis were furious at *The National Intelligence Estimate,* which demonstrated that Iran had halted development of a nuclear warhead in 2003 because it undermined Israeli efforts to secure US collaboration for a military attack on Iran. Sanger spends several paragraphs trying to bolster the Israeli unsubstantiated claims regarding Iran's nuclear program framing the case for a unilateral Israeli attack...which he dates began *"early 2008"* but was stalled by opposition from the US military.

The election of the ultra-militarist Zionist Binyamin Netanyahu, a favorite of the most influential Zionist-American organizations, promises to accelerate Israeli plans for a massive assault on Iran.His appointment of Avidor Lieberman,a notorious zionfascist as foreign minister is a further indication of Israel's militarist posture. In an interview with the *Wall Street Journal,*[11] Netanyahu spoke of Iran as the 'terrorist mother base" and "that Israel cannot accept an Iranian terror base (Gaza) next to its major cities." He then goes on to justify the Israeli murder of civilians because, he claims, the Palestinian resistance ("terrorists") *"hide behind civilians".* The *Wall Street* journalist, one Brett Stephens, in complete awe and wonder at the feet of the Israeli leader, writes approvingly of Netanyahu's justifications for an attack on Iran, *"the threat of a nuclear Iran poses a much greater danger to the world than the economic crises...this poses an existential threat to Israel directly..."* Stephens goes on to sum up Netanyahu's position toward Obama: *"If diplomacy fails and the US does not resort to military force, Israel will decide to go it alone..."*

Israeli leaders have temporarily backed off attacking Iran—launching, instead, the Gaza assault, which has the ancillary benefit of weakening any possible resistance among Palestinians to an Israeli war against their Muslim ally in Tehran. The Israeli war plans toward Iran will be reinforced with the new Obama Presidency. With the rise to power of the ultra-Zionist Dennis Ross as Chief Adviser to Secretary of State Clinton ("We will obliterate Iran") and President Obama, the question of a US-backed

Israeli preemptive attack on Iran looms closer to becoming a reality. Just prior to joining the Obama administration, Ross signed on to a document, which provided a 'roadmap' to war with Iran. Addressing Ross's role in the Obama government, Robert Dreyfuss writing in *The Nation* goes so far as to reveal that "a former White House official says that Ross has told colleagues that he believes the United States will ultimately have no choice but to attack Iran in response to its nuclear program.[12] Zionist infestation of the entire policy-making apparatus of the Obama regime means that any official military or intelligence opposition to an Israeli attack on Iran will be blunted and their spokespersons marginalized.

Zionist Penetration of the Obama Administration

The Obama regime is, if anything, even more penetrated from the top to bottom and from Executive offices to Congress with Zionists in positions to influence every strategic decision having any relation to Middle East policy.

The Jewish Telegraphic Agency,[13] the principle news agency of American Jewish-Zionist publications, and other sources provided a detailed list of the 'pro-Israel' Zionists in strategic Middle East positions in the Obama regime—even before their appointment. . The evidence of Zionist control is overwhelming and the consequences are deadly to any 'balanced' peace negotiations and extremely promising for Israel's war ambitions in the regions:

1. **Dennis Ross** will be an influential adviser on Iran policy. He was appointed Special Advisor for the Gulf and Southwest Asia for Secretary of State Hilary Clinton in February 2009. Ross is an advocate of intensifying sanctions to undermine negotiations and force the military option.

2. **Richard Holbrooke**, appointed as Obama's envoy to Afghanistan, is a prominent Zionist who served as UN envoy under Clinton. He has recently headed an ad hoc group called *United Against a Nuclear Iran*, which advocates military action against Iran if it does not submit to an Israeli-dictated cessation of its legal nuclear energy program. (Holbooke is the one person on this list that, surprisingly, the JTA did not name.)

3. **George Mitchell**, Obama's envoy to the Palestine-Israel conflict, is one of the four founders (presently described as Advisory Board) of the Zionist front group, Bipartisan Policy Center, which proposes a step by step approach, from sanctions to embargo to naval blockade to a military strike on Iran.

4. **Dan Shapiro** and **Puneet Talwar** will collaborate on Middle

East policy at the National Security Council. Shapiro, in consultation with Israel, was "key in shepherding the Syrian Accountability Act through the Senate (a measure that imposed tough sanctions on Syria). Shapiro drafted Obama's cringing, belly-crawling speech to the pre-election annual AIPAC conference in Washington on May 2008. Puneet Talwar will handle Persian Gulf issues—including Iran. He was a staffer of former Senator and current Vice President Joe Biden and was a close collaborator and conduit for AIPAC.

5.   **Eric Lynn** is heading for a White House Middle East policy job. He started his career as an AIPAC intern in 1998 and continued as a staff person for Congressman Peter Deutsch, *"one of the most committed pro-Israel figures in Congress."*[14] Lynn spent a year in Israel, imbibing Zionist military culture and learning Hebrew.

6.   **James Steinberg** and **Jacob 'Jack' Lew** have been named as Clinton's deputies at the State Department. Steinberg has been in a *'strong relation with the pro-Israel community*[15]*'* and was a conduit for Israeli pressure on Arafat to capitulate to Israeli demands. Jack Lew will direct economic stimulus overseas. He is an orthodox-Zionist, who will use American economic resources to back Israeli militarism and reward or punish its adversaries. A former head of a Citigroup investment unit, he holds between $50,000 to $100,000 in Israel State Bonds.

7.   **Samantha Power**, once a critic of Israeli war crimes in 2002 for which the Zionist Power Configuration had her removed from the Obama campaign in March 2008. She was 'rehabilitated' and re-incorporated as a member of the Clinton transition team after an *'abject apology'*, as Jerusalem Telegraph Agency put it, to Israel.

8.   **Cass Sunstein**, a lifetime Zion-Lib (and husband of Samantha Powers), is head of the White House Office of Information and Regulatory Affairs—a key propaganda arm of the Obama regime.

9.   **Rand Beers** was lead national security adviser to Senator Kerry during his presidential campaign of 2004 and 'built close relations' with the pro-Israel political apparatus. As adviser to Homeland Security, he will *'likely be a linchpin as Israel and the US forge a closer alliance'.*[16]

10. **Lee Feinstein and Mara Rudman** are Zionist veterans from the Clinton Administrations. Feinstein is a lead adviser of Secretary of State Clinton and Rudman is Senior Foreign Policy Adviser of President Obama.

11. **Susan Rice**, UN Ambassador appointed by Obama, signed on to a Washington Institute for Near East Policy (WINEP) paper last summer calling for greater Israeli-US coordination for an embargo and military attack on Iran. WINEP is a well-known propaganda mill for Israel's most fanatical, bellicose and unconditional supporters. In her Senate testimony, Rice denounced the United Nation General Assembly's criticism of Israel's Gaza bloodbath.

12. **Stuart Levey**: Undersecretary for Terrorism And Financial Intelligence in the Bush Administration Department of Treasury has been re-appointed by President Obama.[17] Levey is the key government policy maker overseeing, developing, implementing and enforcing the world-wide economic sanctions campaign against Israel's adversaries, namely the Iranian Government, Hamas in the Gaza Strip and Hezbollah in Lebanon.[18] He has worked closely with the Israeli governments in cutting off funding from Arab and Muslim charities and philanthropic organization, while refusing to pursue money-laundering operation which channeled an estimated $50-$60 billion dollars of US funds to illegal Israeli settlements in the occupied Palestinian West Bank.[19]

In cooperation with the Zionist Power Configuration (ZPC), Levey has successfully pressured investment and pension funds in the United States to withdraw their money from companies doing legitimate business in Middle Eastern countries opposed to Israeli criminal violence against the Palestinians. He has traveled throughout Europe, the Middle East and North America, cajoling, threatening and blacklisting countries and companies, which conduct trade with Iran or have dealings with the Hezbollah affiliates in Lebanon or Hamas affiliates in the Gaza Strip. His threats have included economic sanctions and even criminal charges against these companies and governments.

Levey was appointed and re-appointed with the full backing of AIPAC, largely because of his zealous pursuit of Israel's policy of trying to destroy the economy of Iran. Obama's appointment of a Bush holdover, especially a Likud-style hardliner like Levey, is powerful evidence that the new president will continue to confront Tehran aggressively. Even the most feckless Obama supporters should give up any thought that Obama's election would 'open a new page in US-Iranian relations', Obama's June 4, 2009 speech to the Muslim world from Cairo, notwithstanding.

Combined with the appointment of Dennis Ross as Special Middle East Envoy, Levey represents Israel's most powerful policymaker in the Obama Administration. Levey was deeply implicated in secretly obtaining the financial records of banking transactions of millions of Americans and foreigners from a vast international database—an illegal operation which he defended as part of his 'anti-terrorist' operations.[20] Levey's extraordinary services to the State of Israel extend far beyond the borders of the US. He and his staff have been instrumental in blacklisting Iran's leading financial institutions and major industrial groups.[21]

Levey has made significant contribution to the Israeli starvation blockade of the Gaza Strip after the democratic election of the Hamas Party, ensuring that virtually all Western philanthropic funding was cut off from Gaza's civilian educational, health, welfare and civil security programs. By labeling sympathizers of Hamas (including a majority of the voters in Gaza) and opponents of Israeli occupation as *'financiers of terrorism'*, Level publicly boasts of his success in cutting off all aid to the desperate and impoverished Palestinians living under Israeli siege.[22] By labeling all types of aid activity, including providing food and medicine for the sick and hungry, as *'supporting terrorism'*, he has worked tirelessly with the Israelis in eliminating all funds to Gaza, especially funds raised by Palestinian exiles for their besieged compatriots.

According to Levey: "In Israel, I was given an encouraging account of a substantial reduction of funds flowing to Hamas, particularly from the Gulf Region." His main targets are Muslim charities, which operate schools, orphanages, food warehouses, hospitals and clinics, which, he claimed, are 'fertile recruitment grounds allowing terrorists to generate support for their causes and to propagate extremist ideologies'.[23] These are the words of Harvard Law School graduate, Stuart Levey: speaking the language and acting on behalf of the ultra-right wing, racist, Avigdor Liberman, Israel's current Foreign Minister. Accordingly, Levey and his staff have coordinated with the FBI in closing numerous Islamic charity foundations and have successfully prosecuted and jailed many US citizens of Arab descent for contributing to what had been legal charitable foundations before Bush's War on Terror.[24]

On May 27, 2009, five directors of the Holy Land

Foundation, the largest Muslim charity in the US, received sentences ranging up to 65 years in prison. "Holy Land wasn't accused of violence, but of bankrolling schools and social welfare programs the government says are controlled by Hamas. The defendants said they only fed the needy and gave much-needed aid to a volatile region."[25]

Levey's domestic and international campaign against professionals and businessmen of Palestinian, Iranian, Iraqi, Syrian and Saudi descent and scores of European banks, industries and shipping companies, as well as US and Euro-Asian oil companies has been backed by all the major Jewish American organizations.[26] AIPAC;s most recent lobbying efforts to impose sanctions on countries exporting refined petroleum products, including gasoline, to Iran, has the full backing of the US Treasury.[27]

In fact, AIPAC was instrumental in the establishment of Levey's Office of Terrorism and Financial Intelligence as well as his re-appointment by Obama. It is no surprise that Levey has made no effort to follow up any investigation into the multi-billion dollar criminal money laundering scheme to fund illegal settlements in the West Bank involving US Zionists and Israelis, which was first exposed by the Israeli Government Prosecutor, Talia Sasson, in 2005.[28]

No single Zionist official in the Obama Administration or its predecessor has inflicted more damage to the lives and welfare of millions of Palestinians, Iranians and American Muslims than Stuart Levey. No American official has been more effective, energetic and subservient to the interests of the State of Israel than Stuart Level. No member of the US Department of Treasury has ever played such an aggressive role with the major US and European oil producers in preventing them from making legitimate billion-dollar/ billion-euro contracts with Iran. Levey, even more than any leader of the AIPAC, is Israel's most valuable political asset in 'our' USA.

At the head of Obama's foreign policy regime, Vice President Biden *("I am a Zionist")*, Secretary of State Clinton *("demolish Iran")* and Secretary of Defense Gates (a holdover from the Israeli-dominated Bush Administration) have put in place the most Zionist-infested Middle East policy regime in US history. Neither by background, loyalties or commitments is this regime prepared to open serious negotiations with Iran, or to 'broker' an end of Israeli occupation of Palestine—no matter what public face Obama may put on his so-called soft diplomacy with Iran. On the contrary, their close ties with the Zionist Power Configuration and long-term commitment to Israeli militarism and expansionist policies ensure that the Obama regime will proceed toward collaboration with the Jewish State in a military confrontation with Iran. Everyone on Obama's team supported the Israeli carnage in Gaza and endorsed Israel's efforts to destroy the democratically elected Hamas government and prop up the discredited and corrupt quisling clique headed by Abbas.

The Obama Presidency has achieved what many observers thought impossible: It has placed more Zionists in more strategic power positions with a greater commitment to war with Iran than even the Bush Administration. Given Obama's appointments and his own personal subservience to Israeli leaders, it is difficult to imagine the 16 major intelligence services issuing a report refuting Israel's fabrications about Iran's nuclear program, as happened under Bush—particularly now that the ZPC has assured that the Freeman nomination was withdrawn (see chapter 9). What is even more hazardous, given the Zionist stranglehold on the White House, it is unlikely that Obama would block a proposed Israeli air assault on Iran as Bush is reputed to have done.[29]

The Israeli war strategy toward Iran follows the 'salami tactics' of its Nazi forerunner: attacks are designed for maximum destructiveness against civilian infrastructure, against countries and leaders opposed to any Israeli aggression toward Iran. Accordingly, Israel bombed and invaded Lebanon. It bombed Syria. Israel savaged Gaza. Israeli fighters even bombed an arms convoy in Sudan. Its 'lobby' has extended and enforced global economic sanctions through the forceful intervention of a Zionist infested Treasury Department. Obama's top economic adviser, the ultra-Zionist Lawrence Summers, promotes tighter sanctions, boycotts and embargoes against the designated enemies of Israel: policies pointing toward war.

The Dennis Ross Roadmap for War on Iran...

The likelihood that the Obama regime will move the world closer to an offensive war with Iran is not based on idle speculation or selected quotes from his presidential campaign. No one can take seriously President Obama's or Secretary of State Clinton's advocacy of 'negotiations with Iran', when they are accompanied by conditions unacceptable to Iran's sovereignty or national interests. The Obama regime openly threatens war if Iran does not accept unilateral disarmament with intrusive inspection of its strategic defense installations, allowing Israel and the US a unique opportunity for pinpointing vital targets for their first wave of attack.

What conclusively demonstrates Obama's drive to war with Iran is his appointment of the most zealous Zionist militarist, Dennis Ross, to the key strategic position dealing with Iran.

Obama appointed Ross to the post of 'Special Envoy to Iran'. He will act as Czar of US Middle East policy. George Mitchell, Obama's envoy on Israel-Palestine negotiations, is not the favorable appointment some may have presumed (Mitchell is, after all, a founder of The Bipartisan Policy Center mentioned above), but rather reflects a typical 'good cop' (Mitchell) strategy to counter the 'bad cop' (Ross). Ross, who is often called 'Israel's Lawyer', is the ultimate Zionist, a crown prince of the US Zionist Jewish Lobby in all of its major undertakings regarding Iran. Ross is a founding leader of AIPAC, the principle and most powerful Israel First Lobby in Washington. He has been a lifelong and influential ZionCon ideologue, who successfully, under Wolfowitz, led the campaign in favor of the invasion of Iraq. He is among the most prolific and influential writers and propagandists at the Zionist-financed propaganda mill, WINEP (Washington Institute for Near East Policy), which has produced the most bellicose position papers pushing US military intervention in favor of Israel's expansionist ambitions.[30] During the Clinton years, Ross was appointed head of the US 'mediation' committee during the Israeli-Palestinian negotiations (1999-2000). In that position, he acted as 'Israel's lawyer' according to a fellow US Zionist diplomat. He scuttled all possibility of any acceptable compromise by "following Israel's lead." He set up the conditions, which would make Palestinian rejection inevitable while placing the blame on that embittered people. In short, Ross has a profound influence on Obama's politics in relation to Israel.

Ross is a leader in the relatively new Zionist front group, The Bipartisan Policy Center. The 'Center' recently published a report entitled, *"Meeting the Challenge: US Policy Toward Iranian Nuclear Development."* This roadmap for war with Iran was produced by a task force, which included Ross and two other extremist Zioncons, the dual-Israel-US citizen Michal Makovsky and Michael Rubin. Ross' endorsement of the *'Report'* reflects his rejection of any possibility of a negotiated agreement with Iran, which would accept Iran's legal right to a uranium enrichment program as recognized by international treaty.

The fact that Dennis Ross served, until immediately prior to his appointment to the Obama Cabinet in early 2009[31] as the Chairman of the Jerusalem-based Jewish People Policy Planning Institute, under the Jewish Agency, which is an official part of the Israeli Government, proved no barrier to his assuming office, no matter that it might have conflicted with the Foreign Agents Registration Act (FARA), a Federal statute that requires individuals working on behalf of a foreign government to register as such—something Ross has never done.

The *Report* advocates a preemptive Israeli aerial bombing and missile campaign against Iran should the US and Europe fail to strike first. This Dennis Ross-endorsed *Report* proposes a total naval and air blockade and embargo of Iran as a prelude to a US attack on Iran's vital infrastructure. This document called on Obama to '*bring in troops* [raising the question of actual invasion, and not simply aerial strikes] *and material to the region under the cover of the Iraq and Afghanistan conflicts, thus maintaining a degree of strategic and tactical surprise.*' In other words, Obama's forthcoming appointment of Ross to head his regime's Middle East Policy Advisory Group places an unconditional advocate and promoter of genocidal war with Iran in a key strategic foreign policy position.

Secretary of State Hillary Clinton and Dennis Ross will do everything in their power to promote and justify a US-Israeli joint attack on Iran while leaving it to Obama to make the grand public diplomatic gestures needed to convince the public that diplomacy had been truly tried, but proved futile. Ross and Clinton will begin with phony negotiations based on unacceptable ultimatums. This will be followed by acts of war in the form of Gaza-style embargos designed to starve and impoverish the people of Iran, and conclude with a Gaza-style aerial blitzkrieg. Given the extraordinary number of Zionists appointed by Obama in every key level of his government, the possibility of any internal debate or dissent over the Ross roadmap for war in Israel's interest is minimal. Obama has put together a policy-making elite so closely linked and loyal to the Israeli military that it precludes any type of meaningful negotiations with Iran.

Possible External Constraints on Zionist-Israeli-US War on Iran

The only effective deterrent to a Gaza-style Israeli assault on Iran is Tehran's capacity for military retaliation, especially accurate long-range missiles capable of reaching Israel's principle military sites, infrastructure and related support systems. These have been bought and paid for, but the Russians have yet to deliver them. Given the Israeli leaders' lack of any moral constraints and their immersion in a militarist ideology in which brutal force and widespread violence are the primary means of projecting power and securing Israeli public support, a costly massive military counter-attack is probably the most effective deterrent to force its leaders to reconsider Israel's military-driven foreign policy.

Israel's military success in Gaza has created an irrational triumphalist war fever among all of its leaders and their enthusiastic supporters in the million member Jewish-Zionist organizations in the US. This has led them to underestimate the catastrophic costs of a war with Iran. An Israeli-US sneak attack on Iran would unleash major military and political retaliatory action throughout the Middle East. This would certainly inflict major human, military, political and economic losses on many US military installations in the Gulf region. This is especially the case in Iraq and the adjoining client Gulf States, where US military forces are highly vulnerable. An Israeli assault might lead to the destabilization or overthrow of Arab client states. Moreover, Iran may retaliate by successfully launching accurate long-range missiles, which will target major Israeli military complexes and adjoining population centers.

While Israeli militarists adopt a 'defensive' rhetoric, their strategy is to weaken Iran's defense capability and make it more vulnerable to military threats and diplomatic pressure in a lead-up to a pre-emptive aerial assault. International inspections by United Nations agencies are only carried out of Iranian sites but not of US regional military instillations, including their nuclear-armed war ships and submarines, or of Israel's nuclear weapons sites and nuclear weapon laboratories. The one-sided inspections provide a wealth of information on Iranian military capacity and defense locations and of advanced strategic research laboratories. UN inspections prior to the US invasion of Iraq identified key defense installations and Iraqi scientists, their places of work and homes, which were used in bombing missions and the subsequent assassination campaign against top Iraqi scientists. This kind of information was crucial in guiding Israel's bombing and missile assaults and assassination of leaders and their families during its invasions of Lebanon and Gaza.

The Israeli-dictated and US Zionist-implemented economic boycott of Iran is clearly directed toward undermining both Iranian living standards and the performance of their economy, similar to what the Jewish state imposed on Gaza. It is part of the 'softening up' campaign prior to its all out attack.

To date, however, despite a sustained effort by all of the top Zionist functionaries in the US government and the intense pressures of its lobbies on US pension fund managers, the embargo has not crippled the Iranian economy, which has had ample time since the Iranian revolution under Khomeini to adjust to dealing with Western-sponsored economic pressure. Especially with the onset of the recession, the decline of world markets and the growing energy demands of China, there are numerous Western and Asian multinationals eager to trade with Iran and to ignore Israeli and US Zionist pressures.

Israel's genocidal war on Gaza has finally forced important cracks in the overseas Zionist monopoly over Jewish opinion, both worldwide and in the United States. While the leading Jewish communal organizations and their spiritual spokespeople continue to support each and every crime from the bombing of Red Cross ambulances and clinic to United Nations schools, food and medical supplies warehouses and refugee centers, this has finally provoked vigorous opposition among leading Jewish intellectuals, writers and other professionals.

New organizations and personalities have emerged within the

Jewish community, which have forcibly repudiated Israel's genocide. Some Jewish activists have taken bold direct actions, occupying Israeli consular offices in a few major cities and calling for a total boycott of Israeli goods and academic exchanges. Others have confronted Zionist apologists in public forums and press conferences. While the number and influence of Jewish critics of Zionist war crimes is small, their importance lies in their giving legitimacy to and encouraging millions of otherwise intimidated and silent Jews and Gentiles to 'come out' against Israel. As a result, an unprecedented number of people in the West have voiced their horror and opposition to the Zionist military juggernaut and expressed their support for economic boycotts against Israel. On November 25, the President of the United Nations General Assembly called for international sanctions to be imposed on the state of Israel. [32] As the Israeli assault on Gaza proceeded, GA President Miguel d'Escoto-Brockmann was to label Israel's actions genocidal.[33]

The global Boycott, Sanction and Divestment Campaign appears to finally be making an impact. As reported in the *Jerusalem Post*:

> Local exporters are losing foreign markets and customers because of the global economic crisis and growing anti-Israel boycott of locally made products following Operation Cast Lead, the Israel Manufacturers Association said Sunday.
> "In addition to the problems and difficulties arising from the global economic crisis, 21 percent of local exporters report that they are facing problems in selling Israeli goods because of an anti-Israel boycott, mainly from the UK and Scandinavian countries," said Yair Rotloi, chairman of the association's foreign-trade committee."[34]

Even the mighty AIPAC seems to view itself as losing its grip on power:

> Howard Kohr opened the [annual AIPAC] conference admitting that there was now a huge, international campaign against the policies of Israel. He painted a picture of 30,000 people marching in Spain, Italian trade unionists calling for a boycott of Israeli products, the UN Human Rights Council passing 26 resolutions condemning Israel, an Israeli Apartheid Week that is building a global boycott, divestment and sanctions campaign.
> This global movement, he warned, emanates from

the Middle East, echoes in the halls of the United Nations and the capitals of Europe, is voiced in meetings of international peace organizations, and is spreading throughout the United States-from the media to town hall meetings, from campuses to city squares. "No longer is this campaign confined to the ravings of the political far left or far right," he lamented, "but increasingly it is entering the American mainstream."[35]

While Jewish and Gentile mass opposition neither stopped nor weakened Israel's massacre of Gaza civilians, it has laid the political and organizational basis to launch a massive campaign against the US Zionist war plans against Iran.

One of the most effective threats to Israel's genocidal war drive is the launching of investigations into Israeli war crimes, the establishment of tribunals to try Israeli military and political leaders for their crimes against humanity.[36] Israeli leaders have advised their soldier-criminals they will be provided with legal protection. The leaders have expressed concern that they themselves may be subject to citizen arrests and tried by overseas courts. Several governments (Jordan, Norway, Spain) are filing war crimes charges before the International Criminal Court in The Hague. The problem with laying charges on Israeli war criminals is where to draw the line between military-political leaders who directed the war crimes and the field officers, who implemented the policies violating the Geneva Conventions. Or identifying the officials who specifically barred medical and emergency workers for over four days from evacuating wounded and starving civilians, including small children, from the site of a horrific Israeli massacre of Gaza civilians. What about the great masses of Israeli Jewish citizens who were so elated by the bombing of whole civilian neighborhoods that some Israelis set up observation posts with picnic baskets to survey the ongoing carnage? The same Israelis "delighted in the images, splashed across the front pages, of smiling Israeli soldiers riding homes on tanks in victory post."[37]

Mass Israeli elation, political intoxication and embrace of the perpetrators of the killing of unarmed people may be repugnant to world opinion, but it is not a sufficient offense to merit an international tribunal. However it is subject to the same moral repudiation, which many of us felt toward the German people who celebrated Hitler's savage bombing of Soviet, Polish and Balkan cities. Even if the Zionist-controlled White House succeeds in using its veto on the United Nations Security Council to prevent a war crimes investigation of Israeli leaders, the presentation of charges and possible arrests in several European countries will force the Israeli leaders to reflect on their pariah status and might inhibit their push for a murderous war with Iran.

Israelis currently dismiss out of hand the opprobrium of world opinion as irrelevant to its ongoing military offensive. This causes the Jewish state to overlook the importance of world opinion in eroding strategic political support that is essential for any state's functioning—as even the mighty United States has found out—in the future. Many observers believe hundreds of millions of Arab citizens and multitudes of non-Arabs and non-Muslims are coming to believe that Israel and its overseas Zionist Fifth column *will only understand the language of force* since they routinely practice state terrorism to impose their interests on captive, impoverished peoples. As a result, many analysts argue that it is understandable that the weapons of choice for the victims of Israel will inevitably rely on sustained, organized and militarized people's resistance. In these circumstances the current crop of anemic, impotent, collaborationist Arab leaders and regimes may be overthrown and a new combative and consequential leadership could emerge, one which consults and draws its mass support from the deepest feelings of national dignity and moral rectitude, reflected in a profound hatred of Zionist imposed humiliations.

Conclusion

Israel's Gaza war is leading its leaders and its strategically placed overseas agents in the US political system to *overreach* and to pursue a new war with Iran, as part of a regional strategy to secure imperial power. The Obama Administration and the newly elected Israeli prime minister share more than overlapping policymakers and long term commitments to military-driven empire building. They have made it clear that they will proceed in setting in motion a series of diplomatic and economic moves destined to prepare the stage for launching a genocidal war against Iran.

The only deterrent to new wars of extermination is actions, which increase the political, economic and military costs for Israeli aggression. Only when Israeli casualties mount, when Zionist exploiters and bankers suffer losses, when its academics and tourist sites are boycotted, then and only then will the Israelis and their US acolytes begin to rethink their blind adherence to militarist policies.

Unfortunately it may take some military shocks as well.

Addendum

Because Iran refused to even consider opening a dialogue with Obama in the presence of israel's principal mouthpiece directing US policy toward Iran, the White House was forced to shift Ross to a more discrete but still influential position in the National Security Council.

Endnotes

1   See Appendix I.
2   Nathan Guttman, "Olmert's Boast of "Shaming Rice" Provokes Diplomatic Furor," *Forward*, January 15, 2009.
3   *Forward*, January 15, 2009.
4   *Forward*, January 15, 2009.
5   *Forward*, January 15, 2009.
6   See, inter alia, Appendix I, Bibliography of Genocidal/Apartheid Acts Inflicted by Israel in the Palestinians During the Al Aqsa Intifada, in Francis A. Boyle, *Palestine, Palestinians and International Law*, Clarity Press, Inc., Atlanta, 2003, pp. 178-200. Contains listing of 7 Security Council Resolutions, 43 UN General Assembly Resolutions, Statements by the UN High Commissioner for Human Rights, Human Rights Watch, Amnesty International, B-tselem, and Palesine Human Rights Center—just for the period to publication date in 2003, alone.
7   See James Petras, *Zionism, Militarism and the Decline of US Power*, Clarity Press, Atlanta, 2008.
8   *Times on Line*, January 7, 2009
9   David Sanger, "US Rejected Aid for Israeli Raid on Iranian Nuclear Site", *The New York Times*, January 10, 2009
10   Aluf Benn and Amos   "US to Sell IAF Smart Bombs for Heavily Fortified Targets, *Haaretz*, September 14, 2008, cited by Fire Dog Lake at <http://firedoglake.com/2009/01/11/nyts-sanger-sure-gets-it-wrong-us-did-sell-israel-bombs-for-iran-attack>, which also drew attention to their use in Gaza, as reported in Yaakov Katz, "Israel Uses New US-Supplied Smart Bomb," *Jerusalem Post*, December 28, 2009.
11   Brett Stephens, "Iran is the Terrorist 'Mother Regime", *Wall Street Journal*, January 24, 2009.
12   See Robert Dreyfuss, "Dennis Ross's Iran Plan," *The Nation*, April 8, 2009.
13   Ron Kampeas, "Waiting for Obama to Fill Out the Mideast Policy Machine", Jewish Telegraphic Agency, January 20, 2009.
14   Ibid.
15   Ibid
16   *Jewish Telegraph Agency,* January 20, 2009.
17   US Department of Treasury Press Room, February 2, 2009
18   US Department of Treasury, "Biography of Stuart Levey", June 22, 2007; *Chicago Tribune* April 30, 2009.
19   "$50-$60 Billion Laundered from US nonprofits into illegal West Bank colonies creates threat of terrorism backlash", The Israel Lobby Archive, at <http://www.irmep.org/ila/moneylaunder/> The link provides a documented history of Department of Justice and Treasury response to nonprofit money-laundering to the West Bank, including briefs by others.
20   Eric Lichtblau and James Risen, "Bank Data Is Sifted by U.S. in Secret to Block Terror ," *The New York Times* June 23, 2006.
21   Treasury Department *Press Room* January 29, 2007.
22   Department of Treasury Office of Public Affairs, May 4, 2005.
23   Ibid
24   Ibid
25   "Muslim Charity Leaders Sentenced in Federal Court," CBS, May 27, 2009, < http://cbs11tv.com/local/holy.land.foundation.2.1021018.html>
26   Jewish Telegraph Agency, April 27, 2009
27   Grant Smith, *"From Irgun to AIPAC: Israel Lobby's US Treasury Department: Follies Hurt Americans"* Institute for Research in Middle East Policy (IRMEP), September 11, 2008.
28   Ibid
29   See "Bush Protested Planned Israeli Strike on Iran," FOXNews, January 10, 2009.

30   WINEP's Presidential Task Force on the Future of U.S.-Israel Relations issued the June 2008 report "Strengthening the Partnership: How to Deepen U.S.-Israel Cooperation on the Iranian Nuclear Challenge."

31   See "About Us", Jewish People's Policy Planning Institute, < http://www.jpppi.org.il/JPPPI/Templates/ShowPage.asp?DBID=1&LNGID=1&TMID=138&FID=355>

32   Allison Hoffman, "UNGA Head Accuses Israel of Apartheid," Jerusalem Post, November 25, 2008 http://www.jpost.com/servlet/Satellite?pagename=JPost/JPArticle/ShowFull&cid=1226404827209

33   The UN General Assembly President's remarks were made in an interview with Al-Jazeerah, see <http://english.aljazeera.net/news/americas/2009/01/200911321467988347.html> They were widely carried on the internet, but it appears that not a single Anglo-American mainstream media source reprinted them.

34   Sharon Wrobel, "Exporters Suffer Anti-Israel Boycotts," *Jerusalem Post*, March 30, 2009.

35   Cited in Medea Benjamin, "Who Will Stop the AIPAC Jews Before Its Too Late?" Code Pink, May 6, 2009.

36   *Financial Times*, January 16, 2009 page 5.

37   *Financial Times*, January 26, 2009.

CHAPTER 11

THE POLITICS OF AN ISRAELI EXTERMINATION CAMPAIGN:

BACKERS, APOLOGISTS AND ARMS SUPPLIERS

Introduction

Because of the unconditional support of the entire political class in the US, from the White House to Congress, including both Parties, incoming and outgoing elected officials and all the principle print and electronic mass media, the Israeli Government feels no compunction in publicly proclaiming a detailed and graphic account of its policy of mass extermination of the population of Gaza.

Israel's sustained and comprehensive bombing campaign of every aspect of Palestinian governance, civic institutions and society is directed toward destroying civilized life in Gaza. Israel's totalitarian vision is driven by the vision and practice of a permanent purge of Arab Palestine informed by Zionism, an ethno-racist ideology, promulgated by the Jewish state and justified, enforced and pursued by its organized backers in the United States.

The facts of the most recent Israeli extermination—its 2008 assault on Gaza that preceded the Israeli election—have become known: In the first six days of round the clock terror bombing of major and minor populations centers, the Jewish State murdered and seriously maimed over 2,500 people, mostly dismembered and burned in the open ovens of missile fire. Scores of children and women were slaughtered as well as defenseless civilians and officials.

They have sealed off all access to Gaza and declared it a military, free fire zone, while expanding their target to include the entire population of 1.5 millions semi-starved prisoners. According to the *Boston Globe*:

Israeli military officials said their target lists have expanded

165

to include the *vast support network* on which the Islamist movement relies to stay in power "...we are trying to hit the *whole* spectrum, because *everything is connected* and everything supports terrorism against Israel [my emphasis].[1]

A top Israeli in its secret police apparatus is quoted saying,

"Hamas' *civilian infrastructure* is a very sensitive target".[2]

What the Israeli Jewish politicians and military planners designate as "Hamas" is the entire social service network, the entire government and the vast majority of economic activity, embracing almost the entire 1.5 million imprisoned residents of Gaza.

Israel's 'target' list thus involved the *'total population'*, using the totality of its non-nuclear weaponry and for an *unlimited* time period, as it was then put—until the 'bitter end' according to the Israeli Prime Minister. Israel's defense ministry spokesman emphatically reiterated the Jewish's state's totalitarian war concept emphasizing the targeting of civilians: "Hamas has used ostensibly civilian operations as a cover for military activities. Anything affiliated with Hamas is a legitimate target."

Like all totalitarians in the past, the Jewish state boasts of having systematically pre-planned the extermination campaign—months in advance—up to and including the precise hour and day of the bombing to coincide with inflicting the maximum murder of civilians: The rockets and bombs fell as children were leaving school, as graduating police cadets were receiving their diplomas and as frantic mothers ran out from their homes to find their sons and daughters.

The mass military extermination campaign followed Israel's non-stop total economic embargo and unremitting selective assassination campaign of the previous two years. Both were designed to weaken Palestinian support for Hamas, first via mass hunger, disease, humiliation and violent intimidation and facilitating the proxy power grab by the PLO Quislings under Zionist puppet Abbas. When they discovered that mass hunger and selective Israeli murder only strengthened the population's links to its democratically elected government and the resolve of the Hamas government to resist Israel, the Israeli regime unleashed its entire arsenal of weapons, including its new 'American gifts'—up-to-date 1000 pound 'bunker buster' bombs and high tech missiles, which were used to incinerate large numbers of human beings within their deadly radius and to obliterate the spiritual resources and the physical infrastructure of Palestinian civilization.

Moving directly from its totalitarian vision to its military blueprint to the savaging of Palestinian population centers, the Jewish state destroyed the principal university that had served over 18,000 students (mostly women), mosques, pharmacies, electrical and water lines, power stations, fishing villages, fishing boats and the little fishing port that provided a meager supply of fish for the starving population. They destroyed roads, transport facilities, food warehouses, science buildings, small factories, shops and apartments. They destroyed a women's dormitory at the university. In the words of the Israel leader: *"...because everything is connected to everything..."* it is necessary to destroy each and every facet of life, which allows humans to exist with some dignity and independence.

Here is the final tally of the destruction as recorded by the Palestine Center for Human Rights by January 22, 2009:[3]

Destruction to Civilian Property and facilities

During their offensive on the Gaza Strip, IOF have destroyed the following civilian property and facilities:

- IOF have destroyed at least 2,400 houses, including 490 ones by air strikes.
- IOF have destroyed 28 public civilian facilities, including buildings of a number of ministries, municipalities, governorates, fishing harbors and the building of the Palestinian legislative Council.
- IOF have destroyed 21 private projects, including cafeterias, wedding halls, tourist resorts and hotels.
- IOF have destroyed 30 mosques completely and 15 others partially.
- IOF have destroyed offices of 10 charitable societies.
- IOF have destroyed 121 industrial and commercial workshops and damaged at least 200 others.
- IOF have destroyed 5 factories of concrete and one of juice.
- IOF have destroyed 60 police stations.
- IOF have destroyed buildings of 5 media institutions and 2 health ones.
- IOF have destroyed 29 educational institutions completely or partially.
- IOF have razed thousands of donums of agricultural land.
- IOF have heavily damaged thousands of houses.

The destruction of property is each governorate has been as follows:

Northern Gaza Strip

- IOF have destroyed 650 houses, including 250 ones by air strikes. According to initial estimations, at least another 500 houses have been rendered uninhabitable, and hundreds of others have been heavily damaged.

- IOF have destroyed 4 public facilities.
- IOF have destroyed 2 private facilities.
- IOF have destroyed 85 industrial and commercial workshops.
- IOF have destroyed offices of 2 charitable societies.
- IOF have destroyed 6 security buildings.
- IOF have destroyed 7 educational institutions completely or partially.
- IOF have destroyed 10 mosques and damaged 6 others.
- IOF have razed at least 1,000 donums of agricultural.
- IOF have destroyed 150 cars and 200 agricultural tools.

Gaza City

- IOF have destroyed 1,100 houses, including 80 ones by air strikes. According to initial estimations, hundreds of others houses have been partially destroyed and hundreds of others were heavily damaged.
- IOF have destroyed 5 public facilities, including buildings of ministries and the Palestinian Legislative Council.
- IOF have destroyed 8 hotels completely or partially.
- IOF have destroyed 8 private enterprises, including cafeterias and wedding halls.
- IOF have destroyed 5 media institutions, 7 educational ones, 2 health ones and 3 charitable ones.
- IOF have destroyed 18 industrial and commercial workshops.
- IOF have destroyed 10 security buildings.
- IOF have 10 mosques completely or partially.
- IOF have razed hundreds of donums of agricultural land (under documentation).

Central Gaza Strip

- IOF have destroyed 220 houses, including 52 ones by air strikes.
- IOF have destroyed 2 public facilities (building of municipalities.
- IOF have 6 mosques completely or partially.
- IOF have destroyed 2 workshops.
- IOF have destroyed 19 security buildings.
- IOF have razed at least 200 donums of agricultural land.
- IOF have damaged dozens of houses.

Khan Yunis

- IOF have destroyed at least 230 houses, including 28 by air strikes.
- IOF have destroyed 4 public facilities.
- IOF have destroyed offices of 4 charitable societies
- IOF have destroyed 10 industrial and commercial workshops.
- IOF have destroyed 15 security buildings.
- IOF have destroyed 2 mosques and damaged 5 others
- IOF have razed at least 150 donums of agricultural land.
- IOF have damaged 8 educational institutions.

Rafah

- IOF have destroyed 160 houses, including 80 ones by air strikes. At least 300 houses have been also damaged.
- IOF have destroyed 12 public facilities.
- IOF have destroyed 2 private enterprises.
- IOF have destroyed 2 mosques and heavily damaged another 4 ones.
- IOF have destroyed 6 industrial and commercial workshops and damaged 15 stores.
- IOF have heavily damaged 7 educational institutions.
- IOF have destroyed offices of a charitable society.
- IOF have destroyed 10 security buildings.
- IOF have razed at least 300 donums of agricultural land.

The Israeli totalitarian leaders knew with confidence that they could act and they could kill with impunity, locally and before the entire world, because of the influence of the US Zionist Power Configuration in and over the US White House and Congress. They knew they had the full backing of all the major Israeli political parties (Right, Left and Center), trade unions, mass media and especially public opinion. Israeli state terror is backed by 81% of Jewish Israelis according to a poll taken by Israel's Channel 10.[4] Israeli totalitarian violence and extermination of Palestinians is extremely popular among the Jewish electorate, and it was hoped that the Gaza carnage would raise support for the Labor Party candidate, Minister Ehud Barak. (Apparently even this demonstration of "toughness" was insufficient, as Israelis went on to elect the even more radically anti-Arab candidate, Benjamin Netanyahu.)

The Israelis knew they would 'succeed' with virtually no casualties because they bombed, burned and dismembered a defenseless population totally lacking the minimum means to defend themselves from F16 bombers,

White phosphorus rains on Gaza

Israeli forces deliberately killed 63 Palestinian police
cadets attending their graduation ceremony.

helicopter gun ships and missile assaults. The vile depravity of the assault on the defenseless population is matched by the utter cowardice of the Israeli military command and its cheering bloodthirsty public ensconced behind their aerial monopoly. They suffered no threats of aerial retaliation, no wounded or dead pilots or helicopter gunners, as wave after wave swept in and over a defenseless imprisoned population in a crowded and besieged ghetto whose population was not even afforded the possibility of flight.

Hundreds of tanks and armored carriers invaded once the cities and towns were leveled. Then and only then, did the Israeli General staff risk the skin of a precious Jewish 'soldier' and risk the anxiety and worry of their kin in Israel and the US.

Overseas Allies: The Presidents of the Major American Jewish Organizations (PMAJO)

From the moment that the Israeli Government decided it would destroy the newly elected Hamas government and punish the democratic electorate of Gaza with starvation and murder, the entire Zionist Power Configuration (ZPC) in the US, including the PMAJO, pulled all stops in implementing the Israeli policy. The PMAJO encompasses the fifty-one Jewish organizations with the largest membership, with the greatest financial clout and the most influential backers (see Appendix I for a list of the member organizations). The most prominent lobbyist within the PMAJO is AIPAC, which has over 100,000 members and 150 full-time operatives in Washington actively pressuring the US Congress, the White House and all administrative agencies whose policies may relate to the interests of the State of Israel.

However Israeli political extends far beyond its non-governmental agencies. Over two score legislators in the Congress and over a dozen senators are committed Zionists who automatically back Israel's policies and push for US funding and armaments for its military machine. Top officials in key administrative positions, in Treasury, Commerce and the National Security Council, senior functionaries in the Pentagon and top advisers on Middle East affairs are also life-long, fanatically committed Zionists, who consistently and unreservedly back the policies of the State of Israel (see Chapter 10).

Equally important, the majority of the largest film, print and electronic media are owned or deeply influenced by Jewish-Zionist media moguls who are committed to slanting the 'news' in favor of Israel. The composition and influence of the ZPC is central to understanding three main characteristics of Israel's power:

1.   Israel can commit what leading United Nations and international

human rights experts have defined as 'crimes against humanity' with total impunity;

2. Israel can secure an unlimited supply of the most technologically advanced and destructive weapons and use them without limit on a civilian population in violation of even US Congressional restrictions on the legal use of US weaponry, and

3. scores of almost unanimous United Nations condemnations of the construction of genocidal apartheid barriers against a native population, starvation embargoes and the current extermination campaign in Gaza are always vetoed by the US representative.

While many critics of Israel's genocide in Gaza are willing to also condemn what they call 'the complicity' of Washington or 'the United States', they do so *without* clearly identifying the actual socio-political forces influencing policymakers or the 'dual' political loyalties and identities of the 'American' politicians who have long-standing and deep allegiances to Israel. As a consequence, most critics fail to counter, protest or even identify the ideology and politics of the organized power configurations which define US complicity with Israel. They are unwilling to name and shame those who intimidate critics of Israel, who write and mouth the pro-Israel editorials in the mass media, and who filter out any criticism, any truth…even when Israel engages in sustained bloody extermination campaigns. It is a failure of political analysis that is almost stunning in its absence.

The ZPC and the Israeli War of Extermination in Gaza

The ZPC played a major role in all stages of Israel's extermination campaign against Gaza, including a sustained propaganda effort. The ZPC orchestrated a massive successful campaign through the extensive network of American mass media, which it controls and/or influences. It fabricated an image of the Hamas administration in Gaza as a terrorist organization, which allegedly seized power through violence—totally denying Hamas' rise to power through internationally supervised, democratic elections and its defense of its electoral mandate against an attempted US-Israeli-backed PLO military takeover. The entire Zionist Jewish leadership has backed Israel's land grabs, its ghetto wall around Palestinians, the hundreds of road blocks, the Jewish settlers violently taking over Palestinian homes in the West Bank and East Jerusalem, and the criminal, genocidal Israeli economic embargo on Gaza designed to systematically starve the Palestinians into submission.

Throughout the two years of this Israeli extermination campaign, American Zionists played a major role in leading the servile US government at home and abroad in backing each totalitarian measure. The vast majority of local synagogues became bully-pulpits defending the starvation and degradation of 1.5 million Palestinian refugees in Gaza caged on all sides by deadly force and the 'walling off' into economically and socially devastating cantons of the 4.5 million West Bank Palestinian population under foreign occupation—though of course describing this reality in different terms. The US Congress shamelessly followed the Zionist lead, backing every single criminal measure taken by the State of Israel and approving dozens of resolutions, which in most cases were entirely written by AIPAC lobbyists acting in effect as unregistered agents of the Israeli government (contrary to US federal statute, which requires foreign agents and lobbyists to be registered as such).

Israel's demands for the most up-to-date US warplanes, including F-16s, Apache helicopter gun ships, and 1,000 pound bombs were secured by dint of effort of the AIPAC lobbyists and their clients in the US Congress. In other words, the American ZPC created the *ideological cover* and *military instruments* for Israel's 'total war' against the defenseless Palestinian population. Equally important, prominent Zionist leaders in the US Congress and members of the foreign policy establishment blocked or vetoed any international criticism of Israel—securing its impunity and immunity from any of the Congressional sanctions usually enacted against criminal states. In other words, Israeli policymakers operated with the knowledge that there would be no negative economic, diplomatic and military repercussions to their launching the planned Gaza extermination campaign because they knew, in advance, that 'their people' were in total control of US Middle East policy to the extent of their actually repeating verbatim each and every propaganda lie in defense of Israel's total war against the entire population of Gaza.

Defending Israel's War of Extermination

The Zionist-controlled US print media, in particular *The New York Times* and the *Washington Post*, systematically fabricated an account that fit perfectly with Israel's official line defending its massive assault on Gaza. They omitted any historical account of the hundreds of Israeli armed incursions and 'targeted' assassinations of Palestinian leaders and officials (even in their own homes) which repeatedly violated the 'ceasefire' agreed by Hamas and provoked its retaliation in self-defense of its people. They omitted the years of an Israeli-enforced starvation embargo of food and essentials that threatened the lives of 1.5 million Palestinians and led to the desperate efforts of the elected Hamas leadership to secure supplies for the people's survival via tunnels across the Egyptian border and through largely harmless missile attacks against Israel to pressure the Jewish state to negotiate an end of the criminal blockade.

The Conference of President of the Major American Jewish Organizations, and the vast majority of Jewish communal groups and congregations gave enthusiastic and unanimous support to Israel's total war, its extermination campaign against the captive Palestinian population of Gaza. Even as images and reports of the massive destruction, killing and wounding of over 2,500 defenseless Palestinians filtered in the mass media (the final count was to be higher, as noted above), not a single *major* Jewish organization broke ranks; only individuals and small groups protested. All the 'Majors' persisted in the *politics of the Big Lie:* hospitals, mosques, universities, roads, apartments, pharmacies and fishing ports were all labeled 'Hamas targets' whose destruction was thereby justifiable, above and beyond all common sense and reasonable proportionality. An effort was made to equate the systematic all-out assault by uncontested helicopter gunships against 1.5 millions civilians with accounts of Hamas' homemade missiles falling ineffectively near Israeli towns. However, for the average viewer, the comparative threats and demonstrations of damage were so visibly and overwhelmingly disproportionate that the "balanced accounting" required of the media whenever criticism of Israel arises actually became occasions for Israel's further exposure.

Favored Themes of the Israeli Big Lie

A close reading of the most important propaganda organ of the PMAJO, *The Daily Alert*, reveals the propaganda tack taken by the leadership of the pro-Israel power configuration.

The style is the Big Lie, reminiscent of totalitarian regimes.

1. *Denying Israeli war crimes and fabricating accounts that minimize the Jewish State's killings. The Daily Alert* (January 22, 2009) claimed that Israel killed only 600 Palestinians and "most were fighters." The Daily Alert denied on-site reports by major human rights workers, Red Cross officials, Palestinian and international doctors and medical workers and journalists, who risked their lives (and some died) documenting the nearly 1,300 deaths, over 2/3 of which were children, women and non-combatants.[5] Human Rights Watch on Thursday, April 23, branded Israeli probes into the recent Gaza war as an attempt to cover up Israeli war crimes perpetrated in the densely-populated coastal enclave. "The conclusions are an apparent attempt to mask violations of the laws of war by Israeli forces in Gaza," HRW Deputy Director Joe Stork said in a statement.

2. *Repeating Israeli propaganda justifying the bombing of the United Nations-run schools* by claiming the schools were 'infiltrated by Palestinian terrorists' among the thousands of refugees (*The Daily Alert,* January 22, 2009). There was not a single armed resistance fighter found among the 40 bodies recovered from the rubble by the United Nations workers, International Red Cross and Palestinian medical crews at the girls' elementary school; all were children, teachers and refugees.[6] Every organization and individual eyewitness refutes the Zionist-American apology of the Israeli bombing of the school, including the entire European Union.[7] The most bizarre fabrication printed in the *Daily Alert* is a headline, which read: "*Hamas Shot from Civilian Neighborhoods*" over an article by Rod Nordland (*Newsweek*), which, in fact, reports the opposite, "Everyone of the residents interviewed in eastern Jabeliya insisted that there had been no provocation from the area, no resistance fighters and no rocket launchings."

3. "*Israel Doing its Best to Help Gazans*", (*Daily Alert*, January 16, 2009). The third lie is a whopper. In fact, Israel blocked all medicine and medical equipment from entering Gaza, bombed hospitals, shot up ambulances, murdered doctors and medical aid workers and blocked all shipment of water, food and fuel. The Israelis bombed the main United Nations food and medical supply warehouse, destroying its entire contents. The US Zionists defended this bombing by citing Olmert's blood libel that the destruction of thousands of tons of food was a "response to fire coming from the building." The United Nations Secretary General Ban Ki-Moon was outraged by this barefaced lie as he visited the still smoldering UN warehouse to view the destruction while US Secretary of State Rice crawled before the Israelis, begging them to "avoid (a repeat of) such incidents." (*Daily Alert,* January 16, 2009)

4. "*Saving Gaza by Destroying the Heart of Terror*" (*Daily Alert,* January 16, 2009). The Jewish propaganda sheet reproduces an article by the ultra-nationalist Natan Sharansky, who advocates expelling all Palestinian Arabs from 'Greater Israel'. "Terrorism is a cancer that can't be cured through "proportional" treatments," Sharansky asserted in the original article published in *Bloomberg*,[8] forced to address the "proportionality issue" by the unavoidable public perception that disproportional violence was in fact being perpetrated by Israel against the Palestinians. What he was in actuality defending was the destruction of over 10,000 houses, damaging over 40,000 homes, roads,

hospitals, power installations, water and sewage installations, 121 industries and commercial workshops, 30 mosques, 29 educational institutions, farms, poultries, dairies, small fishing vessels and the fishing port (see the above report).

5. *"Israeli Pilot Tries to Avoid Hitting Civilians"*, (*Daily Alert*, January 14, 2009). Photos published in all the international mass media refute this Zionist propaganda claim. The ghostly rubble of whole apartment blocks resembles a nuclear strike or an earthquake, according to the BBC reporters who finally made it into Gaza. Numerous European Parliamentary representatives and other on-site visitors from throughout the world were shocked by the devastation. Not only did Israeli pilots target all civilian targets, but their ground troops assassinated unarmed civilians holding white flags and in some cases even small children attempting to flee. Surviving Palestinian children tell of their fathers executed in front of their families.

The Big Lie promoted by the leading Zionist organizations resonates from the Rabbinical pulpits to their members and beyond: Informal phone surveys with rank and file members of local Zionists groups echo the same lies and apologies, almost verbatim. In a word, neither facts, nor reports, nor universal condemnation, nor even challenges by dissident rabbis, Jewish notables, writers and activists have made a dent on the major Jewish organizations and their agents in influential positions in the new Obama administration. They *are* the willing accomplices to mass murder in Gaza. They *are* active promoters of a pre-emptive aerial assault on Iran. They will unconditionally apologize for any crime against humanity that Israel perpetrates. Their academic apologists at Harvard such as Alan Dershowitz defend Israeli genocide as part of a 'Just War'. In the face of universal condemnation they continue to cite the Holocaust as camouflage for Zionist carnage in the Middle East, and claim that they and their State are the Moral People, or even further, as claimed by Ehud Barak, "The IDF is the most moral army in the world"[9] entitled to decide and judge, what is just and what is sacred Truth—irrespective of world opinion.

The Israeli leaders are perfectly aware of the 'free hand' with which their 'Fifth Column' operates, up to and including their prominent role in defense of genocide. Israeli leaders are assured that even when they launch a bigger, bolder and more destructive war (including the possibility of pre-emptive nuclear strike) against Iran or Syria/Lebanon, they can count on the million-member US Zionist lobby securing White House and US Congressional support. Israeli leaders now know for a fact that the anti-war movement will once again engage in inconsequential protests against the 'shadows of power' and not the real power wielders and warmongers embedded in the Zionist Power Configuration.

To bolster its propaganda efforts, *The Daily Alert* systematically works to convey the impression of widespread support, and to slander and minimize commentary that is adverse, including:

1. Citing selected statement from Israel's allies and clients in government (Washington, Germany and the UK) blaming Hamas for the conflict without mentioning the vast majority of countries in the United Nations General Assembly condemning Israel's brutality.
2. Reproducing Israeli slanders against any and all international human rights leaders and organizations that condemn the Jewish state's policy of genocide against the native Palestinians. In this regard, *The Daily Alert* is the foremost 'genocide denier' in the United States and, perhaps outside of Israel, in the world..
3. Defending every Israeli bombing mission, every day, every hour, of every building, every home, and every economic, religious and educational institution in Gaza as 'defensive' or a 'reprisal'.
4. Quoting US writers, journalists and editors who praise and defend Israel's 'total war' without identifying their long-standing affiliation and identification with Zionist organizations, thereby giving a false image of a wide spectrum of opinion supporting the assault. This includes quoting some of the most notorious, unconditional, perennial apologists of Israeli violence as if they were unbiased intellectuals, including Benny 'Nuke Tehran' Morris, Marty Peretz and Amos Oz. Never has even the most moderate Jewish or Gentile critic of Israel's massive extermination campaign appeared in any issues of *The Daily Alert*.

The Propaganda Role of Jewish Religious Organizations

Major Jewish religious organizations play a very influential role as conduits of Israeli propaganda and are an important force within the principal Zionist umbrella organizations (e.g. Conference of Presidents of Major American Jewish Organizations or CPMAJO). Fully one-fifth of the Conference (see appendix for a full list) is made up of clerical-Zionist organizations, whose principle political function is promoting Israeli goals through direct intervention in US politics at all levels.

A memo from one group, the United Synagogue of Conservative Judaism, issued on January 3, 2009, outlines their detailed strategy in defense of Israel's Gaza massacre:

Every congregation should issue a statement supporting Israel. Solicit statements from elected officials at the city, state or provincial, or federal levels. Solicit statements from local religious, ethnic and other prominent personalities. Monitor and respond to media coverage. Whenever possible, enlist non-Jews as well as public officials and prominent spokespeople to demonstrate their support for Israel.

The memo then proposes a series of *"talking points on the situation in the Gaza Strip"* that repeats *verbatim* the propaganda fabrications of the Israeli political-military high command: Affirming Israel's peaceful intentions, blaming Hamas as the aggressor and claiming that *"Israel, as always, is doing everything within its powers to limit non-combatant casualties in Gaza."* The Jewish clerics in the United Synagogues reassure their faithful congregants of the rightfulness of ignoring the carnage, shielding them from more unpleasant truths readily available on the internet or discernable from any thoughtful viewing of even the limited western television coverage—shielding them from the more than 5000 civilian casualties and the 1,300 deaths, of which three quarters are women, children and unarmed civilians, from the demolition of sixty schools, tens of thousands of homes and the dozen mosques, from the condemnations of war crimes by the United Nations, Red Cross and every Israeli and Palestinian human rights group.

The strategy paper issued by the religious Conservative Jews is very similar to that followed by the entire network of 51 religious and secular groups affiliated with the 'Presidents'. This highlights the way in which a highly disciplined, well-financed minority captures and multiplies its power far beyond its own membership, 'leveraging' influential Gentiles, the mass media at all levels and public figures into a powerful juggernaut in defense of Israeli genocide in Gaza today and for war against Iran tomorrow.

Where is the Outcry?

The principal American Jewish organizations have bombarded the US Congress, influencing, intimidating and purchasing the craven so-called 'representatives' of the American people, the media and public notables with lies in defense of Israel's total war to exterminate a people. Their public, brazen, open and willful promotion of the acts of a state designed to destroy an entire people can be considered complicity in genocide and a crime against humanity.

And yet these willing accomplices, these 'willing executioners' of state mass murder go uncontested within the US political class. One of their leading mouthpieces in the Obama Administration, Chief Presidential

Adviser David Axelrod, even cited an Obama campaign speech defending Israeli assaults on the people of Gaza.

Israel arrogantly repudiated all calls to end this mass murder, because Israel knows that 'its people' are still in control of US policy toward the Middle East and will use their power in the new president's administration to block any condemnation of this crime.

To date the entire human rights and anti-war movements have failed to even mention, let alone challenge, the most powerful propaganda and political organizations, which influence US policy and manipulate the mass media in favor of Israel's extermination campaign. They will play no restraining role on Israel's totalitarian policies as long as its principal US backers are free to lie, manipulate and defend each and every crime.

The official Jewish peace movements found themselves between a rock and a hard place. As Daniel Louban outlined it:

> Powerful and traditionally conservative organizations such as the American Israel Public Affairs Committee (AIPAC) and the Conference of Presidents of Major American Jewish Organizations expressed unqualified support for the offensive, stressing that it was a justifiable and necessary act of self-defense and dismissing concerns about disproportionate use of force or potential long-term political effects.
>
> Dovish groups such as J Street, Americans for Peace Now, Brit Tzedek v'Shalom, and Israel Policy Forum also condemned Hamas rocket attacks and stressed Israel's right to self-defense But they warned of the malign political effects of military escalation, and most called for an immediate cease-fire. But it was the reaction of those organizations occupying the political middle ground between these two camps that was most noteworthy, and perhaps most decisive in framing the political debate over the war within the U.S. Almost universally, groups with a general reputation for liberal politics and moderate dovishness sided with the hawks, giving the military campaign their unqualified support and calling for a "sustainable" or "effective"—as opposed to "immediate"—cease-fire. [10]

There is little hope for an independent US Congressional policy as long as Israel's war of extermination in Gaza can be defended by the Chairman of the House Foreign Affairs Committee (and Zionist zealot) Congressman Howard Berman in the following terms: *"Israel has a right, indeed a duty, to defend itself in response to the hundreds of rockets and mortars fired from Gaza over the past week. No government in world would sit by and allow its citizens to be subjected to this kind of indiscriminate bombardment. The loss of innocent life is a terribly tragedy and the blame for that tragedy lies with Hamas."* Thus Congressman Berman cynically omits the 2 years of Israel's embargo, the daily 'targeted' assassinations of Palestinians, the 'targeted' missile attacks against civilians, the land, sea and air blockades and the blatant 'targeted' destruction of the infrastructure of Gaza. No government, indeed a democratically elected Islamist government, can stand by while its people are starved and murdered into submission. But according to the respected Congressmen Bermans of the world, only the lives of Jews matter, not the growing thousands of murdered, dismembered and mutilated citizens of Gaza—they do not count as people!

What is to be Done

Israel's crimes against humanity demand a public response: social action, which will force it to cease and desist from its campaign to exterminate the people of Gaza. Because the Jewish state has assaulted a vast array of Palestinian social institutions, which resonate with those in our own society, we can and should mobilize them to condemn and boycott their counterparts in Israel:

1. We should urge the entire academic community to denounce Israel's bombardment of the Islamic University of Gaza and the total destruction of all of its science facilities. An organized boycott of Israeli universities and all academic exchanges, especially scientific, should become university policy throughout the country. Special attention should be paid to the 450 US university presidents, who in the recent past, denounced a call by British academics for a boycott and who remain silent and complicit in the face of Israel's total physical annihilation of all ten faculties for 20,000 Palestinian university students.

2. All American health workers, doctors, nurses, technicians, should organize and denounce Israel's medical embargo against the 1.5 million Palestinians crowded into the Gaza Strip. They must condemn Israel's bombardment of Gaza's Children's Hospital, the neighborhood pharmacies and the attacks on any transport of those critically wounded Palestinian victims of its aerial and missile attacks. Medical personnel should raise the fundamental ethical issues regarding the collaboration of US medical personnel and programs with the Jewish State's 'total war' policies of extermination.

3. All citizens should demand the end of all US military aid to Israel, especially F-16 fighter planes, Apache attack helicopters, missiles, 1000 pound 'bunker buster' bombs used by the Israeli armed forces on the civilian infrastructure of Gaza and the murder and maiming of Palestinians, civilians, civil servants, police and national militia. In pursuit of a cutoff of US military aid to Israel, every effort should be made to target and denounce the most forceful, aggressive and successful Zionist advocates and lobbyists who influence the elected members of the US Congress and White House on foreign military aid budgets. No progress in ending US military aid for Israel's ethnic cleansing will succeed unless the peace movement and others appalled by Israel's mass murder tackle the Zionist lobby head on. This includes boycotts, rebuttals and demonstrations against AIPAC, the Jewish Anti-Defamation League and the other 50 leading American Jewish organizations, which initiate and secure US governmental endorsement of Israel's extermination policies.

4. US religious institutions should forcefully denounce Israel's crimes against humanity, including its demolition of 5 mosques, uniting all faiths (Christian, Muslim, Buddhist, etc.) and especially reaching out to the tiny minority of rabbis and observant Jews willing to forthrightly denounce the totalitarian practices of the Israeli state.

5. Port and long shore workers, sailors and other maritime workers and officials should boycott the handling of all trade with Israel and denounce its Navy's violent illegal assault, in international waters, of civilian fishing boats and vessels carrying humanitarian aid to Gaza. No ships carrying Israeli products should be loaded or unloaded as long as Israel maintains its criminal military blockade of the port facilities of Gaza.

6. Tens of millions of US citizens subject to the one-sided pro-Israel bias of the electronic and print media, the lop-sided presentations of Zionist 'op-ed' writers, 'news' reports and the self-styled Middle East experts, should demand equal time, coverage and reportage for non-Zionist specialists, analysts and commentators. We should demand an end to euphemisms and fabrications, which convert victims into aggressors and exterminators into victims.

7. We should wage a battle of ideas everywhere (in every public forum) against the efforts by the Zionist Power Configuration to monopolize discussion over the Israeli policy of genocide, to censor, intimidate and slander critics of Israeli apartheid—as

UN General Assembly President Manuel d'Escoto-Brockmann so aptly calls Israel's Ghetto Wall surrounding Palestinian villages. The outpouring of public protest over Israel's war of extermination is an enormous step forward in countering the Zionist monopoly of the mass media and encouraging action on the part of the tens of millions of Americans who clearly recognize and privately despise Israel's crimes against humanity and resent the local Zionist elite's thuggery against those who speak out. Mass pressure on elected representatives may sway some to reconsider their abject servility to their Zionist 'contributors' and their 'Israel First' Congressional colleagues.

8. A patriotic nationwide campaign should demand that all instruments of the Israel lobby, especially AIPAC, come clean and register as foreign agents of the State of Israel. This might undermine the Lobby's appeal to American Jews, reduce its influence over Congress, open up judicial processes and investigations over its abuse of tax-exemptions and money-laundering, and lead to revelations and convictions over its treasonous procurement of confidential US state documents for a foreign power. There is a powerful political and legal basis for denial of the 'Lobby's' tax-exempt status and domestic legality, apart from the transparent and overwhelming evidence that all Zionist organizations act as transmission belts for Israeli state policies: In the early 1950s up to 1963, the forerunner of AIPAC was obliged to register as a foreign agent of the State of Israel. More recently, an Israeli prosecutor presented evidence that the Israeli-Jewish Agency and its US counterparts were laundering billions of dollars especially for the funding of Israeli colonial settlements on occupied Palestinian land, condemned as illegal under international law. Congressional hearings, law suits and further published research would reveal the role of the Lobby as a Fifth Column forwarding the interests of the State of Israel, even when these are against the interests of the people of the United States.

Until we curtail the pervasive and disproportionate power of the Zionist Power Configuration in all of its manifestations—in American public and civic life—and its deep penetration of American legislative and executive offices in furtherance of Israeli interests, we will fall short of preventing Israel from receiving the arms, funding and political backing to sustain its wars of ethnic extermination, and the United States will continue to be seen, as it presently is in the eyes of much of the world, as complicit in Israeli acts of genocide.

Appendix
The 51 Member Organizations of the
Conference of Presidents of Major American Jewish Organizations

1. Ameinu
2. American Friends of Likud
3. American Gathering/Federation of Jewish Holocaust Survivors
4. American-Israel Friendship League
5. American Israel Public Affairs Committee
6. American Jewish Committee
7. American Jewish Congress
8. American Jewish Joint Distribution Committee
9. American Sephardi Federation
10. American Zionist Movement
11. Americans for Peace Now
12. AMIT
13. Anti-Defamation League
14. Association of Reform Zionist of America
15. B'nai B'rith International
16. Bnai Zion
17. Central Committee of American Rabbis
18. Committee for Accuracy in Middle East Reporting in America
19. Development Corporation for Israel/State of Israel Bonds
20. Emunah of America
21. Friends of Israel Defense Forces
22. Hadassah, Women's Zionist Organization of America
23. Hebrew Immigrant Aid Society
24. Hillel: The Foundation of Jewish Campus Life
25. Jewish Community Centers Association
26. Jewish Council for Public Affairs
27. Jewish Institute for National Security Affairs
28. Jewish Labor Committee
29. Jewish National Fund
30. Jewish Reconstructionist Federation
31. Jewish War Veterans of the USA
32. Jewish Women International
33. MERCAZ USA, Zionist Organization of the Conservative Movement
34. NA'AMAT USA
35. NCSJ: Advocates on behalf of Jews in Russia, Ukraine, the Baltic States and Eurasia
36. National Council of Jewish Women
37. National Council of Young Israel

38. ORT America
39. Rabbinical Assembly
40. Rabbinical Council of America
41. Religious Zionist of America
42. Union for Reform Judaism
43. Union of Orthodox Jewish Congregations of America
44. United Jewish Communities
45. United Synagogue of Conservative Judaism
46. WIZO
47. Women's League for Conservative Judaism
48. Women of Reform Judaism
49. Workmen's Circle
50. World Zionist Executive, US
51. Zionist Organization of America

Endnotes

1   *Boston Globe*, December 30, 2008.
2   Ibid.
3   Palestine Center for Human Rights, Press Release, Ref: 19/2009, Date: 22 January 2009, Time:08:15GMT.
4   *Financial Times*, December 30, 2008.
5   According to Human Rights Watch, "Israel/Gaza: International Investigation Essential", January 27, 2009 "The fighting in Gaza from December 27, when Israel began its military operation, until Israel and Hamas unilaterally declared ceasefires on January 18, left some 1,300 Palestinians dead and more than 5,000 wounded, 40 percent of them children and women. In addition, the casualties included an undetermined number of male civilians not taking part in hostilities. Over the same period, Palestinian rocket fire killed three Israeli civilians and wounded more than 80. Ten Israeli soldiers were killed."
6   "Israel's Day of Carnage: 40 dead as Israelis Bomb Two UN Schools," *The Guardian*, January 7, 2009.
7   Barak Ravid and Akiva Eldar, "UNRWA: Army Admitted Bombed School Did Not Harbor Militants", *Haaretz*, January 11, 2009.
8   Natan Sharansky, "Save Gaza by Destroying the Heart of Terror," *Bloomberg News*, January 15, 2009.
9   Yitzhak Laor," The Most Moral Army in the World. Fact", *Haaretz*, April 14, 2009.
10   Daniol Louban, US Jewish Peace Lobby Isolated In Gaza", IPS, January 19, 2009.

CHAPTER 12

IRANIAN ELECTIONS
THE 'STOLEN ELECTIONS' HOAX

> "Change for the poor means food and jobs, not a relaxed
> dress code or mixed recreation...Politics in Iran is a lot more
> about class war than religion."
> *Financial Times* **Editorial, June 15, 2009**

Introduction

There is hardly any election, in which the White House has a significant stake, where the electoral defeat of the pro-US candidate is not denounced as illegitimate by the entire political and mass media elite. In the most recent period, the White House and its camp followers cried foul following the free (and monitored) elections in Venezuela and Gaza, while joyously fabricating an 'electoral success' in Lebanon despite the fact that the Hezbollah-led coalition received over 53% of the vote.

The recently concluded, June 12, 2009 elections in Iran are a classic case: The incumbent nationalist-populist President Mahmoud Ahmadinejad (MA) received 63.3% of the vote (or 24.5 million votes), while the leading Western-backed liberal opposition candidate Hossein Mousavi (HM) received 34.2% or (13.4 million votes). Iran's presidential election drew a record turnout of more than 80% of the electorate, including an unprecedented overseas vote of 234,812, in which HM won 111,792 to MA's 78,300. The opposition led by HM did not accept their defeat and organized a series of mass demonstrations that turned violent, resulting in the burning and destruction of automobiles, banks, public building and armed confrontations with the police and other authorities. Almost the entire spectrum of Western opinion makers, including all the major electronic and print media, the major liberal, radical, libertarian and conservative web-sites, echoed the opposition's claim of rampant election fraud. Neo-conservatives, libertarian conservatives and Trotskyites joined the Zionists in hailing the opposition protestors as the advance guard of a democratic revolution. Democrats and Republicans condemned the incumbent regime, refused to recognize the result of the vote and praised the demonstrators' efforts to overturn the electoral outcome. *The New York Times*, CNN, *Washington Post*, the Israeli Foreign Office and the entire leadership of the Presidents of the Major American Jewish Organizations called for harsher sanctions against Iran and announced Obama's proposed dialogue with Iran as 'dead in the water'.

The Electoral Fraud Hoax

Western leaders rejected the results because they *'knew'* that their reformist candidate could not lose…For months they published daily interviews, editorials and reports from the field *'detailing'* the failures of Ahmadinejad's administration; they cited the support from clerics, former officials, merchants in the bazaar and above all women and young urbanites fluent in English, to prove that Mousavi was headed for a landslide victory. A victory for Mousavi was described as a victory for the 'voices of moderation', at least the White House's version of that vacuous cliché. Prominent liberal academics deduced the vote count was fraudulent because the opposition candidate, Mousavi, lost in his own ethnic enclave among the Azeris. Other academics claimed that the 'youth vote'—based on their interviews with upper and middle-class university students from the neighborhoods of Northern Tehran were overwhelmingly for the 'reformist' candidate.

What is astonishing about the West's universal condemnation of the electoral outcome as fraudulent is that not a single shred of evidence in either written or observational form has been presented either before or a week after the vote count. During the entire electoral campaign, no credible (or even dubious) charge of voter tampering was raised. As long as the Western media believed their own propaganda of an immanent victory for their candidate, the electoral process was described as highly competitive, with heated public debates and unprecedented levels of public activity and unhindered by public proselytizing. The belief in a free and open election was so strong that the Western leaders and mass media believed that their favored candidate would win.

The Western media relied on its reporters covering the mass demonstrations of opposition supporters, ignoring and downplaying the huge turnout for Ahmadinejad. Worse still, the Western media ignored the class composition of the competing demonstrations – the fact that the incumbent candidate was drawing his support from the far more numerous poor working class, peasant, artisan and public employee sectors while the bulk of the opposition demonstrators was drawn from the upper and middle class students, business and professional class.

Moreover, most Western opinion leaders and reporters based in Tehran extrapolated their projections from their observations in the capital—few venture into the provinces, small and medium size cities and villages where Ahmadinejad has his mass base of support. Moreover the opposition's supporters were an activist minority of students easily mobilized for street activities, while Ahmadinejad's support drew on the majority of working youth and household women workers who would express their views at the ballot box and had little time or inclination to engage in street politics.

A number of newspaper pundits, including Gideon Rachman of the *Financial Times*, claim as evidence of electoral fraud the fact that Ahmadinejad won 63% of the vote in an Azeri-speaking province against his opponent, Mousavi, an ethnic Azeri. The simplistic assumption is that ethnic identity or belonging to a linguistic group is the only possible explanation of voting behavior rather than other social or class interests. A closer look at the voting pattern in the East-Azerbaijan region of Iran reveals that Mousavi won only in the city of Shabestar among the upper and the middle classes (and only by a small margin), whereas he was soundly defeated in the larger rural areas, where the re-distributive policies of the Ahmadinejad government had helped the ethnic Azeris write off debt, obtain cheap credits and easy loans for the farmers. Mousavi did win in the West-Azerbaijan region, using his ethnic ties to win over the urban voters. In the highly populated Tehran province, Mousavi beat Ahmadinejad in the urban centers of Tehran and Shemiranat by gaining the vote of the middle and upper class districts, whereas he lost badly in the adjoining working class suburbs, small towns and rural areas.

The careless and distorted emphasis on 'ethnic voting' cited by writers from the *Financial Times* and *The New York Times* to justify calling Ahmadinejad 's victory a 'stolen vote' is matched by the media's willful and deliberate refusal to acknowledge a rigorous nationwide public opinion poll conducted by two US experts just three weeks before the vote, which showed Ahmadinejad leading by a more than 2 to 1 margin— even larger than his electoral victory on June 12. This poll revealed that among ethnic Azeris, Ahmadinejad was favored by a 2 to 1 margin over Mousavi, demonstrating how class interests represented by one candidate can overcome the ethnic identity of the other candidate.[1] The poll also demonstrated how class issues, within age groups, were more influential in shaping political preferences than 'generational life style'. According to this poll, over two-thirds of Iranian youth were too poor to have access to a computer and the 18-24 year olds *"comprised the strongest voting bloc for Ahmadinejad of all groups"*.[2] The only group, which consistently favored Mousavi, was the university students and graduates, business owners and the upper middle class. The 'youth vote', which the Western media praised as 'pro-reformist', was a clear minority of less than 30% but came from a highly privileged, vocal and largely English speaking group with a monopoly on the Western media. Their overwhelming presence in the Western news reports created what has been referred to as the 'North Tehran Syndrome', for the comfortable upper class enclave from which many of these students come. While they may be articulate, well dressed and fluent in English, they were soundly out-voted in the secrecy of the ballot box.

In general, Ahmadinejad did very well in the oil and chemical producing provinces. This may have be a reflection of the oil workers' opposition to the 'reformist' program, which included proposals to 'privatize' public enterprises. Likewise, the incumbent did very well along the border provinces because of his emphasis on strengthening national security from US and Israeli threats in light of an escalation of US-sponsored cross-border terrorist attacks from Pakistan and Israeli-backed incursions from Iraqi Kurdistan, which have killed scores of Iranian citizens. Sponsorship and massive funding of the groups behind these attacks is an official policy of the US from the Bush Administration, which has not been repudiated by President Obama; in fact it has escalated in the lead-up to the elections.

What Western commentators and their Iranian protégés have ignored is the powerful impact which the devastating US wars and occupation of Iraq and Afghanistan had on Iranian public opinion: Ahmadinejad's strong position on defense matters contrasted with the pro-Western and weak defense posture of many of the campaign propagandists of the opposition.

The great majority of voters for the incumbent probably felt that national security interests, the integrity of the country and the social welfare system, with all of its faults and excesses, could be better defended and improved with Ahmadinejad than with upper-class technocrats supported by Western-oriented privileged youth who prize individual life styles over community values and solidarity.

The demography of voting reveals a real class polarization pitting high income, free market oriented, capitalist individualists against working class, low income, community based supporters of a 'moral economy' in which usury and profiteering are limited by religious precepts. The open attacks by opposition economists of the government welfare spending, easy credit and heavy subsidies of basic food staples did little to ingratiate them with the majority of Iranians benefiting from those programs. The state was seen as the protector and benefactor of the poor workers against the 'market', which represented wealth, power, privilege and corruption. The Opposition's attack on the regime's 'intransigent' foreign policy and positions 'alienating' the West only resonated with the liberal university students and import-export business groups. To many Iranians, the regime's military buildup was seen as having prevented a US or Israeli attack.

The scale of the opposition's electoral deficit should tell us is how out of touch it is with its own people's vital concerns. It should remind them that by moving closer to Western opinion, they removed themselves from the everyday interests of security, housing, jobs and subsidized food prices that make life tolerable for those living below the middle class and outside the privileged gates of Tehran University.

Amhadinejad's electoral success, seen in historical comparative perspective should not be a surprise. In similar electoral contests between nationalist-populists against pro-Western liberals, the populists have won. Past examples include Peron in Argentina and, most recently, Chavez of Venezuela, Evo Morales in Bolivia and even Lula da Silva in Brazil, all of whom have demonstrated an ability to secure close to or even greater than 60% of the vote in free elections. The voting majorities in these countries prefer social welfare over unrestrained markets, national security over alignments with military empires.

The consequences of the electoral victory of Ahmadinejad are open to debate. The US may conclude that continuing to back a vocal, but badly defeated, minority has few prospects for securing concessions on nuclear enrichment and an abandonment of Iran's support for Hezbollah and Hamas. A realistic approach would be to open a wide-ranging discussion with Iran, and acknowledging, as Senator Kerry recently pointed out, that enriching uranium is not an existential threat to anyone. This approach would sharply differ from the approach of American Zionists, embedded in the Obama regime, who follow Israel's lead of pushing for a preemptive war with Iran and use the specious argument that no negotiations are possible with an 'illegitimate' government in Tehran which 'stole an election'.

Recent events suggest that political leaders in Europe, and even some in Washington, do not accept the Zionist-mass media line of 'stolen elections'. The White House has not suspended its offer of negotiations with the newly re-elected government but has focused rather on the repression of the opposition protesters (and not the vote count). Likewise, the 27-nation European Union expressed 'serious concern about violence' and called for the *"aspirations of the Iranian people to be achieved through peaceful means and that freedom of expression be respected"*.[3] Except for Sarkozy of France, no EU leader has questioned the outcome of the voting.

The wild card in the aftermath of the elections is the Israeli response: Netanyahu has signaled to his American Zionist followers that they should use the hoax of *'electoral fraud'* to exert maximum pressure on the Obama regime to end all plans to meet with the newly re-elected Ahmadinejad regime.

Paradoxically, US commentators (left, right and center) who bought into the electoral fraud hoax are inadvertently providing Netanyahu and his American followers with the arguments and fabrications: Where they see religious wars, we see class wars; where they see electoral fraud, we see imperial destabilization.

Endnotes

1   *Washington Post,* June 15, 2009.
2   Ibid.
3   *Financial Times* June 16, 2009 p. 4.

CHAPTER 13

THE NEW AGRO-INDUSTRIAL NEO-COLONIALISM

TWO, THREE, MANY MASS REVOLTS

"The deal South Korea's Daewoo Logistics is negotiating with the Madagascar Government looks rapacious...The Madagascan case looks neo-colonial...The Madagascan people stand to lose half of their arable land." **Financial Times Editorial, November 20, 2008**

"Cambodia is in talks with several Asian and Middle Eastern governments to receive as much as $3 billions US dollars in agricultural investments in return for millions of hectares of land concessions..."
Financial Times, November 21, 2008

"We are starving in the midst of bountiful harvests and booming exports!"
Unemployed Rural Landless Workers, Para State, Brazil (2003)

Introduction

Colonial style empire building is making a huge comeback, and most of the colonialists are latecomers, elbowing their way past the established European and US predators.

Backed by their governments and bankrolled with huge trade and investment profits and budget surpluses, the newly emerging neo-colonial economic powers (ENEP) are seizing control of vast tracts of fertile lands from poor countries in Africa, Asia and Latin America, through the interme-diation of local corrupt, free-market regimes. Millions of acres of land have been granted—in most cases free of charge—to the ENEP who, at most, promise to invest millions in infrastructure to facilitate the transfer of their plundered agricultural products back to their own home markets and to pay an ongoing wage of less than $1 dollar a day to the destitute local peasants. Projects and agreements between the ENEP and pliant neo-colonial regimes are in the works to expand imperial land takeovers to cover additional tens of millions of hectares of farmland in the very near future. The great land sell-off/transfer takes place at a time and in places where landless peasants are growing in number, and small farmers are being forcibly displaced by the neo-colonial state and bankrupted through debt and lack of affordable credit. Millions of organized landless peasants and rural workers struggling for cultivatable land are criminalized, repressed, assassinated or jailed and their families are driven into disease-ridden urban slums. The historic context, economic actors and methods of agro-business empire building bear similarities to and differences with the old-style empire building of the past centuries.

Old and New Style Agro-Imperial Exploitation

During the previous five centuries of imperial domination the exploitation and export of agricultural products and minerals played a central role in the enrichment of the Euro-North American empires. Up to the 19th century, large-scale plantations and latifundios, organized around staple crops, relied on forced labor—slaves, indentured servants, semi-serfs, tenant farmers, migrant seasonal workers and a host of other forms of labor (including prisoners)—to accumulate wealth and profits for colonial settlers, home country investors and the imperial state treasuries.

The agricultural empires were secured through conquest of indigenous peoples, importation of slaves and indentured workers, and the forcible seizure and dispossession of communal lands, and ruled through colonial officials. In many cases, the colonial rulers incorporated local elites ('nobles', monarchs, tribal chiefs and favored minorities) as administrators and recruited the impoverished, dispossessed natives to serve as colonial soldiers to be led by white Euro-American officers.

Colonial-style agro-imperialism came under attack by mass-based national liberation movements throughout the 19th and first half of the 20th centuries, culminating in the establishment of independent national regimes throughout Africa, Asia (except Palestine) and Latin America. From the very beginning of their reign, the newly independent states pursued diverse policies toward colonial-era land ownership and exploitation. A few of the radical, socialist and nationalist regimes eventually expropriated, either partially or entirely, foreign landowners, as was the case in China, Cuba, Indochina, Zimbabwe, Guyana, Angola, India and elsewhere. Many of these 'expropriations' led to land transfers to the new emerging post-colonial bourgeoisie, leaving the mass of the rural labor force without land or confined to communal land. In most cases the transition from colonial to post-colonial regimes was underwritten by a political pact ensuring the continuation of colonial patterns of land ownership, cultivation, marketing and labor relations (described as a "neo-colonial" agro-export system). With few exceptions most independent governments failed to change their dependence on export crops, diversify export markets, develop food self-sufficiency or finance the settlement of rural poor onto fertile uncultivated public lands.

Where land distribution did take place, the regimes failed to invest sufficiently in the new forms of rural organization (family farms, co-ops or communal 'ejidos') or imposed centrally-controlled large-scale state enterprises, which were inefficiently run, failed to provide adequate incentives for the direct producers, and were exploited to finance urban-industrial development. As a result, many state farms and cooperatives were eventually dismantled. In most countries great masses of the rural poor continued to be landless and subject to the demands of local tax collectors, military recruiters and usurious moneylenders until they were evicted by land speculators, real estate developers and national and local officials.

Neo-Liberalism and the Rise of New Agro-Imperialism

Emblematic of the new style agro-imperialism is the South Korean takeover of half (1.3 million hectares) of Madagascar's total arable land under a 70-90 year lease in which the Daewoo Logistics Corporation of South Korea expects to pay nothing in return for a contract to cultivate maize and palm oil for export.[1] In Cambodia, several emerging agro-imperial Asian and Middle Eastern countries are 'negotiating' (with hefty bribes and offers of lucrative local 'partnerships' to local politicians) the takeover of millions of hectares of fertile land.[2] The scope and depth of the new emerging agro-imperial expansion into the impoverished countryside of Asian, African and Latin American countries far surpasses that of the pre-20th-century colonial empires. A detailed account of the new agro-imperialist countries and their neo-colonial colonies has recently been compiled on the website of GRAIN.[3]

The driving forces of contemporary agro-imperialist conquest and land grabbing can be divided into three blocs:

1. The new rich Arab oil regimes, mostly among the Gulf States (in part, through their 'sovereign wealth funds').
2. The newly-emerging imperial countries of Asia (China, India, South Korea and Japan) and Israel
3. The earlier imperial countries (US and Europe), the World Bank, Wall Street investment banks and other assorted imperial speculator-financial companies.

Each of these agro-imperial blocs is organized around one to three 'leading' countries: Among the Gulf imperial states, Saudi Arabia and Kuwait; in Asia, China, Korea and Japan are the main land grabbers. Among the US-European-World Bank land predators, there are a wide range of agro-imperialist monopoly firms buying up land ranging from Goldman Sachs and Blackstone in the US to Louis Dreyfuss in the Netherlands and Deutschbank in Germany. Upward of several hundred million acres of arable land have been or are in the process of being appropriated by the world's biggest capitalist landowners in what is one of the greatest concentrations of private landownership in the history of empire building.

The process of agro-imperial empire building operates largely through political and financial mechanisms, preceded, in some cases, by military coups, imperial interventions and destabilization campaigns to establish pliable neo-colonial 'partners' or, more accurately, collaborators, disposed to cooperate in this huge imperial land grab. Once in place, the Afro-Asian-Latin American neo-colonial regimes impose a neo-liberal agenda which includes the break-up of communally-held lands, the promotion of agro-export strategies, and the repression of any local land reform movements among subsistence farmers and landless rural workers demanding the redistribution of fallow public and private lands. The neo-colonial regimes' free market policies eliminate or lower tariff barriers on heavily-subsidized food imports from the US and Europe. These policies bankrupt local market farmers and peasants, thereby increasing the amount of available land to 'lease' or sell off to the new agro-imperial countries and multinationals. The military and police play a key role in evicting impoverished, indebted and starving farmers and preventing squatters from occupying and producing food on fertile land for local consumption.

Once the neo-colonial collaborator regimes are in place and their 'free market' agendas are implemented, the stage is set for the entry and takeover of vast tracts of cultivable land by the agro-imperial countries and investors.

Israel is the major exception to this pattern of agro-imperial conquest, as it relies on the massive sustained use of force against an entire nation to dispossess Palestinian farmers and seize territory via armed colonial settlers—in the style of earlier Euro-American colonial imperialism.[4]

The sellout usually follows one of two paths or a combination of both. Newly emerging imperial countries take the lead or are solicited by the neo-colonial regime to invest in 'agricultural development'. One-sided 'negotiations' follow in which substantial sums of cash flow from the imperial treasury into the overseas bank accounts of their neo-colonial 'partners'. The agreements and the terms of the contracts are unequal: The food and agricultural commodities are almost totally exported back to the home markets of the agro-imperial country, even as the 'host country's' population starves and is dependent on emergency shipments of food from imperial 'humanitarian' agencies. 'Development', including promise of large-scale investment, is largely directed at building roads, transport, ports and storage facilities to be used exclusively to facilitate the transfer of agricultural produce overseas by the large-scale agro-imperial firms. Most of the land is taken rent-free or subject to 'nominal' fees, which go into the pockets of the political elite or are recycled into the urban real estate market and luxury imports for the local wealthy elite.

Except for the collaborationist relatives or cronies of the neo-colonial rulers, almost all of the high paid directors, senior executives and technical staff come from the imperial countries in the tradition of the colonial past. An army of low salary, educated, 'third country nationals' generally enter as middle level technical and administrative employees—completely subverting any possibility of vital technology or skills transfer to the local population. The major and much touted 'benefit' to the neo-colonial country is the employment of local manual farm workers, who are rarely paid above the going rate of US$1-2 dollars a day and are harshly repressed and denied any independent trade union representation.

In contrast, the agro-imperial companies and regimes reap enormous profits, secure supplies of food at subsidized prices, exercise political influence or hegemonic control over collaborator elites and establish economic 'beachheads' to expand their investments and facilitate foreign takeover of the local financial, trade and processing sectors.

Target Countries

While there is a great deal of competition and overlap among the agro-imperial countries in plundering the target countries, the tendency is for the Arab petroleum imperial regimes to focus on penetrating neo-colonies in South and Southeast Asia. The Asian 'Economic Tiger' countries concentrate on Africa and Latin America, while the US-European multinationals exploit the former communist countries of Eastern Europe and the former Soviet Union as well as Latin America and Africa.

China, probably the most dynamic agro-imperial country today, has invested in Africa, Latin America and Southeast Asia to ensure low cost soybean supplies (especially from Brazil), rice production in Cuba (5,000 hectares), Burma, Cameroon (10,000 hectares), Laos (100,000 hectares), Mozambique (with 10,000 Chinese farm-worker settlers), the Philippines (1.24 million hectares) and Uganda. Japan has purchased 100,000 hectares of Brazilian farmland for soybean and maize. Its corporations own 12 million hectares in Southeast Asia and South America.

The Gulf States are projecting a $1 billion dollar fund to finance land grabs in North and Sub-Saharan Africa. Bahrain has acquired land in Pakistan, the Philippines and Sudan to supply itself with rice. Kuwait has grabbed land in Burma, Cambodia, Morocco, Yemen, Egypt, Laos, Sudan and Uganda. Qatar has taken over rice fields in Cambodia and Pakistan and wheat, maize and oil seed croplands in Sudan as well as land in Vietnam for cereals, fruit, vegetables and raising cattle. Saudi Arabia has been 'offered' 500,000 hectares of rice fields in Indonesia and hundreds of thousands of hectares of fertile land in Ethiopia and Sudan.

The World Bank (WB) has played a major role in promoting agro-imperial land grabs, allocating $1.4 billion dollars to finance agro-business takeovers of 'underutilized lands'. The WB conditions its loans to neo-colonies, like the Ukraine, on their opening up lands to be exploited by foreign investors.[5] Taking advantage of neo-liberal 'center-left' regimes in Argentina and Brazil, agro-imperial investors from the US and Europe have bought millions of acres of fertile farmlands and pastures to supply their imperial homelands, while millions of landless peasants and unemployed workers are left to watch the trains laden with beef, wheat and soy beans head for the foreign MNC-controlled port facilities and on to the imperial home markets in Europe, Asia and the US.

At least two emerging imperial countries, Brazil and China, are subject themselves to imperial land grabs by more 'advanced' imperial countries and have become 'agents' of agricultural colonization. Japanese, European and North American multinationals exploit Brazil even as Brazilian colonial settlers and agro-industrialists have taken over wide swathes of borderlands in Paraguay, Uruguay and Bolivia. A similar pattern occurs in China where valuable farmlands are exploited by Japanese and overseas Chinese capitalists at the same time that China is seizing fertile land in poorer countries in Africa and Southeast Asia.

Present and Future Consequences of Agro-Imperialism

The re-colonization by emerging imperialist states of huge tracts of fertile farmland of the poorest countries and regions of Africa, Asia and Latin America is resulting in a deepening class polarization between, on the one hand, wealthy rentier Arab oil states, Asian billionaires, affluent state-funded Jewish settlers and Western speculators and, on the other hand, hundreds of millions of starving, landless, dispossessed peasants in Sudan, Madagascar, Ethiopia, Cambodia, Palestine, Burma, China, Indonesia, Brazil, the Philippines, Paraguay and elsewhere.

Agro-imperialism is still in its early stages—taking possession of huge tracts of land, expropriating peasants and exploiting the landless rural workers as day laborers. The next phase which is currently unfolding is to take control over the transport systems, infrastructure and credit systems, which accompany the growth of agro-export crops. Monopolizing infrastructure, credit and the profits from seeds, fertilizers, processing industries, tolls and interest payments on loans further concentrates de facto imperial control over the colonial economy and extends political influence over local politicians, rulers and collaborators within the bureaucracies.

The neo-colonized class structure, especially in largely agricultural economies, is evolving into a four-tier class system in which the foreign capitalists and their entourage are at the pinnacle of elite status representing less than 1% of the population. In the second tier, representing 10% of the population are the local political elite and their cronies and relatives as well as well-placed bureaucrats and military officers, who enrich themselves through partnerships ('joint ventures') with the neo-colonials and via bribes and land grabs. The local middle class represents almost 20% and is in constant danger of falling into poverty in the face of the world economic crises. The dispossessed peasants, rural workers, rural refugees, urban squatters and indebted subsistence peasants and farmers make up the fourth tier of the class structure with close to 70% of the population.

Within the emerging neo-colonial agro-export model, the 'middle class' is shrinking and changing in composition. The number of family farmers producing for the domestic market is declining in the face of state-supported foreign-owned farms producing for their own 'home markets'. As a result market vendors and small retailers in the local markets are falling behind, squeezed out by the large foreign-owned supermarkets. The loss of employment for domestic producers of farm goods and services and the elimination of a host of 'commercial' intermediaries between town and country is sharpening the class polarization between top and bottom tiers of the class structure. The new colonial middle class is reconfigured to include a small stratum of lawyers, professionals, publicists and low-level functionaries of the foreign firms, and public and private security forces. The auxiliary role of the 'new middle class' in servicing the axis of colonial economic and political power will make them less nation-oriented and more colonial in their allegiances and political outlook, more 'free market' consumerist in their life style and more prone to approve of repressive (including fascistic) domestic solutions to rural and urban unrest and popular struggles for justice.

At the present moment, the biggest constraint on the advance of agro-imperialism is the economic collapse of world capitalism, which is undermining the 'export of capital'. The sudden collapse of commodity prices is making it less profitable to invest in overseas farmland. The drying up of credit is undermining the financing of grandiose overseas land grabs. The 70% decline in oil revenues is limiting the Middle East Sovereign Funds and other investment vehicles of Gulf oil foreign reserves. On the other hand, the collapse of agricultural prices is bankrupting African, Asian and Latin

American elite agro-producers, forcing down land prices and presenting opportunities for imperial agro-investors to buy up even more fertile land at rock-bottom prices.

The current world capitalist recession is adding millions of unem- ployed rural workers to the hundreds of millions of peasants dispossessed during the expansion period of the agricultural commodity boom during the first half of the current decade. Labor costs and land are cheap, at the same time that effective consumer demand is falling. Agro-imperialists can employ all the Third World rural labor they want at $1 dollar a day or less, but how can they market their products and realize returns that cover the costs of loans, bribes, transport, marketing, elite salaries, perks, CEO bonuses and investor dividends when demand is in decline?

Some agro-imperialists may take advantage of the recession to buy cheaply now and look forward to long-term profits when the multi-trillion dollar state-funded recovery takes effect. Others may cut back on their land grabs or more likely hold vast expanses of valuable land out of production until the 'market' improves—while dispossessed peasants starve on the margins of fallow fields.

The new agro-imperialists are banking on the new imperialist states committing resources (money and troops) to bolster the neo-colonial gen- darmes in repressing the inevitable uprisings of the billions of dispossessed, hungry and marginalized people in Sudan, Ethiopia, Burma, Cambodia, Brazil, Paraguay, the Philippines, China and elsewhere. Time is running out for the easy deals, transfers of ownership and long-term leases consum- mated by local neo-colonial collaborators and overseas colonial investors and states. Currently imperial wars and domestic economic recessions in the old and emerging imperial countries are systematically draining their economies and testing the willingness of their populations to sacrifice for new-style colonial empire building. Without international military and economic backing, the thin stratum of local neo-colonial rulers can hardly withstand sustained, mass uprisings of the destitute peasantry allied with the downwardly mobile lower middle class and growing legions of unemployed university-educated young people.

The promise of a new era of agro imperial empire building and a new wave of emerging imperial states may be short-lived. In its place we may see a new wave of rural-based national liberation movements and ferocious competition between new and old imperial states fighting over increasingly scarce financial and economic resources. While downwardly mobile workers and employees in the Western imperial centers gyrate be- tween one and another imperial party (Democrat/Republican, Conservative/ Labor) they will play no role for the foreseeable future. When and if they break loose…they may turn toward a demagogic nationalist right or toward a currently invisible (at least in the US and Europe) 'patriotic nationalist' socialist left. In either case, current imperial pillage and the subsequent mass rebellion will start elsewhere with or without a change in the US or Europe.

Endnotes

1   *Financial Times,* November 20, 2008 page 3.
2   *Financial Times,* November 21, 2008 page 7.
3   http://www.grain.org (November 22, 2008).
4   Stephen Lendman, "Another Israeli West Bank Land Grab Scheme", Counterpunch. Org. October 10, 2008; *Guardian,* October 10, 2008.
5   See GRAIN.org, supra endnote 3.

CHAPTER 14

REGIONAL WARS AND WESTERN PROGRESSIVE OPINION

COMMISERATE WITH THE VICTIMS CONDEMN THOSE WHO RESIST!

We know in some detail of the willing and gratuitous support that tens of millions of American citizens have bestowed on the White House and Congressional perpetrators of crimes against humanity. The Clinton Administration was freely re-elected in 1996 after deliberately imposing a starvation embargo on Iraq and mounting a relentless, unopposed bombing campaign on that devastated country for four straight years, leading to the documented deaths of over 500,000 Iraqi children and countless more vulnerable adults. The majority of US citizens re-elected George W. Bush after he launched wars which caused the deaths of over a million Iraqi civilians, of scores of thousands of Afghanis, and thousands of Pakistanis.

We know Americans continued to support George W. Bush after he gave full support to Israel's murderous attacks on Palestinian civilians and the blockade of vital food, water and fuel to the occupied territories, not to mention its frequent bombing of Lebanon and Syria, which culminated, during Bush's second term, in the horrific Israeli bombing campaign against Lebanese cities and villages killing thousands of civilians.

We know this brutality received the unconditional support of the Presidents of the 51 Major American Jewish Organizations and their thousands of affiliated community groups (totaling over one million members). We know that in order to accomplish each and every Israeli assassination of a Palestinian, each dispossession of Palestinians from their land and homes and the uprooting of their orchards, vineyards and the poisoning of their wells, there has been a systematic campaign to obliterate Americans' democratic freedoms of speech and assembly—especially our right to publicly condemn Israel and expose its agents operating among US power brokers.

Through hard experience the majority of the American public has come to recognize the pitfalls of militarism and is slowly coming to realize the profound threats posed by the entrenched Zionist Power Configuration to our 'four freedoms'.

That is all to the good. However, these advances in public opinion have been far from sufficient. The American public has just elected a new president who promises to escalate the imperialist military presence in Afghanistan and fill key posts in his regime with known militarists and Zionists from the previous regime of President 'Bill' Clinton—yet a large percentage of the domestic (and world) population appear content to remain self-deceived in the comforting notion that Barack Obama will lead us to peace, rather than involving us in continued and even escalating warfare.

The almost complete disappearance of the peace movement and its absorption into the pro-war Democratic Party through the efforts of the electoral machine of President-Elect Barack Obama escaped public notice. Likewise, the vast majority of US 'progressive' opinion-makers embraced, with occasional mild reservations, the Obama candidacy and, in effect, became part of Obama's 'broad coalition', thereby joining hands with billionaire Zionist zealots and Wall Street financial swindlers, Clintonite 'humanitarian' militarists, impotent millionaire trade union bureaucrats and various and sundry upwardly mobile 'minority' politicians and vote hustlers. Whether or not progressives were intoxicated by the empty presidential campaign rhetoric of 'change', they willingly sacrificed their most common sense understanding of how the American electoral system truly functions as it dishes up candidates for public "choice". Instead, in becoming engaged in the service of what they would presumably say is at least the 'lesser evil'—as if their voices, when it came to policy choices, might be expected to outweigh those of the heavy-hitter funders who underpinned Obama's campaign—they also surrendered their most elementary principles. Those who should know better have, "lesser evil" proviso or no, objectively thereby embraced the evils of new imperial wars, complicity with Israel's colonial savagery and the deepening immiseration of the American people.

The US progressive intellectuals show no such (im)moral scruples when it comes to their stance in relation to anti-imperial resistance movements in Asian (especially in the Middle East), Africa and Latin America.

US Progressives and Third World Resistance Movements

Among the most prominent progressive intellectuals (PPIs) in the US and Europe—writers, bloggers and academics—there is nary a single one who exhibits the same 'pragmatism' that they purport to practice in choosing 'lesser evil' politicians in the US or Europe, with regard to political choices in highly conflicted countries. Can we find a single PPI who will argue that they support the democratically-elected Hamas in Palestine or Hezbollah in Lebanon, or the popularly supported nationalist Muqtada al-Sadr in Iraq, the anti-occupation Taliban in Afghanistan or even the right, recognized under international law, of the Iranian people to the peaceful development of nuclear energy because—whatever their defects—these are 'lesser evils' compared to those Western governments who, after all, have attacked and occupied their countries and are slaughtering their peoples, with a view to seizing their resources and/or setting up neo-colonial regimes?

Let us consider the issue in greater detail. PPIs justified their support for Obama on the basis of his campaign rhetoric in favor of peace and justice, even as he voted for Bush's war budgets and foreign aid programs funding the murder of hundreds of thousands of Iraqis, Afghanis, Palestinians, Colombians, Somalis and Pakistanis, and the dispossessing and displacement of at least 10 million people from their towns, farms and homes. The very same PPI reject and refuse to apply the 'lesser evil' criteria in support of Hamas, the democratically-elected Palestinian administration in the Gaza, which is in the forefront of the struggle against the brutal Israeli colonial occupation—because it is 'violent' (which means it retaliates against almost daily Israeli armed assaults), seeks a 'theocratic state' (similar to the theologically defined 'Jewish' state of Israel), represses dissidents (in the form of occasional crackdowns on CIA-funded Fatah functionaries and militias).

At best the PPIs take an interest only in the Palestinian *victims* of Israel's genocidal embargo of food, water, fuel and medicine; they protest against overt racist assaults by Israel's colonial Judeo-fascist settlers when they assault school girls on their way to school or elderly farmers in their orchards; they protest the arbitrary and deliberate delays at Israeli military checkpoints, which cause the deaths of acutely ill Palestinians, cancer victims, women in labor, men with heart attacks and people in need of kidney dialysis by preventing them from reaching medical facilities. But when, in effect, Hamas takes steps in retaliation to Israeli violence, steps which are even sanctioned in international law as their right as victims of occupation, such as attacks on Israeli soldiers, those actions are fulsomely condemned.

In other words the PPI support the Palestinians as *victims* but condemn them as *fighters* who challenge their executioners. The PPI's *support for victims* is a cost-free posture, providing credibility to their 'progressive' label, and indeed makes them aptly fit the "bleeding heart" label appended to them by their opponents. Their opposition to the fighters assures the establishment that the PPI's criticism does not seek to adversely affect the US empire-building and its Israeli allies by saying that there are indeed out there—on the other side—"lesser evil" alternatives which should be embraced.

The most outspoken, self-proclaimed progressive 'libertarians' and 'democrats' in the Western world claim to support national self-determination and oppose imperial conquests, yet they unfailingly reject the real-existing mass popular movements that are demanding self-determination and leading the struggle against imperial conquest and foreign occupation in order to achieve this right. Almost without exception they denounce national resistance movements for not fitting their idealized notions of perfect justice, peaceful tolerance and secular, democratic principles, which they feel a resistance movement should embody. Is it bad faith, or mere political naiveté and stupidity? Yet the PPI do not impose such criteria before advocating support for candidates in their own countries. While Hezbollah is flatly rejected as too 'clerical' by the PPIs, British progressives supported Tony Blair, the leader of the Labor Party and his role as bloody accomplice to Clinton, Bush, Sharon and a whole host of servile puppet regimes in Iraq, Afghanistan, Somalia and elsewhere.

In terms of military aggression—and deaths, loss of limbs and homes—the 'lesser evil' Democrats and European Social Democrats and Center-Left politicians have a far worse record than that the Taliban, Hezbollah, Hamas and Sadrist forces. More to the point, they fail to honestly address the reality that the living conditions and safety of the vast majority of the people in Iraq, Afghanistan, Lebanon and Somalia—by any standard— were vastly better under the independent if authoritarian rule of Saddam Hussein, the clerical Taliban in Afghanistan, the Islamic Councils in Somalia than under the US-EU military occupations and client regimes. And indeed, the same holds true for democratic Iran and Venezuela—recognized targets of Western regimes, though not yet invaded.

Some of the PPIs avoid the real and difficult choices by pretending that there are 'third choices' just on the horizon in countries currently under imperial and colonial conquest and occupation. They reject both the imperial armies and the anti-imperial resistance in the name of abstract progressive libertarian principles. The shameless cant and hypocrisy of their position is clear when the same issue is posed in terms of political choices within the imperial mother country. Here the PPIs had a thousand and one arguments to back one (Obama) of the two major imperial war party presidential candidates; here 'realism' and 'lesser evil' arguments come to the fore. And what 'choices' are made! The same libertarians and democrats who condemned the Taliban for its destruction of ancient religious monuments support "lesser evil" Democratic candidates, like Obama, who openly proposed to escalate the US military occupation in Afghanistan and intensify the killing fields in South Asia.

There are profound moral and political dilemmas in making political choices in a world in which destructive imperial wars are led by liberal electoral politicians and vigorously resisted by clerical and secular authoritarian movements and leaders. But the historical record of the past three hundred years is clear: Western parliamentarian imperialism and its contemporary legacy has destroyed and undermined far more lives and livelihoods in far more countries over a greater time span than even the worst of the post colonial regimes. Moreover, the colonial wars, pursued by 'lesser evil' electoral regimes and politicians, have had a profoundly destructive impact on those very 'democratic values' in the Western countries that the PPIs profess to defend.

The PPI, by choosing the 'lesser evil'—in the most recent instance, supporting Barack Obama—have condemned themselves, on the one hand, to *political impotence* in the making of Washington's policies, and on the other hand, to *political irrelevance* to the struggles for national liberation. The service they do in drawing wider public attention to the horrors of victimization is countered by the assistance rendered to their purportedly "lesser-evil" Western governments by serving as credible proponents of the myth that *there is no alternative.*

CHAPTER 15

OBAMA'S
ANIMAL FARM

BIGGER, BLOODIER WARS EQUAL
PEACE AND JUSTICE

"The Deltas are psychos...You have to be a certified psychopath to join the Delta Force...", a US Army colonel from Fort Bragg once told me back in the 1980s. Now President Obama has elevated the most notorious of the psychopaths, General Stanley McChrystal, to head the US and NATO military command in Afghanistan. McChrystal's rise to leadership is marked by his central role in directing special operations teams engaged in extrajudicial assassinations, systematic torture, bombing of civilian communities and search and destroy missions. He is the very embodiment of the brutality and gore that accompanies military-driven empire building. Between September 2003 and August 2008, McChrystal directed the Pentagon's Joint Special Operations (JSO) Command which operates special teams in overseas assassinations.

The point of the 'Special Operations' teams (SOT) is that they do not distinguish between civilian and military oppositions, between activists and their sympathizers, and the armed resistance. The SOT specialize in establishing death squads and recruiting and training paramilitary forces to terrorize communities, neighborhoods and social movements opposing US client regimes. The SOT's *counter-terrorism* is terrorism in reverse, focusing on socio-political groups between US proxies and the armed resistance. McChrystal's SOT targeted local and national insurgent leaders in Iraq, Afghanistan and Pakistan through commando raids and air strikes. During the last 5 years of the Bush-Cheney-Rumsfeld period, the SOT were deeply implicated in the torture of political prisoners and suspects. McChrystal was a special favorite of Rumsfeld and Cheney because he was in charge of the 'direct action' forces of the 'Special Missions Units. *'Direct Action'* operatives are the death squads and torturers, and their only engagement with the local population is to terrorize, and not to propagandize. They engage in 'propaganda of the dead', assassinating local leaders to 'teach' the locals to obey and submit to the occupation. Obama's appointment of McChrystal as head reflects a grave new military escalation of his Afghanistan war in the face of the advance of the resistance throughout the country.

The deteriorating position of the US is manifest in the tightening circle around all the roads leading in and out of Afghanistan's capital, Kabul, as well as the expansion of Taliban control and influence throughout the Pakistan-Afghanistan border. Obama's inability to recruit new NATO reinforcements means that the White House's only chance to advance its military-driven empire is to escalate the number of US troops and to increase the kill ratio among any and all suspected civilians in territories controlled by the Afghan armed resistance.

The White House and the Pentagon claim that the appointment of McChrystal was due to the *'complexities'* of the situation on the ground and the need for a 'change in strategy'. *'Complexity'* is a euphemism for the increased mass opposition to the US, *complicating* traditional carpet 'bombing and military sweep' operations. The new strategy practiced by McChrystal involves large scale, long term *'special operations'* to devastate and kill the local social networks and community leaders, which provide the support system for the armed resistance.

Obama's decision to prevent the release of scores of photographs documenting the torture of prisoners by US troops and 'interrogators' (especially under command of the 'Special Forces') is directly related to his appointment of McChrystal, whose 'SOT' forces were highly implicated in widespread torture in Iraq. Equally important, under McChrystal's command the DELTA, SEAL and Special Operations Teams will have a bigger role in the new 'counter-insurgency strategy'. Obama's claim that the publication of these photographs will adversely affect the 'troops' has a particular meaning: the graphic exposure of McChrystal's *modus operandi* for the past 5 years under President Bush will undermine his effectiveness in carrying out the same operations under Obama.

Obama's decision to re-start the secret *'military tribunals'* of foreign political prisoners held at the Guantanamo prison camp, is not merely a replay of the Bush-Cheney policies, which Obama had condemned and vowed to eliminate during his presidential campaign, but part of his larger policy of militarization and coincides with his approval of the major secret police surveillance operations conducted against US citizens. As Jeremy Scahill noted in "Little Known Military Thug Squad Still Brutalizing Prisoners at Gitmo Under Obama":

As the Obama administration continues to fight the

release of some 2,000 photos that graphically document U.S. military abuse of prisoners in Iraq and Afghanistan, an ongoing Spanish investigation is adding harrowing details to the ever-emerging portrait of the torture inside and outside Guantánamo. Among them: "blows to [the] testicles;" "detention underground in total darkness for three weeks with deprivation of food and sleep;" being "inoculated … through injection with 'a disease for dog cysts;'" the smearing of feces on prisoners; and waterboarding. The torture, according to the Spanish investigation, all occurred "under the authority of American military personnel" and was sometimes conducted in the presence of medical professionals…

Less than two weeks later, on Jan. 22, newly inaugurated President Obama issued an executive order requiring the closure of Guantánamo within a year and also ordered a review of the status of the prisoners held there, requiring "humane standards of confinement" in accordance with the Geneva Conventions.

But one month later, the Center for Constitutional Rights released a report titled "Conditions of Confinement at Guantánamo: Still In Violation of the Law," which found that abuses continued. In fact, one Guantanamo lawyer, Ahmed Ghappour, said that his clients were reporting "a ramping up in abuse" since Obama was elected, including "beatings, the dislocation of limbs, spraying of pepper spray into closed cells, applying pepper spray to toilet paper and over-force feeding detainees who are on hunger strike," according to Reuters. [1]

Putting McChrystal in charge of the expanded Afghanistan-Pakistan military operations means putting a notorious practitioner of military terrorism—the torture and assassination of opponents to US policy—at the center of US foreign policy. Obama's quantitative and qualitative expansion of the US war in South Asia means massive numbers of refugees fleeing the destruction of their farms, homes and villages; tens of thousands of civilian deaths, and the eradication of entire communities.

The UN High Commissioner for Refugees warns the exodus of refugees from the Swat Valley region of Pakistan might be the largest displacement of people since the 1994 genocide in Rwanda. Officials estimate the tally of refugees fleeing the North West Frontier Province exceeds 2 million people. [2]

All of this will be committed by the Obama Administration in the quest to *'empty the lake (displace entire populations) to catch the fish (armed insurgents and activists)'*.

Obama's restoration of all of the most notorious Bush Era policies and the appointment of Bush's most brutal commander is based on his total embrace of the ideology of *military-driven empire building.* Once one believes (as Obama does) that US power and expansion are based on military conquests and counter-insurgency, all other ideological, diplomatic, moral and economic considerations will be subordinated to militarism. By focusing all resources on successful military conquest, scant attention is paid to the costs borne by the people targeted for conquest or to the US treasury and the domestic American economy. This has been clear from the start: In the midst of a major recession/depression with millions of Americans losing their employment and homes, President Obama increased the military budget by 4% —taking it beyond $800 billion dollars.

Obama's embrace of militarism is obvious from his decision to expand the Afghan war despite NATO's refusal to commit any more combat troops. It is obvious in his appointment of the most hard-line and notorious Special Forces General from the Bush-Cheney era to head the military command in subduing Afghanistan and the frontier areas of Pakistan. What lies ahead for Pakistan may be further clarified by plans to build a new "super-embassy" in Islamabad, rivaling that in Baghdad, termed its "largest and most expensive ever" at $700 million:[3]

> The U.S. is embarking on a $1 billion crash program to expand its diplomatic presence in Pakistan and neighboring Afghanistan, another sign that the Obama administration is making a costly, long-term commitment to war-torn South Asia, U.S. officials said Wednesday.
>
> The White House has asked Congress for and seems likely to receive $736 million to build a new U.S. embassy in Islamabad, along with permanent housing for U.S. government civilians and new office space in the Pakistani capital.[4]

It is just as George Orwell described in *Animal Farm*: The Democratic Pigs are now pursuing the same brutal, military policies of their predecessors, the Republican Porkers, only now it is in the name of the *people* and *peace.* Orwell might paraphrase the policy of President Barack Obama, as *'Bigger and bloodier wars equal peace and justice'.*

Endnotes

1   Alternet, May 16, 2009.

2   Declan Walsh, "Swat refugee number largest since 1994 Rwandan genocide," *The Guardian*, May 19, 2009.

3   Fox News Channel, "U.S. Embassy in Iraq Largest, Most Expensive Ever", January 5, 2009.

4   Saheed Shah and Warren Stroebel "Iraq Redux? Obama Seeks Funds for Pakistan Super-Embassy", McClatchy, May 27, 2009.

CHAPTER 16

OBAMA'S FOREIGN POLICY FAILURES

Introduction

President Obama's greatest foreign policy successes are found in the reports of the mass media. His greatest failures go unreported, but are of great consequence. While some might argue that it is still too soon to make any assessment of Obama's foreign policy after he has had only five months at the helm, the policy priorities addressed below seem doomed to ongoing failure due to key limitations that cannot be surmounted without changes in US policy orientation—which seem unlikely to be forthcoming.

Our survey of the major foreign policy priorities of the White House reveals a continuous series of major setbacks, which call into question the principal objectives and methods pursued by the Obama regime.

These setbacks are, in order of importance:

1. Washington's attempt to push for a joint economic stimulus program among the 20 biggest economies at the G-20 meeting in April 2009;

2. Calls for a major military commitment from NATO to increase the number of combat troops in conflict zones in Afghanistan and Pakistan to complement the additional 21,000 US troop buildup;

3. Plans to forge closer political and diplomatic relations among the countries of the Americas based on the pursuit of a common agenda, including the continued exclusion of Cuba and isolation of Venezuela, Bolivia and Ecuador;

4. Weakening, isolating and pressuring Iran through a mixture

of diplomatic gestures and tightening economic sanctions to surrender its nuclear energy program;

5. The application of pressure on North Korea to suspend its satellite and missile-testing program in addition to dismantling its nuclear weapons program.
6. Securing an agreement between Israel and the Palestinian Authority for a 'two-state solution', in which Israel agrees to end and dismantle its illegal settlements in exchange for recognition of Israel as a 'Jewish State'
7. Pressuring the government of Pakistan to increase its military role in attacking the autonomous Northwest provinces and territories along the Pakistan-Afghan border in support of the US war against Islamic resistance movements, especially among the Pashtun people (over 40 million strong), in both Afghanistan and Pakistan
8. Securing a stable pro-US regime in Iraq capable of remaining in power after a withdrawal of the majority of US occupation troops

What is striking about Obama's objectives is the continuities with the previous administration of George W. Bush, even as the mass media proclaims 'significant changes'.[1]

Failure of Stimulus Proposals at the April 2009 G-20 Summit

Like his predecessor Bush, Obama's first economic priority is to pour trillions of Federal Reserve-borrowed dollars into the financial system as *opposed* to directing state resources toward reviving popular demand, reconstructing the manufacturing sector, creating a universal health system and directly employing the 5 million workers who, due to the financial crisis, became unemployed in the last year. Obama's economic regime is totally dominated by Wall Street bankers and completely devoid of any representatives from labor, manufacturing and the health sector.[2] In essence, Obama has reinforced and deepened the *'finance-centered'* model of capitalist development, which demands that the G-20 countries follow financial stimulus plans—ignoring job creation through the financing of public investments focused on manufacturing.

For Obama, *'economic stimulus'* means reconstructing the power of finance capital, even if it means running huge budget deficits, which undermine other public investments. The *'theory'* justifying the finance-centered focus is based on the belief that the US world empire is built on the recovery of the supremacy of finance capital—to which the industrial powers should submit.[3] The conflicts at the G-20 summit and the ultimate failure of Obama to secure support for his so-called 'stimulus' proposal was that he was promoting a financial centered 'stimulus' while the rest of the economic powers—with the exception of the UK—were concerned with 'stimulating' manufacturing, employment and commodity exports.[4] Labor and manufacturing in Europe—especially in Germany and France—have far more weight in shaping economic policy than they do in the United States.[5]

The incompatibility of the finance-dominated regime of Obama with European, Asian and Latin American regimes reflects the latter's more sectorally diversified ruling class, has led to the White House failure to secure a 'coordinated' stimulus policy.

Summit of the Americas: US Faces Isolation and Divergences

Conflicts of interest prevented Washington from securing any favorable economic agreements at the 'Summit of the Americas' Conference in April. The breakdown of the US finance-centered empire and its negative impact on all of the countries of the Americas undermined Obama's efforts for reassert US hegemonic leadership.[6] The White House already knew the futility of any effort to revive a regional free trade agreement. Worse still, Washington's argument for the advantages of 'globalization' were seriously undermined by Obama's promotion of 'financial protectionism' in which US subsidiary banks in Latin America were directed to channel their financial resources back to the home office, drying up financing and credit for Latin American exporters. In other words, under the stress of the economic depression, 'globalization' led to the reverse flow of financial resources out of Latin America, prejudicing US influence and leverage while increasing regional ties and economic nationalism among the Latin American countries.

The result was that the Obama regime's financial-centered empire had nothing to offer and everything to lose in any deep diagnosis of the impact of the recession/depression. The While House had nothing to offer in the way of expanding markets, capital flows or in stimulating productive investments to create employment. In these dire circumstances, the Obama regime preferred and indeed was forced to resort to vacuous platitudes and systematic evasions of the most pressing economic issues in order to create the illusion of 'good feeling' among the participants.[7] Rather than 'project power' in the hemisphere, Washington was reduced to reiterating bankrupt policies justifying the Cuban embargo in splendid isolation.[8]

The decline of US power based on its crisis-ridden finance-centered empire is evident in its inability to sustain its traditional client rulers or to destabilize adversarial presidents. Even as the Summit was transpiring, in Bolivia a group of armed mercenaries, contracted by US-backed economic elites in the separatist province of Santa Cruz to overthrow the Morales regime, were captured or killed by the Bolivian military.[9] After three years of

US financing and deep involvement with regional elites engaged in political and economic warfare against Evo Morales, and after suffering several electoral defeats, Washington and its regional allies could only muster a tawdry hotel shoot-out between Eastern European contract hit-men and the Bolivian army, ending in ignominious defeat.

The political weakness of the Obama regime is even more evident in the major electoral defeats it has suffered in Ecuador, where President Correa was re-elected with over 52% of the vote—a 22% margin over the nearest pro-Washington candidate, Lucio Gutierrez.[10] In Nicaragua, Bolivia, Venezuela, El Salvador and Honduras, the electorate voted decisively for left and center-left candidates, defeating right-wing US-supported candidates. The only exception was Panama where a right-wing millionaire was elected in May 2009. Though few of the center-left regimes pursue economic-nationalist policies, they do exercise a degree of independence in their foreign and domestic policies, especially with regard to relations with Venezuela and Cuba, trade, investment, state intervention and opposition to the dictates of the IMF.

Moreover the financial collapse in the US and the accompanying economic depression has led to a major crisis and conflict between North and South America with profound long-term consequences. The implosion of cross-border lending resulting in US (and European) banks returning capital to their domestic markets is depressing regional and world finance for the foreseeable future.[11] Wall Street's financial crash is a self-inflicted strategic blow to financial *'globalization'* (imperialism). Between April-December 2008, US financial institutions 'repatriated' $750 billion dollars from their overseas subsidiaries. Foreign holdings of US banks are shrinking as a share of their total balance sheets—especially hitting Latin American regimes dependent on US capital flows. Unable to secure credit, US investors in Latin America have curtailed their overseas activity. The process of *'de-capitalization'* of Latin America has accelerated with US and European *'state-intervention'* into the banking sector, which has led to *'financial protectionism'* where the *'state'* banks push for domestic lending at the expense of foreign operations.[12] This especially harms countries like Brazil, Mexico and Argentina, where repatriating US (and Spanish) financial institutions own a significant percentage of their domestic banks. The withdrawal of capital to the imperial states, financial protectionism and the decline of US official financing means that Obama's 'recovery plan' is based on the de-capitalization of Latin America and the drying up of credit for exporter/importers, exacerbating the recession.

The policy implications are readily visible: Obama has few economic assets to pressure Latin America and many liabilities to address. Given the low priority assigned to Latin America in the current crisis, Washington must rely on local elites, which have been weakened economically by Wall

Street and the IMF's declining presence and are now more dependent on state intervention to confront the drop in export market demand. Obama's economic priorities and financial protectionist policies go directly against any *'harmonization of interest'* and strengthen nationalist, regionalist and statist political and economic policies and governments in Latin America.

The *'historic movements'* in opposite directions between the US and Latin America are exacerbated by Obama's commitment to military-centered empire building. While Latin America's civilian regimes are desperately looking for new markets, credits and investments to buttress their declining capitalist systems and forestall domestic social challenges from below, Obama projects the US empire through militarism. Obama's failed policies in Latin America are the result of *structural relations* dependent on financial markets (and their breakdown) and global militarism. Over time the diverging composition of regimes and socio-economic policies will become more acute as the recession deepens into a major depression in Latin America. One consequence of this divergence can be seen in the increasing trade between Latin America and the Arab countries, which has tripled since 2005.[13]

The most striking indicator of the United States' declining economic presence and political influence in Latin America is found in the trade figures of Brazil, Latin America's biggest and most industrialized country. In April 2009, total trade between Brazil and China amounted to $3.2 billion dollars, while its trade with the US was $2.8 billion.[14] This was the second straight month that China surpassed the US as Brazil's biggest trading partner, ending 80 years of US primacy. Just as the US pours hundreds of billions of dollars into military-driven empire building, China has steadily pursued its overseas economic empire via billion dollar trade and joint investment agreements with Brazil in oil, gas, iron ore, soya and cellulose. China has already displaced the US as Chile's primary trading partner, and is increasing its share of trade with Venezuela, Bolivia, Ecuador and Argentina—and even with staunchly US clients, like Colombia, Peru and Mexico. Two further indicators of changing orientation within Brazil itself were Brazil's recent decision to purchase $10 billion of IMF Bonds in preference to US Treasury bonds,[15] and its participation in the June 2009 conference in Yekaterinburg, where de-dollarization figured strongly on the agenda.

> ...the six SCO countries and BRIC countries intend to trade in their own currencies so as to get the benefit of mutual credit that the United States until now has monopolized for itself. Toward this end, China has struck bilateral deals with Argentina and Brazil to denominate their trade in renminbi rather than the dollar, sterling or euros[16]

The US request to attend the meeting was rejected.

As regional wars and economic depression cause the US to retreat from Latin America, the region's ruling classes look to Asia, especially China, to meet their trade and investment requirements.

Sooner rather than later, issues of superior economic production and growth trump pure military power in shaping the hierarchy of nations in the world economy. This process of an upwardly mobile economic power displacing a crisis-ridden world military power as the chief interlocutor is now being played out in Latin America. While the transition may have begun well over a decade before his administration, the policies of President Obama are accelerating the shift in Latin America away from US dominance.

NATO Conference: Obama's Military Escalation in Search of Allies

On April 4, 2009 Obama attended the NATO Conference in Strasbourg in order to push for allied support for expanding the war in South Asia. South Asia, and especially the Afghan-Pakistani (Af-Pak) border regions, has become the centerpiece of Obama's foreign policy. This is the area where the US is most vulnerable to strategic military and political losses, and where he has had the most difficulty winning material and manpower support from the NATO allies.

Even prior to taking office, Obama had emphasized the *'strategic'* importance of winning the war in Afghanistan, reversing the advances of the Taliban and other resistance fighters, and establishing a stable pro-Washington client regime in Kabul. To that end, Obama has since announced a massive escalation of combat troop deployment (over 21,000) to Afghanistan, an additional $80 billion dollars in funding to the already $750 billion dollars allocated for the Pentagon, and has pursued an aggressive policy of pressuring European and Asian allies for substantial addition of combat troops and financial aid. At the April NATO conference, Obama's proposals were bluntly rejected.[17] The principal allies agreed to send 5,000 additional troops in temporary and non-combat roles, including 3,000 to *'monitor'* elections in August 2009 and then to withdraw; two thousand to act as *trainers* and *'advisers'* in non-conflict-ridden surroundings.[18] What Obama fails to recognize is that the NATO countries do not consider Afghanistan an area of strategic importance to European security. They do not see the forces engaged as a threat to their safety; they do not see the prospect for a quick, low-cost victory. They do not relish following Obama's proposed to extend the war into Pakistan—which is thus multiplying resistance to his plans. They do not want to alienate the vast majority of their own population and destabilize their own power.

European and most Asian allies are not willing to pour scarce resources and military personnel into a losing war, in a non-strategic region at a time of deepening economic recession. They do not see the sense in it. They do not have anything like a comparable military-industrial complex which must be fed or shrivel. Obama on the other hand, following Bush and various other predecessors, with a vast military-industrial bureaucracy embedded in military-driven empire building, talks diplomacy while vigorously pursuing wars of conquest. His attempts to elevate the local conflict into a threat to world security based on the presence of a tiny number of fighters in the mountains of the Hindu Kush, is hardly convincing. Obama's failure to recognize that the Taliban and other groups have access to vast contiguous and porous borders with ethnic, clan and religious allies capable of sustaining prolonged guerrilla warfare, leads him to extend the frontiers of warfare and escalate the number of US troops. The expansion of the war in turn multiplies enemies and armed recruits. In Pakistan, this creates a wider swath of armed political opposition, which undermines Obama's client in Islamabad.[19] Under strong pressure from the White House, Pakistan launched a major military campaign in the Swat region causing the mass flight of 2 million refugees while still failing to defeat the Taliban.

Pouring billions of dollars into a prolonged colonial war with little possible economic gain at a time when GDP is declining by 6% and exports by 30% demonstrates the continued centrality of military-driven empire building and Obama's role as 'willing executioner'.[20]

The divergence between Europe/NATO and the US/Obama is structurally rooted in their conflicting visions of world power: The former emphasize financing their economies to recover and expand exports while the latter operates under the delusion that prolonged colonial wars in remote regions of the world are essential for the 'stability' of world capitalism. Obama's failure to secure NATO support for the Af/Pak expansion underlines his complete political and military isolation in one of the primary areas of his administration's policy goals. This means that the US will shoulder the entire cost of a war in Afghanistan, which has spilled over into Pakistan, and bear worldwide condemnation as thousands of civilian casualties mount and millions of refugees flee the air and ground wars.[21]

Iran: The Zionist Presence and Lost Opportunities

Obama's *stated* policy approach to Iran was to *'turn a new page'*, open negotiations without prior conditions in order to secure an agreement to end Iran's alleged nuclear weapons program, and its alleged support for 'terrorist' organizations, namely Hamas and Hezbollah. In addition, Obama hopes to secure co-operation in the US war in Afghanistan as well as propping up the Maliki client regime in Iraq.[22]

From the very start, Obama's policy got off on the wrong foot. He appointed two of the most pro-Israel and virulent enemies of Iran to key posts in Treasury and the State Department. Stuart Levey was reappointed as Under Secretary for Terrorism and Financial Intelligence in the Treasury Department and Dennis Ross (often called 'Israel's Lawyer') has been appointed the State Department's point man on Iran. Stuart Levey has led a worldwide crusade of intimidation and coercion against any business, bank or oil company that has any economic dealings with Iran. Ross, who left an Israeli government-funded think tank to take up his new position in the Obama Administration, endorsed a document in late 2008 supporting the 'military option' against Iran. Ross and Levey are hardly likely to *'open a new page'* in US Iranian relations. More to the point, they fit in with a bellicose policy advocating greater confrontation and increasing the likelihood of a new US-Middle East war.

The appointment of Hilary Clinton as Secretary of State will not favor an opening to Iran. She is on public record as advocating the 'obliteration' of Iran during the Presidential campaign in 2008 and now in office backs 'crippling sanctions' to force Iran to dismantle its nuclear energy program. Her approach follows closely the script of the previous Bush Administration.[23]

The Obama regime has not pursued 'negotiations' despite the highly publicized communications of Obama to Iran and to Muslims in general— Instead it has been actively engaged in securing tougher sanctions against Iran while seeking to dictate the outcomes of any meeting with Tehran.

Under the guiding hand of the Israel-First lobby, AIPAC, Congressional leaders of both parties are backing new and harsher sanctions against companies, *"including Lloyds of London, Total (France) and British Petroleum unless they end their involvement in the export of refined oil to Iran or the construction of refineries in that country".*[24] Vice President Biden, in attendance at the annual Washington DC AIPAC Conference (May 1-3, 2009) supported warlike sanctions against Iran. Clearly Obama's conciliatory rhetoric is in direct contradiction with his hard-line appointments and the harsh sanctions his regime pursues. Obama's appointment of hard-core Zionists linked directly to Israel to strategic positions reflects the powerful influence which the Zionist Power Configurations exercises over strategic Middle East issues. As a result, Obama's policy toward Iran is skewed in the direction of serving Israel's military interests rather than the broader economic and strategic interests of the US empire.[25]

Obama is pursuing a policy of 'negotiations' on exclusively Zionist terms: By demanding Iran surrender its internationally recognized and closely regulated program of nuclear enrichment, and abandon strategic allies and principles of solidarity with the rights of the Palestinian people or face a US economic blockade, the White House is rejecting any possibility of a peaceful negotiated settlement.

In pursuing an iron-fist policy toward Iran to satisfy the demands of the Zionist Power Configuration acting on behalf of Israel, Obama is missing major diplomatic, economic and political opportunities to stabilize US imperial interests in the region. Through a process of give and take, Washington could secure Iranian co-operation in stabilizing Iraq and Afghanistan. In the past Iran has demonstrated its willingness to support US puppet rulers in Iraq and Afghanistan. In the case of Afghanistan, Iran directly aided the US occupation by attacking fleeing Taliban forces in the Western frontier regions. In contrast, Washington's close relation with Israel strengthens the Taliban in Afghanistan and Muslim resistance to its occupation of Iraq.

While opposing the Israeli government policy of dispossession of the Palestinians, Iran has declared its willingness to accept a 'two-state solution' if "that is what the Palestinians want". The new far-right Israeli regime of Netanyahu/Liebermann, backed by the major American Zionist organizations, openly rejected a 'two-state solution', in repudiation the public position of the Obama government during his May 18, 2009 Washington meeting with Obama.[26]

The US National Intelligence Agencies published its National Intelligence Estimate in November 2007, which publicly refuted Israel's claim that Iran is engaged in weaponizing its enriched uranium. On the ground investigations by the United Nations and international inspectors from the International Atomic Energy Agency, found no evidence of an Iranian nuclear weapons programs.[27] By choosing to endorse Israel's unfounded claims of an *'existential threat'* stemming from the development of nuclear weapons by Iran, the Obama Administration has become an accomplice in Israel's overt preparations for war against Iran. By refusing to use the findings of the international inspectors and its own intelligence agencies to come to terms with Iran's nuclear-energy program, Obama runs the risk of becoming embroiled in a devastating war provoked by the government of Israel.

In a time in which the US exports have declined by over 30% in the first quarter of 2009 and the economy is mired in a prolonged deep recession, the Obama regime prioritized military relations with Israel on highly unfavorable terms. In this regard, overall economic losses from Obama's policy of exclusive dealings with a minor economic player like Israel—has led to the losses of many billions of dollars of potential trade with Iran.[28] Unlike the highly unfavorable US trade balance with Israel and the monstrous $30 billion-dollar 'aid' handout to the Jewish State, Iran offers a major investment outlet and a lucrative market for US petroleum, agro-business, chemical and financial enterprises.

In order to back up Israel's blockade and boycott policies against duly elected Arab leaders, especially Hamas in Gaza and Hezbollah in

Lebanon, Washington is forced to support harsh corrupt dictatorships in the West Bank, Egypt and Jordan simply because they are allied to Israel. If, as the Obama regime claims, electoral processes will stabilize the region, then its commitment to Israel and its allies is destabilizing the region. And indeed, such calls remain fraudulent in the face of US refusal to recognize the governments (such as Hamas) that result from same.

Instead of pursuing new policies toward Iran designed to secure imperial interests in the region, the Obama regime chooses confrontation which undermines its *'conciliatory rhetoric'* and, worst, has led to increasing tensions. New sanctions against gasoline export as a provocation to a new, expanded war cannot be in US interests, as it will surely send the US into an even deeper depression. No matter: as AIPAC put it, urging its membership to push Congress to proceed:

> The Iran Refined Petroleum Sanctions Act (H.R. 2194 in the House and S. 908 in the Senate) could have a dramatic effect on Iran's economy—Tehran imports nearly 40 percent of its gas and diesel needs—by limiting Iran's ability to import and produce refined petroleum products by requiring the president to impose sanctions on companies helping Iran in these areas.[29]

As for gaining the cooperation of the world in sanctioning Iran, "just a few examples of how the effort to isolate Iran has been undercut" are listed in Fact Sheet #63, "Failure of Iran Sanctions", published by the Jewish Virtual Library, which inter alia includes recent Iranian deals with Russia, China, Germany, Italy, Switzerland, Turkey, Austria, Malaysia, and various Gulf emirates.[30]

North Korea: The Unmasking of a Policy

The Obama regime has undermined the tentative nuclear disarmament agreements reached between the Bush Administration and the North Korean Government. The original agreement was based on reciprocal concessions, in which North Korea agreed to dismantle its nuclear weapons program in exchange for economic and energy aid from the US, Japan, China, South Korea and Russia. The North Koreans complied with the agreement, but the economic aid was not forthcoming, in large part because of demands by the US to include intrusive inspections.[31] The incoming Obama administration did not take any initiative to move aid programs forward. On the contrary, in response to an experimental rocket launch of a satellite, Secretary of State Hilary Clinton called for and secured a *condemnation* of North Korea's legal right to space technology and called for the implementation of new economic sanctions.[32] These harsh reprisals caused the North Koreans to end negotiations and to re-start their nuclear weapons program, raising military tensions in the peninsula and undermining the peace process.[33] In the brief period of three months, the Obama White House has succeeded in ramping up a new arena of military confrontation.

Afghanistan-Pakistan: Extending Warfare and Destabilizing a Client

In response to the resurgence of the Afghan resistance and the expansion of its influence beyond its southern strongholds, Obama opened *new* fronts of conflict in Pakistan by engaging in systematic bombing of villages and communities. As a result, Pakistani fighters and their Afghan allies have drawn increasing popular support extending their influence throughout the Northwest Territories. By pressuring the weak and unpopular Zadari regime to intensify military operations against Pakistanis opposed to the US bombing raids, the Obama regime has eroded what little support it had within the state apparatus.[34] Over 2 million Pakistanis in the region have been driven from their homes by the military offensive.[35] Obama's Pakistan policy is an extension of its failed Afghan military strategy of targeting entire civilian areas (in this case the over 40 million-strong Pashtuns) influenced or controlled by the anti-US resistance in the hope of eliminating some Taliban fighters among the thousands of civilian deaths.

The result is predictable: The Pakistan Army, the main prop of the weak US client President Zadari, becomes increasingly compromised as a *tool* for furthering US colonial war aims and surrendering *sovereignty* in the face of systematic US cross-border attacks. By forcing the divided and over-extended Pakistani regime to engage in large-scale warfare against its fiercely independent citizens in the Northwest Territories, Pakistani cities and towns will have to contend with the catastrophe of over 2 million internal refugees who have been driven from their homes and communities. Obama increases the possibility of a military revolt by nationalist-Islamist soldiers and officers, which would shift the entire balance of power in the region (and beyond) against Washington.[36] Instead of 'containing' and limiting the area of combat in Afghanistan, Obama's Pakistan policy has widened the front and implicated a large but fragile client state in an extended war which could bring about its downfall—not unlike US policy which led to the overthrow of the Shah of Iran.[37]

Obama's escalation in Afghanistan precludes a negotiated national settlement with the Taliban, which confines it to Afghanistan in exchange for limiting its role as a safe haven for Al Qaeda. Under increased US attack, the Taliban have internationalized their fight beyond their contiguous borders with Pakistan raising the specter of the US extending deeper into that country in support of their failed client in Islamabad.

Israel-Palestine Policy

White House policy toward the Israeli occupation of Palestine has been characterized by ritual reiteration of policy (a *'Two-State Solution'*), indecisive and inconsequential attempts to formulate a coherent strategy and capitulation to Israel's continued territorial expansion.[38] Obama is faced with an openly annexationalist newly-elected far-right government; even as Netanyahu accedes to mouthing the language of a *'two-state solution'*, he encircles it with preconditions and actions which are in direct repudiation of it. Washington *passively* submits to Israeli rebuffs. Obama's Middle East policy appointees from top to bottom are mostly *Israel-Firsters*. The Obama regime and the Democratic Party leadership in the Congress are indebted to the Zionist lobby, which rejects any attempt to even 'pressure' Israel—thus disarming any of the possible economic or military levers which could be used to pry concessions from the Netanyahu-Leiberman regime. Worse still, Washington supports the Israeli blockade of Gaza ruled by the democratically-elected Hamas government in power, thus strengthening Israel's iron grip on the Palestinians.

One of President Obama's most egregious foreign policy failures took place during his May 18, 2009 meeting in Washington with Israeli Prime Minister Benyamin Netanyahu. After having made as Israeli-Palestinian *'two-state'* settlement one of his major foreign policy goals, Obama failed to even secure a verbal commitment from the Israeli extremist leader.[39] After 4 hours of discussion, Netanyahu rejected Obama's offer to consider a time limit on diplomatic overtures to Iran (with the implicit threat of a military option) in exchange for the Likud Prime Minister mouthing the 'three words': *'two state solution'!* Worse still from the White House view, Netanyahu insisted that any *negotiations* with the Palestinians were conditional on their recognition of Israel as a *Jewish State*, thus disenfranchising the 1.5 million Palestinian Muslim and Christians who remained after the mass expulsions.

As if to flaunt his disdain for Obama's call for a freeze on new settlements, Netanyahu's regime accelerated plans for 20 new Jewish housing settlements in the occupied West Bank—precisely on the day of their meeting. Worst of all, Obama came out of the meeting displaying his utter impotence—he could not even make a 'show' of having any influence on the extremist Jewish Prime Minister. Netanyahu's brazen and public repudiation of Obama was based on his clear understanding that the power of the US Zionist Power Configuration over Congress and in the Executive branch guaranteed that Obama would not counter Israeli extremism by threatening to decrease US financial or military or even diplomatic aid to the Jewish state. After weeks of rumors and stories of Obama's *'willingness'* to confront or pressure Netanyahu to accept a two state solution, the end result was a humiliating public debacle in which Obama secured absolutely nothing.

Following his meeting with Obama, Netanyahu (the visitor) went to the US Congress with his power base among a huge majority of members of the House and Senate and top Zionist Jewish leaders, where almost the entire elected US representative body re-affirmed its unconditional support for Israeli policy—strictly on Netanyahu's terms. The impotence and failings of President Obama in his dealing with Netanyahu were not lost on the entire world (especially the Arab world). Hamas Spokesman, Fawzi Barhoum summed up the general perception thus: *"The statements (about a two-state solution) by Obama are nothing but wishes on which we do not much count".*[40]

The Obama regime 'immersion' in Zionist-Israeli politics blinds it to the favorable opportunities for a grand accord in the region—or indeed, the possibilities of a grand accord *against* it, sweeping through the Muslim populations of the region, irrespective of efforts to exacerbate a Sunni-Shi'a divide. Hamas leaders have shut down all rocket retaliatory attacks on Israel and called for a 10-year ceasefire.[41] The Arab League (including the Gulf States) has reiterated its willingness to recognize Israel and open diplomatic relations in exchange for an end to the occupation of the West Bank and blockade of Gaza. The European Union has opened dialog with Hamas and Hezbollah while postponing extending 'special' economic status to Israel. Even Iran has agreed to accept a Palestinian settlement based on the *Two-State Solution.*

Faced with major shifts and concessions, the Obama regime remains impotent. It is unable to put any muscle behind its proposals; it struggles even to set conditions for the resumption of peace negotiations. In the meantime, the Zionist Power Configuration inside and outside presses forward with new and more dangerous sanctions against Iran. During the AIPAC Conference in Washington (May 1-5), six thousand Israel-Firsters set their goal on securing Congressional majorities in favor of provocative blockades and sanctions against companies which export refined petroleum products into Iran.[42] The *Iran Refined Petroleum Sanctions Act (IRPSA)* currently in the Congress and authored by AIPAC operatives is viewed as a weapon the crush the Iranian economy and overthrow the government. By attempting to entice AIPAC and Israel with the claim that a peace agreement with Palestine would lead to a 'consensus' to confront Iran, the Obama regime surrenders its diplomatic option to Iran in favor of Israel's militarist approach—without securing any changes in its policy toward Palestine.

Consequences of Obama's Failed Policies

Early on the Obama regime's foreign policy has suffered a series of important setbacks on major policy issues.

Its G-20 economic initiatives to secure or support proposals to coordinate stimulus policies based on financial bailouts and larger deficits were rejected. The re-vitalization of the IMF via an injection of $750 billion dollars was not welcomed by the *'emerging market'* countries because of the IMF's harsh conditions. The NATO summit spurned Washington's demands for more combat troops to Afghanistan. Of the 5000 troops promised, three-fourths are to serve for the duration of the Afghan Presidential election (August 2009) and the rest as trainers and advisers far from the frontlines.

The Summit of the Americas was a fiasco for Washington. It was completely isolated in its defense of US policy toward Cuba, the Cuban Embargo and its designation of Cuba as a 'state supporter of terrorism'. Obama offered nothing in the way of new policies in the face of the US-induced regional economic recession. At the same time the Latin American countries turned elsewhere—to Iran and China, as well as within the region, for opportunities to stimulate their economies. Obama's bellicose posturing toward North Korea reversed six years of negotiations, resulting in the revival of tensions and the reassembly of Pyongyang's nuclear weapons program. The escalation of the US/NATO war in Afghanistan and its extension into Pakistan undermines US clients in the region and makes it likely that the US military will find itself in an unending colonial war with no possibility of a victory.

Obama's deep ties to American Zionist policies and organizations and their loyalties to the new far rightwing Israeli annexationist regime precludes the pursuit of any policy which could open the way toward a 'two-state' resolution of the conflict. The hard line White House position of escalating sanctions against Iran and the buildup of Israeli long-distance offensive weapons precludes any meaningful new initiatives toward Tehran.[43] The result of these failed policies is that already, in a brief five months into the Obama administration, Washington is increasingly politically isolated: Alone in fighting wars in Sough Asia; alone in aiding and abetting Israeli intransigence; alone among its fellow nations in the *Western Hemisphere* in its imposition of an embargo against Cuba. Political isolation means the political and economic costs of Obama's military-driven empire building will be borne almost exclusively by the US Treasury and citizenry—at a time of unprecedented peacetime deficits and a deepening recession.

Obama's focus on foreign military adventures, domestic financial bailouts and promoting the IMF has caused the countries of Latin America to turn away from their big traditional partner in Washington and sign up for major trade and investment agreements elsewhere. Brazil welcomed a hundred member delegation of business leaders form Iran, headed by its Prime Minister and composed of a wide array of business and banking leaders to seal multi-billion and co-investment deals. In late May, President Da Silva promoted a big increase in trade and investment with its biggest trading partner—China. The response by Secretary Clinton was pathetic: Instead of recognizing the economic eclipse of the US and seeking to increase its economic presence, she cited the threat of Iranian terrorism— among oil, agribusiness and banking executives.[44]

Obama's continued backing for rightwing regional leaders in Bolivia and Ecuador against reformist presidents has contributed to the latters' repeated electoral victories and the political isolation of the US. Obama's rhetoric of 'opening up' to Venezuela, accompanied by harsh attacks on the dangers of *'Chavismo'*, including unfounded charges of its complicity in drug trafficking, has led to Venezuela's growing trade and joint investment links with China, Iran and Russia.

Failed policies have consequences. The pursuit of long-term large-scale overseas military commitments in a time of economic depression is self-destructive, self-isolating and doomed to failure. Satisfying Israeli illegal colonial aspirations and military goals sacrifices hundreds of billions of dollars in trade with Iran, the Gulf States and South Asian economies.

The greatest problem is not that the Obama regime is pursuing wars that will lead to defeats (which is true), but that the entire notion of pouring resources into military-driven empire building at a time of deepening recession is leading to hundreds of thousands of deaths and millions of refugees throughout the world, while destroying the livelihoods and social safety net of millions of American citizens, and any lingering shreds of American moral credibility.

Endnotes

1   *American Conservative* April 14, 2009.
2   *Financial Times*, April 2, 2009, p.11.
3   *Financial Times*, April 15, 2009, p.9.
4   *Financial Times*, April 2, 2009 p.4.
5   *Financial Times*, March 26, 2009 p. 1.
6   See *Economic Commission for Latin America: Report to Summit* April 17-19, 2009.
7   *La Jornada* April 20 2009.
8   *La Jornada* April 17, 2009.
9   *La Jornada* April 20 2009.
10   *La Jornada* April 27, 2009.
11   *Financial Times* April 30, 2009 p. 7.
12   *Financial Times* April 30, 2009 p.7.
13   *Al Jazeera* March 31, 2009.
14   *Telegraph (UK)* May 10, 2009.
15   Bloomberg, Thursday, Jun. 11, 2009 03:36AM EDT, cited in Report on Business, *Globe and Mail*, June 11, 2009. <http://www.theglobeandmail.com/report-on-business/brazil-earmarks-10-billion-for-imf-bonds-minister/article1177391/>

16   Michael Hudson, "De-Dollarization: Dismantling America's Financial-Military Empire: The Yekaterinburg Turning Point", Globalresearch.ca, June 13, 2009.
17   *Financial Times,* April 2, 2009 p.7.
18   *Financial Times,* April 8, 2009 p.2.
19   *Financial Times,* May 6, 2009 p.1; see also Gareth Porter, "*Errant Drone Attacks Spur Militants in Pakistan* IPS April 16, 2009.
20   BBC News, April 2, 2009.
21   BBC News, May 7, 2009.
22   *Financial Times,* March 6, 2009 p. 5.
23   *Financial Times,* April 23, 2009 p.3
24   *Financial Times,* April 23, 2009 p.3
25   *Financial Times,* February 24, 2009 p. 13.
26   BBC News May 19, 2009.
27   IAEA Report On Iran February 19, 2009.
28   BBC News April 29, 2009.
29   "Take Action: Support Tougher Iran Sanctions", AIPAC website at <http://www.aipac.org/694.asp>
30   Fact Sheet #63, Failure of Iran Sanctions, published by the Jewish Virtual Library at <http://www.jewishvirtuallibrary.org/jsource/talking/63_Sanctions.html>
31   *Financial Times,* April 15, 2009.
32   *Financial Times,* April 13, 2009 p. 4.
33   *Al Jazeera,* April 14, 2009.
34   *Financial Times,* April 2, 2009 p. 7.
35   BBC News May 19, 2009.
36   BBC News May 8, 2009.
37   *Financial Times,* April 27, 2009 p.5.
38   BBC News April 18, 2009.
39   BBC News May 19, 2009.
40   *Al Jazeera,* May 19, 2009.
41   *The New York Times,* May 4, 2009.
42   *Jerusalem Post,* May 1, 2009.
43   *Financial Times,* March 23, 2009 p.3.
44   www.presstv.com, May 2, 2009.

Index

Clinton, Hillary 46, 50, 51, 52, 54, 55,
    56, 60, 66, 75, 86, 127, 131,
    132, 135, 138, 140, 141, 150,
    151, 152, 155, 156, 157, 158,
    205, 206, 208, 222, 224, 229
Clintons, Hillary and Bill 52
Cohen, David 140
collaborators 69, 75, 84, 85, 86, 101,
    124, 152, 199, 200
collateralized debt obligations 20
Colombia 73, 74, 77, 81, 82, 85, 86,
    87, 90, 91, 93, 98, 99, 100,
    101, 110, 125, 126, 219
colonialism 32, 43, 50, 53, 55, 56,
    60, 84, 88, 98, 108, 113, 125,
    129, 131, 135, 137, 139, 187,
    196, 197, 198, 199, 200, 201,
    202, 203, 206, 207, 208, 209,
    221, 225, 228, 229
colonial wars 56, 60, 113, 209, 221
commodities 20, 24, 28, 44, 60, 66,
    71, 199
competition 19, 22, 23
corporate flight 59
corporations 24, 34, 59, 82, 94, 96, 101
    , 102, 122, 129, 200
credit freeze 66, 93
crimes against humanity 161, 177, 185,
    186, 187, 205
Cuba 75, 77, 89, 91, 92, 97, 99, 125,
    126, 197, 200, 215, 218, 228

D

Daily Alert 179, 180, 181, 182
death squads 210
debt trap 80
de-coupling 30
deficit 25, 62, 67, 92, 96, 129, 194
Democratic Party 46, 52, 130, 206, 226
depression 16, 18, 21, 22, 24, 26, 27, 2
    8, 29, 32, 33, 35, 36, 217, 218,
    219, 220, 224, 229
derivatives 21, 25, 34
d'Escoto-Brockmann, Miguel 160, 187
diplomacy 87, 90
disinvestment 26, 29

E

Eastern Europe 19, 29
economic recovery 29, 31, 35, 36
Ecuador 73, 76, 85, 88, 90, 91, 92, 93,
    105, 107, 125, 215, 218, 219,
    229
Egypt 123, 145, 201, 224
elections 49, 50, 51, 52, 57, 60, 70, 73,
    75, 76, 81, 82, 86, 88, 100, 101,
    105, 107, 108, 109, 110, 111,
    112, 113, 123, 127, 137, 138,
    139, 141, 150, 152, 153, 154,
    165, 177, 190, 191, 194, 228,
    229
Emanuel, Rahm 51, 54
embargo 77, 91, 92, 137, 151, 153,
    158, 159, 166, 177, 178, 185,
    205, 207, 217, 228
enemy combatants 127, 128
England 21, 22; see also United Kingdom
equality 37, 38, 39, 40
Ethiopia 201, 203
Europe 19, 23, 24, 29, 32, 44, 45, 62,
    64, 67, 70, 72, 77, 78, 85, 87,
    88, 95, 110, 120, 127, 128, 145,
    153, 157, 161, 194, 198, 199,
    200, 201, 203, 204, 206, 207,
    217, 221
exploitation 17, 19, 20, 21, 23, 24, 28, 3
    0, 31, 36, 38
exports 20

F

falling profits 19, 31
Fatah 207
FBI 142, 154
Federal Reserve 35, 216
finance capital 20, 21, 31, 60, 216
financial instruments 19, 20, 36, 44,
    46, 58
flight of manufacturing 34
food 27, 30, 39, 87, 94, 95, 96, 99,
    113, 154, 159, 167, 178, 180,
    190, 193, 194, 198, 199, 200,
    205, 207, 212
foreign investment 70, 79
foreign policy 35, 51, 83, 84, 86, 90,
    91, 104, 108, 130, 132, 139, 141,
    146, 148, 155, 158, 178, 194,
    212, 215, 220, 226, 228
foreign reserves 70
freedom of speech 109
Freeman, Charles 46, 55, 132, 133,
    134, 135, 140, 141, 143, 156
free market 16, 17, 21, 27, 30
free market ideology 21, 71

G

G-20 95, 97, 215, 216, 228
Gates, Robert 51, 52, 55, 56, 131,
    149, 155
Gaza 125, 130, 131, 133, 140, 141,
    143, 144, 145, 146, 147, 148,
    150, 153, 154, 156, 158, 159,
    160, 161, 162, 163, 165, 166,
    167, 168, 169, 174, 176, 177,

V

Venezuela 73, 74, 76, 77, 78, 81, 84,
85, 86, 89, 90, 91, 92, 95, 96,
97, 98, 99, 105, 107, 108, 110,
112, 113, 120, 125, 126, 128,
145, 190, 194, 208, 215, 218,
219, 229
Vietnam 30
Volker, Paul 52, 54
voters 50, 102, 110, 113, 138, 154,
192, 193; see also elections

W

wages 19
Wall Street 27, 34, 40, 41, 42, 43, 44,
46, 47, 48, 49, 51, 53, 54, 58,
59, 60, 61, 62, 67, 103, 104,
150, 163, 198, 206, 216, 218
war crimes 53, 130, 148, 152, 160,
161, 179, 183
wars 31, 33, 34, 49, 50, 51, 52, 54,
55, 56, 57, 60, 61, 67, 68, 69,
77, 84, 85, 86, 91, 102, 104,
113, 121, 122, 126, 127, 129,
139, 142, 143, 144, 146, 147,
162, 187, 193, 195, 203, 205,
206, 208, 209, 210, 213, 220,
221, 228, 229
welfare state 38, 51, 59
West Bank 130, 131, 141, 153, 155,
163, 177, 178, 204, 224, 226,
227
White House 26, 27, 51, 52, 53, 54,
58, 60, 90, 91, 92, 119, 132,
133, 134, 140, 142, 143, 147,
149, 150, 151, 152, 156, 161,
162, 165, 169, 176, 181, 186,
190, 191, 194, 205, 211, 213,
215, 217, 221, 222, 225, 226,
228
workers 19, 20, 22, 23, 24, 26, 27, 28,
29, 31, 32, 33, 34, 37, 38, 39,
45, 50, 57, 64, 66, 68, 70, 71,
72, 73, 76, 81, 82, 83, 88, 90,
93, 94, 95, 96, 98, 105, 108,
109, 114, 116, 119, 127, 129,
161, 179, 180, 185, 186, 192,
193, 197, 199, 200, 201, 202,
203, 216
working class 22, 24, 36, 64, 105, 109,
112, 192, 193
working conditions 37, 38
World Bank 53, 75, 94, 198, 199, 201
World Conference Against Racism 131
world depression 16, 18, 21, 22, 28
World Trade Organization 20
WWII 69, 75

Y

Yugoslavia 55, 75

Z

Zadari, Asif Ali 123, 225
Zimbabwe 197
Zinni, General Anthony 131
Zionism 41, 42, 43, 46, 47, 49, 54, 60,
61, 69, 122, 125, 126, 127, 129,
130, 131, 132, 133, 134, 135,
136, 137, 138, 139, 140, 141,
142, 143, 144, 145, 146, 147,
148, 149, 150, 151, 152, 153,
155, 156, 157, 158, 159, 160,
161, 162, 163, 165, 166, 169,
176, 177, 178, 180, 181, 182,
184, 186, 187, 188, 189, 194,
206, 221, 222, 223, 226, 227,
228
Zionist power configuration 60, 129, 130,
131, 132, 133, 134, 135, 136,
137, 138, 139, 141, 149, 153,
156, 176, 177, 178